Mother and Sons, Inc.

THE MIDDLE AGES SERIES

Ruth Mazo Karras, Series Editor
Edward Peters, Founding Editor

A complete list of books in the series
is available from the publisher.

MOTHER AND SONS, INC.

Martha de Cabanis
in Medieval Montpellier

KATHRYN L. REYERSON

PENN

UNIVERSITY OF PENNSYLVANIA PRESS

PHILADELPHIA

Published by
University of Pennsylvania Press
Philadelphia, Pennsylvania 19104-4112
www.upenn.edu/pennpress

Printed in the United States of America on acid-free paper
10 9 8 7 6 5 4 3 2 1

Library of Congress Cataloging-in-Publication Data

Names: Reyerson, Kathryn, author.
Title: Mother and Sons, Inc.: Martha de Cabanis in medieval Montpellier /
Kathryn L. Reyerson.
Other titles: Middle Ages series.
Description: 1st edition. | Philadelphia: University of Pennsylvania Press,
[2017] | Series: The Middle Ages series | Includes bibliographical
references and index.
Identifiers: LCCN 2017013304 | ISBN 9780812249613 (hardcover: alk.
paper)
Subjects: LCSH: Cabanis, Martha de, active 1328–1342. | Women
merchants—France—Montpellier—Biography. |
Widows—France—Montpellier—Biography. | Guardian and
ward—France—Montpellier—History—To 1500 | Montpellier
(France)—Economic conditions.
Classification: LCC HF3554.6.C3 R49 2017 | DDC 381.092 [B]—dc23
LC record available at https://lccn.loc.gov/2017013304

To the memory of Gretchen Asmussen

CONTENTS

Introduction

This is the story of Martha de Cabanis, a medieval woman of the mercantile milieu in the southern French town of Montpellier, a large commercial center of coastal Languedoc. Martha married, as did most of her contemporaries, but she was widowed early in the 1320s and left with three young sons, aged eleven, eight, and four. The extant written evidence records her actions as a widow and a guardian to her children and offers a window on the world of such a woman in that time and place.

Mother and Sons, Inc. falls within the wider historiography on medieval widows. In 1989, the Settimana di Studi of the Istituto di storia economica F. Datini in Prato, Italy, had women in the medieval economy as its theme. Odile Redon and others bemoaned the lack of focus on women as widows.[1] In the ensuing decades, the situation has changed dramatically. Many of the newer works on women focus on the fate of medieval widows. Provence, Languedoc, Roussillon, and the Crown of Aragon have seen studies that deal, among other issues, with the role of the widow as guardian of her minor children and with the economic agency of widows.[2] These works represent a useful continental counterpoint to the impressive literature on women in medieval Britain.[3]

In the course of the present study, I will compare Martha's experience with that of widows and wives who have enjoyed detailed development in recent monographs and articles. From my own pen on the history of Montpellier, there are the elite widow Agnes de Bossones, guardian of her three young daughters, traceable through a lengthy widowhood; the real estate rentier and widow Maria Naturale, an in-law of Martha; and Maria Lamberti, another elite widow and guardian of her son, faced with financial challenges at her husband's death.[4] Also treated is the married in-law of Martha, Bernarda de Cabanis, a mercer. Rebecca Winer has brought to life the experience in the town of Perpignan in Roussillon of the elite woman Raimunda de Camerada, widow of Pere, vicar, royal bailiff, and king's lieutenant, in lengthy litigation after her husband's death, and Sança, widow of Duran de Pererar.[5] For the Crown of Aragon Marie Kelleher has written of Romia, widow of Pere de Grenolosa, stripped of the *mas* (rural estate) under her control at one point in her widowhood, and Blanca, widow of Guillem des Prat, in litigation over her late husband's estate.[6] For Marseille, Susan McDonough has given us Silona Filholine, often in court to defend her assets.[7] And in a northern European comparison, Shennan Hutton has traced the career of Mergriete Scettorf of Ghent, first as the wife of Frank van der Hamme, a well-to-do baker, then as a widow, and finally after she remarried.[8]

Much of our knowledge of medieval women comes from normative sources, legal codes and treatises, royal and municipal legislation, and prescriptive works, that is, literature that laid down authoritative rules or directions for how things should be done. These sources paint a somewhat negative view of what women could do in what was undeniably a man's world, the patriarchal and patrilineal society of the High and Late Middle Ages. But is this the whole picture? Documents of practice in notarial registers give us a window on daily life that requires revision of that rather stark portrait.[9] This book traces the activities of one woman, Martha de Cabanis, wife and then widow of the merchant and mercer Guiraudus de Cabanis, using notarial evidence. Much of the past is unrecoverable, but occasionally there remain rich pockets of information that help us see a bit more clearly. It is important to complement the information from normative sources through examination of documents of practice. This case study of Martha attempts to do that through the invaluable legal and economic sources that have survived to shed some light on the urban inhabitants of Montpellier.[10]

Still, the documentary record for Martha disappoints. We do not have Martha's marriage/dowry contracts or her last will and testament or the will of her husband Guiraudus, though we know he wrote one because there remains the trace of a receipt for payment of a testamentary bequest. Beyond this, we do not know the terms of Guiraudus's will though it is likely he named Martha as guardian of their three sons. She held that role two years after Guiraudus's death in 1326, when she first appeared in the documents in 1328, and then in the 1330s, and into the 1340s.

There remain no letters or diaries for Martha. The *ricordanze* of Florence come the closest to diary-like family records for the Middle Ages.[11] One wishes for a counterpart to the Paston letters of fifteenth-century England or to those of Margherita Datini to her husband Francesco di Marco in the late fourteenth century, but there are none.[12]

However, comparatively speaking, in terms of survivals of evidence for other medieval women, there remains considerable information about Martha's activities, particularly in the area of business, commerce, and real estate. What has survived for Martha are formal contractual documents, most of them surviving in one notarial register of 1336–42, written by Guillelmus Nogareti, and a few scattered in other registers of Johannes Holanie.[13] Like legal records, economic records tend to be formulaic, terse, and impersonal. Yet it is possible to tease out something of Martha's personality from the contracts that survive. For her family life and her personal possessions, the general historical context can provide insights. Her spiritual life remains an unknown.

The story of Martha de Cabanis fits within the legal culture of the kingdom of Aragon/Majorca and of southern Europe, specifically within the region of Roman law/written law that was the legacy of Greco-Roman antiquity. Medieval society was a patriarchy, whether for peasant women or for urban women like Martha.[14] Judith Bennett drew on Adrienne Rich and Allan Johnson for meaningful definitions of patriarchy. Rich saw it as "a familial-social, ideological, political system in which men—by force, direct pressure, or through ritual, tradition, law, and language, customs, etiquette, education, and the division of labor, determine what part women shall or shall not play, and in which the female is everywhere subsumed under the male."[15] For a more recent definition of patriarchy, Bennett quoted Johnson: "A society is patriarchal to the degree that it promotes male privilege by being *male dominated, male identified,* and *male centered.*"[16] The challenge of medieval women was to maneuver within the constraints of their society to achieve their aims. For the south of France, the particular brand of patriarchy owed a lot to Roman law heritage, but its influence was not universal.

While Roman law did not readily allow a widowed mother to be the guardian of her children, in Montpellier such was often the practice. One of the most prominent capacities in which women such as Martha appeared in business transactions was as guardian (*tutrix*) of younger children (under fourteen) or curator (*curatrix*), in the sense of advisor and caretaker, of older children.[17] In this role and as executors of their husbands' estates, women were involved in the payment of debts, acquittals, real estate acts, in commerce, in finance, and in the apprenticeship of their children.

Martha encountered several challenges as a widowed mother with young children for whom she would act as guardian. Marie Kelleher has outlined three choices a widow faced on the loss of her husband. One, she could enter a new marriage or join a religious community. Second, she could leave her dowry and dower in the marital estate for entry into her husband's lineage, deepening her links with his family. Third, she could set up an independent household. Regardless of her choice, Kelleher emphasized, "a widow had a legal claim to the ownership and management of her dowry and dower [in Montpellier termed *augmentum* (augment)] after her husband's death."[18] Martha appeared to operate independently after her husband's death, but there is reason to believe she stayed in the family home. When we come upon her two years after her husband's death and then more consistently ten years into widowhood, there are no male relatives surrounding her. Those relatives I have hypothesized in Chapter 3 did business with her sons but were not involved in her household. As a result, it is likely that Martha was the head of household. She would never remarry.

This book is the story of what Martha did and what she may have done. Like many historians, I am fond of notarial registers because they contain a wealth of information about life in the Middle Ages. My study examines Martha in her various roles as daughter, wife, mother, and widow. Her challenges would be many: to raise and train her sons to carry on their father's business; to preserve that business until they were ready to take over; and to invest for herself. For this study of Martha's life, however, I will need to go beyond the notarial evidence, to speculate a bit, to contextualize, to recreate the urban setting in which she lived, with as much depth and complexity as possible for areas of her life that escape us.[19] Martha's experience provides valuable information on the world of elite mercantile women in fourteenth-century Montpellier.

The most privileged status for medieval women was that of widow.[20] For the first time in their lives, women were freed from the oversight of male family members, husbands and fathers, in particular, though male relatives could continue to offer advice.[21] Widows might rely on others to represent them and to advise them in economic matters, but the decisions were theirs. Widows of Martha's station, the urban mercantile elite, could, if they chose, in the first half of the fourteenth century, be actively involved in the world of business. Just how the widow Martha maneuvered within the legal constraints of social, economic, and personal status lies at the heart of my investigation. The present study addresses the life of Martha, with attention to the broader historical context, and in comparison with men, in order to analyze and interpret her experiences and to take account of gender differences.[22]

Martha enjoyed many advantages, as her late husband, Guiraudus de Cabanis, was a mercer and merchant who belonged to an extended merchant family and was a successful businessman.[23] Guiraudus very likely thought enough of Martha's abilities to make her guardian of their sons in his will. She would serve in the capacity of guardian while her sons were under fourteen, the practical age of majority in the south of France, and then as curator until they were in their early twenties. Guiraudus had a well-structured business entourage and loyal partners Martha could rely on.[24] Guiraudus's colleagues shared his confidence in Martha's abilities, and they clearly respected and supported her. As the widow of a prominent merchant, she profited from her high status but also from her engagement in the world of business.

Martha's life falls squarely in the first half of the fourteenth century, long after the center of gravity shifted from towns in the south of France dominated by noble courts of the dukes of Aquitaine, the counts of Toulouse, the viscounts of Narbonne, and the lords of Montpellier to an urban civilization of non-noble townspeople, still open to the cosmopolitan influences of the Mediterranean world but without the glamorous noble men and women of the twelfth and early thirteenth centuries who figured in the historical documents as well as the legends of epic, romance, and lyric poetry.[25] For Montpellier, there was a long line of seigneurial ladies, the *dominae* of the lordship of Montpellier (Ermessendis of Melgueil, Sybilla de Mataplana, Mathilda, duchess of Burgundy, among them), climaxed by Eudoxia Comnena, daughter of a Byzantine emperor and wife of the last Guilhem lord of Montpellier, Guilhem VIII, and later rejected by him.[26] Their daughter, the tragic Marie of Montpellier, was abused by three husbands, the third being Peter II of Aragon, whom she rebuked roundly in her heart-wrenching will before her death in 1213.[27] Women of the urban elite like Martha could look back on the heritage of these noble women.

Martha lived a century and more after the illustrious women above. When prescriptive literature emerged in the later Middle Ages, a domestic focus for married women of the urban elite was preeminent.[28] Women of more modest social strata were also subject to the strictures of a society that, in assumptions and practice, privileged men. Older scholarship on women of the urban mercantile elite saw them essentially confined to household oversight and management, with little economic independence.[29] In contrast, case studies of documents of practice such as that on Ragusa by Susan Mosher Stuard and recent studies on the Crown of Aragon and southern France have demonstrated that, even in the most patriarchal societies, women had options.[30]

Revisionist studies have called into question the degree and nature of women's perceived inferiority in the Middle Ages, though in some respects medieval women are still a mystery after decades of modern scholarship.[31] Medieval England is the site of the most focused debate about the handicaps for women resulting from patriarchal strictures. Marjorie McIntosh, who occupies a middle ground favoring greater agency for women, has usefully rehearsed the debate.[32] Caroline Barron and Jeremy Goldberg take a rosy view of women's situation, maintaining that women electing *femme sole* status in England had an identity separate from their husbands and an independent economic and legal situation, with some limitations. On the other side of the debate, Maryanne Kowaleski and Judith Bennett see a continuous pattern of under-rewarded work for women with essentially no independent occupational identity.[33] In her study of women in medieval London, Barbara Hanawalt finds wealthy women had considerable agency, while definitively putting to rest any fiction of a golden age. Scholarship on the Crown of Aragon and southern France has begun to engage with these questions, though from a less polemical standpoint, as the following chapters will show. Marie Kelleher and Rebecca Winer have confronted both the statutory prescriptions regarding women and their actions in practice.

The story of Martha is a history of women informed by but not focused on gender, one important aspect among several of significance for the study of women.[34] Class and economic status mattered greatly as well. The field of women and gender has opened up a reconsideration of the paradigms for women's experience in the medieval era, particularly the patriarchy/patriliny paradigm that views the Middle Ages as a society where men controlled property and held power. Judith Bennett's *History Matters* argues for a continuing patriarchal equilibrium across all time from data based on wages and work.[35] Bennett, among others, makes the case that medieval society was heavily patriarchal and women suffered from very serious disadvantages (social, economic, and legal) that meant that they played a limited role in society. I have argued that, while women were hardly equal to men, they could and did do a great deal more than many historians (and others) have thought, especially under particular circumstances, such as coming from wealthy families and being widowed.[36] My study asserts that Martha was an impressive business-woman as well as the head of a large mercantile household. Martha's lived experience in the first half of the fourteenth century will illustrate just how much women could and did do. Only with a body of case studies can we expand our understanding of the significance of wealth, social status, and gender for urban women in medieval Europe.[37]

This book has three main goals. It seeks to demonstrate the "realized potential" of Martha de Cabanis's agency as representative of elite urban women, particularly as widowed guardians.[38] Martha may have been extraordinary in her business acumen, but she was a woman of her time.[39] The second aim is to offer the reader an entrée into the world of the urban merchant family of the 1330s and 1340s. The crises of the late Middle Ages had begun, but Montpellier still enjoyed a mature medieval urban economy prior to the arrival of the Black Death in 1348.[40] And the third is to help the reader imagine the life of an urban mercantile woman in a large medieval city. Women often worked behind the scenes, escaping notice in the documents, but in the case of Martha we have significant details of her business involvement once a widow and as guardian of her sons.

Throughout the following chapters, politics, economics, and crises will be evoked as they fit into the chronology. Chapter 1 provides an overview of the town of Montpellier and the region in which Martha lived. An introduction to Martha, her family, and her early years with attention to her maternal and paternal lines will follow in Chapter 2. Chapter 3 deals with her marriage to Guiraudus de Cabanis and with her Cabanis in-laws. Chapter 4 evokes the family home, domestic space, and personal possessions. Chapter 5 focuses on Guiraudus's death in the tumultuous 1320s and the beginnings of Martha's widowhood. Chapter 6 addresses Martha's challenge as a widow in the context of the medieval legal environment, examined through statutes and a legal treatise, and sets the scene for her actions as guardian of her sons and on her own. The legal constraints on women's activities provide a context for Martha's actions as widow and guardian, with a resulting dialogue between legal prescriptions and actions in documents of practice. Chapter 7 deals with her role as guardian in actual business practice. Chapter 8 focuses on real property matters. Martha's dealings in real property on her own behalf and as guardian of her sons take us into the creation and maintenance of a landed fortune and her sons' expansion of their real property holdings. Chapter 9 traces the evolution of Martha's role from guardian to collaborator with her sons in business and as the mastermind of commercial, industrial, and real property investments. The medieval luxury trade in textiles was a Cabanis specialty. Martha's engineering for herself and her sons of the acquisition of bourgeois (*burgensis*) status in the Bastide of Beauvais near Toulouse represented a significant coup and a sign of major expansion of Cabanis business in south-western France in 1342. Throughout the book and in conclusion, I will con-sider Martha in light of Montpellier women and medieval European women.

The decades of the 1320s, 1330s, and 1340s were a final moment of pros-perity for the mercantile classes of Montpellier and a last gasp of women's agency before the onset of the late Middle Ages and early modern era, a contested period for women that saw the expansion of Roman law.[41] We lose track of Martha and her sons in the mid-1340s, just prior to the Black Death of 1348 that caused the town to lose upward of three-fourths of its popula-tion.[42] Were they its victims? No information survives to inform us. This book will tell Martha's story as it illuminates the limits of what was possible for elite mercantile women in the context of a patriarchal society, and that was a lot in the period prior to the plague of 1348.

CHAPTER I

Montpellier in the Time of Martha

This town is founded on merchandise and merchants. This is notorious and manifest because the place of Montpellier is the key to the sea in this land.

—A municipal official's comment on Montpellier in 1346

In the first half of the fourteenth century, Montpellier enjoyed a considerable reputation for trade, as the town official suggests above, though its heyday had probably been the thirteenth century. The town was an entrepôt for Mediterranean imports and northern French exports. Martha and her family would be active participants in the mercantile enterprise of Montpellier. Its history was a short one, making Montpellier's commercial reputation all the more impressive.

Martha and her fellow inhabitants lived in a town of recent medieval foundation. In a region of intense Roman colonization, Montpellier first appeared in a donation of 985 CE by the count of Melgueil of a *mansus* to a certain Guillelmus.[1] Over the course of the next two centuries, the Guilhem family built a lordship of some importance but of limited geographic size. After eight generations of Guilhem lords, in 1202–4, Montpellier experienced a communal revolution with the ejection of the illegitimate heir of Guilhem VIII, offspring of a relationship with a Castilian woman coming after Guilhem VIII's repudiation of his wife, the Byzantine princess Eudoxia Comnena. Guilhem VIII tried in vain to get Pope Innocent III to legitimize his children from the illegitimate union. The papal bull *Per venerabilem* provided Innocent's rationale for refusing to intervene in a matter he thought should be decided by the king of France.[2] The bourgeois of Montpellier chose to side

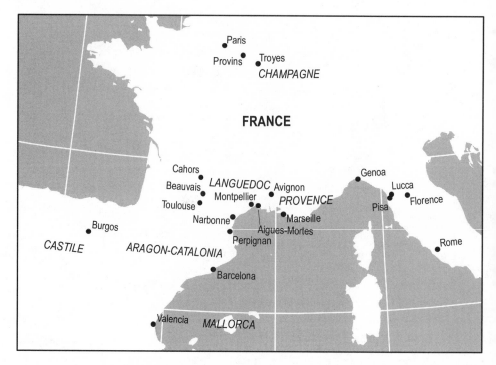

MAP 1. Medieval France and the western Mediterranean.

with Marie of Montpellier, Guilhem VIII's legitimate daughter, in the succession dispute. Marie and her third husband Peter, king of Aragon, became the secular lords of Montpellier.[3] Their heir, James I the Conqueror, was born in Montpellier in 1208. Marie and Peter recognized the prerogatives of the Montpellier commune in a charter of customs of 1204 and subsequent legislation.[4] The charter put in place an urban government of twelve consuls, elected annually, that continued to function during Martha's lifetime with little change before the mid-fourteenth century.[5] The Aragonese and from 1276 the Majorcan dynasties would rule in Montpellier until 1349; for most of the thirteenth century and until 1349, Montpellier existed as a political enclave in the kingdom of France.

The Albigensian crusades against heresy, with their political aftermath, represented a watershed for southern French history in the first half of the thirteenth century.[6] The victory of the northern French led to the installation of the administration of the Capetian king of France in the Midi.[7] The great noble houses of the south, undermined by their relative toleration of deviant beliefs and minority groups, were devastated by the northern conquerors. Montpellier had an orthodox reputation during the Albigensian era, but the legal historian André Gouron has suggested that the political upheaval in Montpellier in the period 1202–4, prior to the outbreak of the Crusades, may have had something to do with heresy.[8] Whatever the religious conditions of Montpellier, the arrival of the king of France in the south would have a significant effect on the lives of the inhabitants. The king established the administrative districts (*sénéchaussées*) of Beaucaire-Nîmes and Carcassonne-Béziers as a result of the treaty of Paris-Meaux of 1229. By the regulations of the system of *apanage*, Toulouse and its region would revert to the French crown after the 1271 death of Alfonse of Poitiers and his wife, the heiress of Toulouse, since they were childless.[9]

During the thirteenth-century expansion of French influence in the south of France, Montpellier remained a city of dual political allegiance, with the dynamic commercial quarter of Montpellier belonging to the king of Aragon/Majorca and the episcopal quarter of Montpelliéret remaining under the bishop of Maguelone.[10] Until the fourteenth century, Montpellier looked more to the realms of Aragon-Catalonia than to the kingdom of the Capetians in France.[11] Thereafter, in the first half of the fourteenth century, the king of Majorca and the king of France shared jurisdiction over the town, resulting for Martha and her fellow inhabitants in a town of two masters, with French influence ever on the rise.

The French king was certainly a presence for Montpellier inhabitants in Martha's era, given his possession since 1293 of the episcopal quarter of the town, Montpelliéret. In 1349 he would purchase of the seigneurial quarter of Montpellier.[12] In the decade and a half leading up to the 1293 purchase, there had been a heated conflict of jurisdiction between the king of Majorca and the king of France in Montpellier. The Aragonese dynasty had split the lands of James I at his death in 1276. The cadet kingdom of Majorca that resulted included Montpellier. In 1282 it was agreed that the king of France had criminal jurisdiction in the *sénéchausée* of Beaucaire-Nîmes in which Montpellier was located. The court of the seneschal was to be a court of last instance for the royal judge of appeals in Montpellier.[13] Because of this agreement, the name of the king of France was authorized to appear on all public acts in Montpellier. His jurisdiction over notarial acts was of major consequence for business transactions in an area where notarial traditions had been strong since the twelfth century. Through this agreement, coinage of the king of France was to receive the same respect in the territory of Montpellier as money of the king of Majorca. Finally, merchants were affected by the initiatives of the French king Philip IV who established in Montpellier in the 1290s the court of the Petit Scel, a court of voluntary jurisdiction for commercial matters, without territorial limitation. Martha and her sons made reference to this court in their documents of procuration.[14]

The purchase of Montpelliéret from the bishop of Maguelone in 1293 made Philip IV the direct overlord of the king of Majorca for his lordship of Montpellier.[15] The king received all temporal jurisdiction over the quarter of Montpelliéret, though the bishop retained jurisdiction over his clergy and still judged the less important crimes committed by his servants. The presence of a rector in Montpelliéret, representing the king of France, with a court system for civil and criminal matters, would not have been lost on active merchants such as Martha and her sons. All feudal rights over the lordship and the château of Lattes were ceded, with the 1293 purchase, to the king of France. Lattes was the traditional port of Montpellier on the lagoons (*étangs*).[16] Other rights passed to the king, such as the bishop's jurisdiction over the Jews. When Philip IV and his successors began to move against the property of the Jews in the early fourteenth century, those Jews who inhabited Montpellier would not be exempt from these actions.[17]

In the 1330s and 1340s, the political situation of France and Majorca grew increasingly complicated. With the beginnings of the Hundred Years War in 1337, Philip VI of France attempted to raise taxes and troops from towns like Montpellier, creating some financial hardship and chaos for the inhabitants.[18] James III, king of Majorca, was losing territory and ultimately his position to the king of Aragon in the mid-1340s, periodically alienating the king of France who was otherwise occupied with English aggression and could provide no assistance to James.[19] These events would have an impact on Martha and her sons, as they affected Montpellier directly.

In the first half of the fourteenth century, the presence of the papal court at Avignon was of great significance for the market of Montpellier and for merchants like Martha and her sons.[20] Montpellier was one of the stops of Clement V in his wanderings before settling in Avignon in 1309. The financial network of the papal court and the considerable number of consumers in Avignon had an impact on the merchants' and changers' professions in Montpellier, as well as in the area of precious metalwork. Montpellier had early relations with towns of the Provençal coast and towns of the Rhône River valley. While there were relations with Avignon before the arrival of the papal

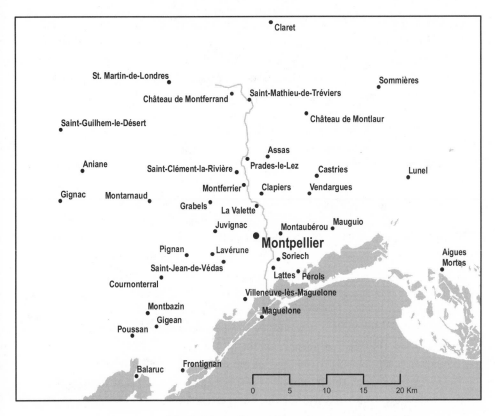

MAP 2. Montpellier and its region.

court in 1309, mentions of the presence of Avignonnais in Montpellier and of Montpelliérains in Avignon multiplied in the first half of the fourteenth century.

Montpellier was located in a region that had experienced deep Roman colonization. The Roman road, Via Domitia (Voie Domitienne)—owing its name to a second-century BCE Roman conqueror—ran south from Beaucaire and Nîmes, crossed the Lez River in the vicinity of Substantion, north of the present Montpellier at about the level of Castelnau, and continued in a western direction to Lavérune, to Béziers, and beyond. This road ran north of the settlement of Montpellier but would be deflected farther south to serve the urban center more fully as the town of Montpellier grew under the lordship of the Guilhem family in the twelfth century.

A second road, also likely predating the medieval era, was the *Cami salinié* or salt road that departed from the Via Domitia above Lunel and ran south to the inland bays below Mauguio, linking the salt-producing areas of Villeneuve-lès-Maguelone, Maguelone, and Vic-la-Gardiole. The only source of salt in the surrounding region was the sea, and the probable antiquity of these saline areas suggests a distant origin for this road.[21]

The town of Montpellier itself was crossed by the *Cami roumieu* or medieval pilgrimage road that originated in Provence and had as its goal the shrine of Santiago de Compostella in Galicia in northwestern Spain.[22] The *Cami roumieu* entered Montpellier by the Nîmes road and exited via the rue de la Saunerie and the road to Béziers. This road brought pilgrimage traffic to Montpellier and stimulated the foundation and prominence of the pilgrimage church of Notre-Dame des Tables. Martha would have been familiar with this venerable road network and with a host of secondary roads in the vicinity, including a road that stretched from Substantion on the left bank of the Lez to the little port of Lattes on the lagoons to the south of town and roads going north, linking Montpellier to the Massif Central and northern France.

Today Montpellier is about seven miles (approximately eleven kilometers) from the Mediterranean. The continual deposit of sand has caused a gradual but progressive distancing of the sea and especially a reconfiguring of the coastline. Between Montpellier and the coast lie a series of lagoons that separate dry land from the sea. At about five kilometers to the south is the old port of Lattes, in existence before the coming of the Greeks to the western Mediterranean basin in the sixth to the fourth centuries BCE. Lattes, on dry land at the edge of marshes and lagoons leading to the sea, served Montpellier and its trade in the period before, during, and after the development of the French royal port of Aigues-Mortes in the second half of the thirteenth century.[23]

It is very difficult, if not impossible, today to reconstruct the topography of the medieval littoral south of Montpellier. Within the space of a lifetime, to say nothing of the centuries separating the fourteenth from the present, there have been natural changes in the lay of the land and in the streambeds.[24] Whatever the exact configuration of the medieval coastline in Martha's day, the fact remains that Montpellier was not a port, necessitating special measures to make possible communication with sea-going vessels. The region was lacking in major natural ports, harboring nothing on a par with Genoa, Marseille, or Barcelona. However, Montpellier's connection with Lattes and, from the mid-thirteenth century, with Aigues-Mortes made it possible for the town to develop a prime role as an international center of Mediterranean imports and exports as well as international financial exchange.

Though not directly on the Mediterranean French coast, Montpellier was very much a part of a maritime environment. Life in Montpellier in the Middle Ages meant life near the sea for women and men. Men were the most directly involved in sea life as fishermen, sailors, pirates, privateers, and traveling merchants.[25] Women tended not to travel on the sea for commercial business, but they might make pilgrimages that took them on the water, and there were certainly many women hangers-on in the crusading ventures of the late eleventh, twelfth, and thirteenth centuries who traversed the Mediterranean. The lagoons separating Montpellier from the coast beyond the port of Lattes were sites of intense fishing operations in the Middle Ages.[26] A maritime environment meant cosmopolitanism, as ideas and products filtered in by sea from distant shores. It also meant that the inhabitants of Montpellier, women and men, were exposed to foreign trends, whether in material culture, business practice, religion, medicine, law, or institutions.

To the north of Montpellier lies a semi-arid region of *garrigues*, with hills of sparse vegetation, interspersed here and there by a peak, such as Pic Saint-Loup, and the towns of Saint-Martin de Londres and Ganges. Beyond lie the Cévennes Mountains with Alès. As one moved north of Montpellier into the *garrigue*, these brush lands were home to aromatic herbs. In the fall, as today, they must have enveloped the town in smells of rosemary, thyme, coriander, basil, and other scents. The *garrigue* land was generally dry and infertile for crops. There were attempts throughout the medieval period to bring isolated areas under cultivation, but these were met with varying success.[27] Sheep and goats were raised in this region and were led north to summer pasturage in the Cévennes Mountains. Livestock from the region of the Montagne Noire around Saint-Pons joined *garrigue* animals for winter grazing on the salt marshes along the coastal plain from Montpellier to Sète.[28]

To the interior and west stretched a series of towns that were the site of regional Languedocian fairs, Villeveyrac, Montagnac, and Pézenas.[29] In the Hérault River valley to the northwest, the origin of the seigneural Guilhem family, are the abbey sites of Aniane and Saint-Guilhem-le-Désert, along with Gignac, and farther north the town of Lodève.[30]

To the northeast of Montpellier, after having traversed the suburb of Castelnau-le-Lez and the town of Lunel, one reaches the old Roman town of Nîmes, about fifty kilometers away. Beyond Nîmes, one enters the Rhône delta and Provence. To the east along the coastal plain lies Mauguio (the medieval Melgueil), the comital capital of the region and the site of the most important local monetary atelier.[31] Aigues-Mortes, built in the mid- and later thirteenth century, lies twenty-six kilometers to the southeast of Montpellier and was accessible via a system of canals and lagoons at the time it served as a regional port.[32] To the southwest, following the coast, are Villeneuve-lès-Maguelone, Frontingnan, Mèze, the lagoon of Thau, and finally Agde, again a port of consequence and the site of a bishopric. The episcopal site of Maguelone, the medieval bishopric of Montpellier, lay near the coast on a narrow band of land in the lagoon off Villeneuve.

The countryside surrounding Montpellier had a semi-arid landscape, ideally suited to vineyards, though the area enjoyed a polyculture with grain growing and market gardening in the Middle Ages. The overall dryness prevented a spring planting of cereals. It is likely that Martha's maternal family possessed vineyards and rural lands. Martha and her sons and the extended Cabanis family had significant investments in vineyards.[33] The vine is favored by Montpellier's climate that is typically Mediterranean with long dry summers and mild winters.[34] While vineyards were cultivated on the hills and in the sandy marshlands, grain was cultivated on the richest lands of the plain.

This cultivation pattern has left its mark in the regional place names. The best examples are two little towns to the west of Montpellier, Cournonsec, a little dry hillside settlement, and Cournonterral, a better-watered territory on the plain. *Terral* means good earth. The biennial rotation system of antiquity—winter wheat alternating with fallow—was still commonly in use during Martha's lifetime. With the disastrous growing years of the first quarter of the fourteenth century, the situation was frequently desperate and famine a common tragedy.[35] Before this, the situation was propitious for town and countryside.

The region and the town experienced considerable prosperity in the twelfth and thirteenth centuries. By Martha's time as a young person in the early fourteenth century, the Mediterranean town of Montpellier had grown in size and prominence from its medieval rural beginnings in the late tenth century.[36] The image of the town in the fourteenth century was one of commercial, financial, and intellectual prowess through the presence of its renowned university.[37] John XXII (1316–34) studied in Montpellier and in his native Cahors before becoming pope. During his papacy, he confirmed statutes for the Faculty of Medicine of Montpellier. Benedict XII (1334–42) accorded new statutes to the Faculty of Law of Montpellier. Urban V (1362–70), born Guillelmus Grimoardi of Gévaudan, received his doctorate in canon law at Montpellier in 1341 and, once pope, would be a benefactor of university life in the town.[38] The presence of the papacy at Avignon in the fourteenth century had a profound impact on Montpellier commercially, artistically, and culturally.[39]

The urban population could count 6,000–9,000 inhabitants about the year 1200, reaching a plateau of around 35,000–40,000 by 1300, significant in size by medieval standards in the era before 1350, though some cities such as Milan had probably 100,000 and Paris 200,000 or more inhabitants.[40] The five decades preceding the Black Death of 1348 were not years of dramatic economic expansion for Montpellier, though some economic resilience can be noted, particularly in the 1330s and 1340s.[41] Montpellier remained a mature urban economy, still prosperous in Martha's era of the first half of the fourteenth century.

Within this population, the urban elite to which Martha belonged represented a relatively small group. If the political elite of Montpellier, based on families with consular participation, yielded 500-plus names, using a conservative multiplying coefficient of 3, 4, or even 5 to account for family members, an upper estimate of 2,500 souls emerges to include the families of consular participants, not a large group in a population of 35,000–40,000.[42] If one includes others called upon for municipal service but not yet serving as consuls, the numbers would be slightly larger. Martha would have known members of this small urban elite of Montpellier to which she belonged. Many of them clustered in the central quarter of town that is the historic district today.[43]

Topographically, Montpellier occupied about forty-five hectares (a little over 111 acres) within the twelfth-century town walls, the Commune Clôture fortifications. In comparison, Narbonne had thirty-seven hectares, while the northern French town of Lille had eighty hectares.[44] Montpellier was perhaps a kilometer in length, within the walls, north to south. The town fortifications ran 3,762 meters, with eleven main gates and additional minor entrances. Along the inside of the walls ran an interior road called the Douze Pans. Outside the fortifications, there was another road called the Douve. It was key for urban defenders to be able to move troops along these paths. Typically, at Montpellier and elsewhere, the walls were encumbered inside by housing, while outside the walls urban trades used the ditches for their work: rope makers spread their cords and wood merchants their lumber.[45]

Two towers of the Commune Clôture survive today: the Tour de la Babette in the southwestern quadrant and the Tour des Pins at the north end of the oval shape enclosed by the city walls.[46] The stone construction of the walls and of significant houses within the town drew on the local quarries of Pignan, Saint-Geniès, and Caunelles.[47] As one approached Montpellier from the sea, the fortifications would likely have been visible. Though the walls are no longer standing, they formed an irregular oval traced by the current urban boulevards.

Comprised of two bourgs, the town of Montpellier recognized a political distinction between the seigneurial quarter of Montpellier and the bishop's sector of Montpelliéret. The two bourgs were spread over three hills: from east to west, there was Montpelliéret, with an elevation of thirty-seven meters; the hill of Notre-Dame or Montpellier at forty-nine meters, with the most important concentration of population; and the Peyrou hill at fifty meters.

The so-called Condamine or central historic section included the area with Notre-Dame des Tables, the signature pilgrimage church, and the first town hall situated on the Herbaria Square.[48] The Herbaria Square was located up the street from Notre-Dame des Tables in a continuation of the central commercial quarter of Montpellier.[49] On one side of the Herbaria Square sat the first town hall.[50] Martha and her husband Guiraudus's family home was near Arc Saint-Nicolas on the rue de l'Aiguillerie in one of the mercers' quarters, not far from the Place Pétrarque today, and a short walk to Notre-Dame des Tables. Martha's sons would later have various holdings in the central business quarters, including houses on the Herbaria Square. The rue de l'Aiguillerie represented a portion of the main east-west axis, the Via Francigena that led across the town from the northeast and Nîmes to Agde and Béziers in the west.

Other quarters such as the Blancaria near the Merdanson stream, the Coirataria, and Castelmoton, which had sheltered Jews before their 1306 expulsion, were distinguished by their own identity in Martha's lifetime.[51] The early suburbs were extensive: the Courreau, the Saunerie, Lattes, Pila Saint-Gély, Villefranche, and Saint-Jacques, with important religious institutions established there. Some of this territory had been incorporated within the late twelfth-century Commune Clôture.[52]

Urban statutes regulated where artisanal activities could take place. Tanning was a particularly dirty process, due to the toxic chemicals involved—tannic acid, dung, and lime. Tanners were in need of water for their trade and often relegated to the outskirts of towns because of the smells associated with their activities. Butchers also saw their activities regulated.[53] The odors

FIGURE 1. Aerial view of Montpellier. Image from the author's collection.

from tanning and butchering were strong and would easily have offended
urban inhabitants. Tawing, which was Martha's father's profession, did not
use acid, but with oil and alum and eggs, it would also have been a messy
operation.[54] Given the presence in Montpellier of a major university, it is
possible that Martha's father was involved in the production of tawed leather
for book binding.

Water was in short supply in Montpellier.[55] Limited numbers of fountains and wells in the town and its suburbs supplied what water there was for
domestic needs. Originally, the central hill of Notre-Dame had a water
supply, drawn from underground wells and springs, which was adequate for
the town's population. But, by the end of the thirteenth century, as early
as 1267, Montpellier had begun to suffer from a lack of drinking water;
the town consuls were proposing new methods to meet the urban water
requirements.[56]

The river system in the immediate vicinity of Montpellier, poor, if
almost inexistent in the dry season, was not conducive to the kind of navigation possible on the Rhône or even on the Hérault at Agde, the Orb at
Béziers, or the Aude at Carcassonne. Two small streams, tributaries of the
Lez, crossed the nucleus of Montpellier, the most prominent being the Merdanson; both were canalized underground in later eras. Already in the Middle
Ages, the guardians of the fortifications (*ouvriers de la Commune Clôture*)
rerouted water courses occasionally. These regional and local rivers tended to
dry up in warm months and to flow or overflow in the rainy months of the
winter and spring.

Merchants and urban inhabitants overall were concerned about the
urban environment, as living space was cramped, water in short supply, and
the streets extremely narrow. Urban statutes regulated rights of way, possession of rainwater, and the passage of light and air. There were building
restrictions in many sets of statutes that governed the extent of overhangs
and the runoff of rainwater. In Montpellier in 1205, statutes provided for the
deputation of two men to supervise the maintenance of the roads, walls of
buildings, gutters, and garbage.[57] Neighbors' complaints abounded in such
tight quarters. In the dense urban center where Martha lived as a married
woman, a widow, and likely as a child, light must have been at a premium,
even at midday.[58]

Municipal officials were responsible for latrine placement, and water use
may also have devolved upon those individuals responsible for the urban
walls. In the archives of the Commune Clôture are occasional permits to

build gutters or drainage canals.[59] In several cases, fines were issued for the illegal construction of latrines and gutters; frequently building permits included the prohibition to construct these. Since the exterior trench of the Montpellier fortifications was undoubtedly used for urban waste disposal, the involvement of the municipality is understandable, from the standpoint of defense but also that of urban hygiene. The defense preparedness of the inner and outer roads of the fortifications would have been of concern to urban inhabitants.[60]

The transmission of information about important events and crises took several forms in Montpellier. Bells were undoubtedly the common method of transmitting information to a medieval urban population en masse. Attacks would have been announced via bells, and fires as well. Bells pierced the day and the night with different chimes, usually of warning or summons. Without newspapers, mass dissemination of news and of official announcements came through town criers who proclaimed information of all kinds throughout the town. In Montpellier, the urban defense organization, the *ouvriers de la Commune Clôture*, used written notices posted at several gates of the town to advertise their *criées de bans*, official pronouncements, also published orally, mentioning all that might be detrimental to the defense of the town and the efficacity of the walls.[61]

Criminals, wrongdoers, and debtors were brought to justice via town criers who summoned them to court to account for their actions or failure to pay. Martha would have heard these summonses at the *trivium* of the court of the king of Majorca; in the Canabassaria (linen quarter); in the canton of the Pelliparia (furriers' quarter); at the old court in Montpelliéret, and elsewhere in town. Rules and regulations regarding government and business were recited annually to recall for merchants and other urban inhabitants the details of local business practice, while criers shared letters and orders from political authorities that imparted import/export information, monetary information, and fiscal demands, usually the result of war planning and operations.[62] Municipal officials took oaths of office at the annual public ceremony ushering in the new municipal administration.

Beyond the pealing of bells, the hustle and bustle in the streets of Montpellier would have been deafening in the center of town, with people hawking goods, the creaking of carts transporting merchandise, and the braying and whinnying of animals of transport.[63] At the central Herbaria Square in Montpellier, day-labor hiring took place during the night, and then, at dawn, hucksters and resellers set up stalls and stands to sell vegetables and chickens.[64] For Martha and her fellow inhabitants, Montpellier was a lively, crowded urban environment.

Although the first half of the fourteenth century brought challenges to the inhabitants of Montpellier, this was still an era of relative prosperity. Martha and her sons would flourish. But I am getting ahead of myself. First, let us meet Martha's family and investigate her early years in Montpellier.

CHAPTER 2

Martha, Her Family, Their Social Rank, and Political Influence

Moreover, I have been able to make this present gift among the living
that I make to you, my daughter, stipulating and receiving, through
the motive of maternal love and because of the final services and
kindnesses you did and are doing for me.

—Martha's mother Jacoba's words to her daughter on 12 February 1342

In one of the few moments of emotion present in the Cabanis register of
the notary Guillelmus Nogareti, Jacoba, Martha's mother, related the reason for her gift of land to her daughter. She stated that she did so out of
maternal love. Even more telling is the fact that she had an afterthought
and clearly asked the notary to elaborate in a footnote to be inserted in the
text that the gift was made on account of the services and kindnesses that
Martha had shown her and was showing her. Martha's was a family with
affective ties.

The concept of family, the cement of medieval society, has been the
subject of debate.[1] It has long been acknowledged that a vision of the family
evolving from an extended form to a nuclear form in the course of the Middle
Ages was in need of revision.[2] In fact, the family followed a life cycle that at
times gave it an extended form, with several generations living under one
roof, and at times a nuclear configuration.[3] How the term *family* is defined
is also at issue.

A family can be formed from blood ties, from marriage alliances, from
adoption, and from the spiritual linkages such as god-parenthood that were

particularly important in the Middle Ages. The French terms of *parentèle*, *lignage*, *lignée* (all reflecting the concept in English of lineage) indicate medieval family ties.[4] The term *familia* (family) was very vague and could include blood relatives, domestic servants, clients, and others associated with the household. The 1205 statutes of Montpellier used the term *familia* to describe the domestic household, defined in the Montpellier statutes as "wife, slaves, freed servants, paid servants, sons and nephews, apprentices or students, pupils, . . . and women who were members of the *familia*."[5] There is no evidence in Montpellier for the existence of large extended familial groupings such as the *alberghi* in Genoa and the *consorterie* in parts of Tuscany, or of urban *lignages*, or the clans that existed in some medieval towns.[6] Jacques Heers noted large groupings of family and clienteles in Bruges, Douai, Strasbourg, and Metz and found some evidence of urban towers at Aix-en-Provence and Avignon, along with the amphitheater fortifications of Arles and Nîmes.[7] There is nothing similar in Montpellier or in Barcelona where Stephen Bensch identified patterns of familial alignment that distinguished Barcelona from many Mediterranean societies.[8] In the case of the family founded by Martha and her husband Guiraudus de Cabanis, apprentices, entourage members, and factors, along with domestic servants and others, may have been added to the list of possible members of their large mercantile household. Relations, networks, and linkages were essential to survival and certainly assisted medieval individuals in facing up to the challenges of the time. These began with family.[9]

In a study that argues for Martha's business prominence, the question of where she got her talent is germane. Her birth family provides some suggestions. Martha came from a commercial/industrial background that was very common in medieval Montpellier. Her parents were Petrus de Tornamira, tawer or bleacher (*blancherius*), and Jacoba, the daughter of Raymundus Franchi, grain merchant. Martha's father's occupation was connected to leather. He shared the last name of, and may have been related to, a very prominent Montpellier family, the Tornamira, whose connections were multiple throughout the south of France and in Majorca.[10] One branch of the family specialized in the law. A Petrus de Tornamira was recorded as a jurist and law professor in the early fourteenth century, having studied at the University of Bologna in the 1260s. His son Marcus and another relation named Johannes were also doctors of law. Petrus the jurist's prominence permitted his daughter to marry within the regional nobility in 1301. Family members were part of the urban nobility as *burgenses* in the early 1340s. Petrus de

Tornamira himself served as assessor for the consuls at least five times in the late thirteenth and early fourteenth centuries.[11]

Homonyms were common in Montpellier. If there was no close family relationship between the legal specialist Petrus and Martha's father, at the very least, they were colleagues in the municipal administration.[12] Petrus de Tornamira, the tawer, was a successful artisan and entrepreneur. He served as town consul at least once in 1295 when he is specifically identified as P. de Tornamira, tawer.[13] He was likely the P. de Tornamira in the consular lists of 1301 and 1311, as lawyers were not admitted to the consulate at this date, though they served in positions such as bailiff (*bayle*) and assessor. Martha's father would have enjoyed high status through his political service. As noted earlier, his profession of tawer may have connected him to leather book binding, for which there must have been a considerable market in a university town like Montpellier.[14]

Since the 1204 charter of customs, town government had been in the hands of the consuls who were responsible for urban defense, fiscal and economic decisions, municipal legislation, and de facto legal jurisdiction. In consulates, the lord retained theoretical jurisdictional prerogatives.[15] In Montpellier there were twelve consuls, drawn from among the most important occupations of the town. The tawers/bleachers (*blancherii*) participated in town government as consuls in the tenth consular position. Tawers were alone at this position, not having to share with any other group (see Table 1). From five tawer candidates one consul would be chosen.

The tawers served in the Tuesday ladder of the Commune Clôture urban defense organization, managed by the Ouvriers de la Commune Clôture.[16] From 1204, defense of the town gates was in the hands of seven groups of trades called ladders (*échelles*). There was one ladder staffed by specific trades for each day of the week in the organization of urban defense. The particular grouping of trades by day of the week was related to the numbers of participants in each occupation, driven by military, not social, considerations.[17]

Consular election was a matter of co-optation and chance. Five electors were drawn from each of the seven ladders of urban defense to make up a group of thirty-five, not eligible for consular election that year; from these a group of seven were chosen by lot. They, along with the outgoing consuls, designated sixty consular candidates, five for each position, from a determined group of occupations given in the schema of consular recruitment. One consul was chosen from among the five for each of the twelve consular positions through a drawing.[18]

Table 1. Consular Recruitment

9 changers 1 pepperer	2 consuls
9 members of the Red Drapery 5 members of the High Drapery both alternate with grain merchants	3 consuls
4 furriers 1 merchant of the rue de la Corregerie	1 consul
3 hemp/linen merchants 1 mercer 1 spice merchant-apothecary of Saint Nicolas	1 consul
4 butchers 1 fish merchant or fisherman	1 consul
2 leathersmiths 2 shoemakers and 1 blacksmith or 2 blacksmiths and 1 shoemaker	1 consul
5 tawers	1 consul
2 wood merchants of the Lattes gate 2 wood merchants of the Peyrou gate 2 masons	1 consul
5 agricultural workers	1 consul

The trade in skins and leather was an important one in Montpellier. The highest quality leather came from Spain as *cordouan*, tooled after the Arabic fashion, but the term *cordouan* came to be applied to luxury-quality leather in general, and there was local production in Montpellier. Thus a thirteenth-century list of taxes of the convent of Saint-Pierre de Lagny, in the Champagne Fair town of Lagny, would mention "cordouan de Montpellier et de Marseille."[19] Montpellier had a significant trade in skins and leather in the late thirteenth and first half of the fourteenth centuries.[20] Leather was imported from Spain, and skins and leather were sold in the town and shipped to the Champagne Fairs. The urban topography reflected the concentration in leather and skins in quarters called the Blancaria (tawing) and the Coirataria (tanning); see Map 3.[21]

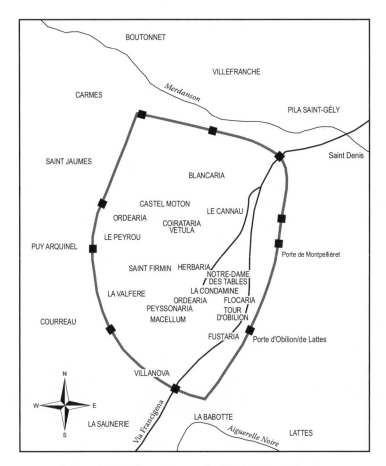

MAP 3. Montpellier: the town, fortifications, and suburbs.

A prestigious trade in the Middle Ages, tawing produced remarkable leather products. The process involved alum or oil that was rubbed into the hide with salt. The hide was then stretched and softened using egg yolks and oil.[22] The process itself was costly, and the final product was a fine white leather, much prized in the Middle Ages. Martha's father was, thus, an important member of the urban elite.

Martha's mother, Jacoba, was the daughter of grain merchant (*orgerius*), Raymundus Franchi. Martha's maternal grandfather, R. Franc, as he is called in the consular lists, was a frequent presence as town consul, with the name appearing first in 1271, then again every few years between 1280 and 1313.[23] In

1331, a R. Franc major (the elder) was listed. It is likely that homonyms were again in play. Whether this is still the same grain merchant is questionable, though he could have been a relative.[24] The Franc or Franchi family of grain merchants was prominent, but it is not possible to say much about specific individuals of Martha's grandfather's generation.[25] In the case of the grain merchants, they competed for three consular positions (three, four, and five of the twelve) with drapers. They were part of the Friday ladder of the urban defense organization.

Grain merchants were involved in provisioning the town from local grain but also, and importantly in times of shortage, from imported grain produced as far away as the Black Sea. Raymundus Franchi may have been wealthy, as he could have made a lot of money in the grain trade in the last decades of the thirteenth century when the town's population was growing and the beginnings of agricultural crisis were visible in Europe. The town chronicle of Montpellier, the official source of information for the town consulate comprised of merchants, artisans, and agricultural workers, recorded brief political news from an early date and, until the thirteenth century, focused local attention on the Hispanic world to which Montpellier was linked. The chronicle was a source of notations of climatic, political, and geographic events, especially from the later thirteenth century on.[26] The beginning of a cooling trend can be noted as early as 1262, when, in the month of January, the chronicle recorded a great snowfall.[27] Martha's father and grandfather would have been alive at this time and certainly startled, as were their co-citizens, to see snow, which almost never falls along the Mediterranean coast of France. Climatic problems continued, and, in 1285, the chronicle made note of food shortages for all of Christendom and the high price of grain.[28] Things only got worse in the fourteenth century when the chronicle noted climatic and natural disasters: an earthquake in Montpellier in 1309 on 29 March; on 21 August, the flood of a tributary of the Lez River, causing damage to houses in the suburbs. In 1313, drought descended on the region, necessitating processions to beg for rain that finally came.[29] The importance of the grain trade cannot be overestimated in an era of agricultural shortages.[30]

It is highly likely that Petrus de Tornamira and Raymundus Franchi became acquainted when serving in consular roles in the 1290s and early 1300s.[31] There were many occasions for these two to interact as members of the governing elite of the town, even though they exercised very different professions. The marriage of Jacoba and Petrus was a prestigious one of the consular elite. Whether they had children beyond Martha is not known.

We have no information about Martha's relationship with her father and only late hints regarding the closeness of Martha with her blood family at the end of her mother's life. There is documented affection between Jacoba and Martha, in the passage quoted at the beginning of this chapter and expressed in an otherwise dry notarial contract of 1342, whereby Jacoba, who was a widow at this time, made a gift while living (*donatio inter vivos*) of land in Boutonnet, a northeastern suburb of Montpellier, to Martha, who used it in a land exchange.[32] Jacoba spoke of her maternal love for Martha and the care she had experienced at Martha's hands. Martha's mother lived independently into the early 1340s, as she had the notary draw up this gift to her daughter in her own house in 1342, though she must have been close to death when she made this contract. End-of-life care can be very involved. There is no indication that Jacoba came to live with Martha, but, in a town of limited topographical extent, Martha may still have been close by and able to provide nursing assistance or to manage this kind of help for her declining mother. We have no indications of siblings for Martha; if she were the only remaining child of her mother or the only one nearby, her assistance would have been critical. It is likely Martha had uncles, brothers of her mother, and cousins, given the continuing recurrence of the name R. Franc in the consular lists. However, there remains no evidence of their interaction or intervention in her life and that of her sons.

If Martha were between fifteen and twenty years of age at the birth of her eldest son in 1315—he was eleven at the death of her husband in 1326—she may have been born between 1295 and 1300.[33] Jacoba at her death in 1342 may have been in her early sixties if she was about fifteen to twenty when Martha was born ca. 1295. Thus, following her mother's example, Martha could easily have lived another twenty years after 1342, into the 1360s. The likelihood is, however, that she died in the 1348 plague, along with her sons.[34]

As a girl growing up in Montpellier at the end of the thirteenth century, Martha would have experienced the last of the medieval heyday of the town.[35] This was a period of economic prosperity and population growth. Where within the town Martha grew up and where her family home was are unknown. Montpellier was a compact town with no neighborhood within the walls very far from another. The quarters of the Coirataria and the Blancaria were within the walls, not far from the central elite quarter near Notre-Dame des Tables and not far from Martha's future home as a married woman and widow near Arc Saint-Nicolas on the rue de l'Aiguillerie.

Martha's background would have been anything but parochial. Montpellier was a cosmopolitan place. Foreign merchants frequented the markets of

Montpellier in large numbers. The notarial registers show them registering many contracts in person in town. With a grandfather in the grain trade and a father in the luxury leather business, Martha would have had broad geographic horizons. The world to which she would have been exposed vicariously included the Champagne Fairs and Spanish outlets for the leather trade and the whole of the Mediterranean world for the grain trade.

We know nothing about girls' childhoods in Montpellier, but we can speculate about Martha's experiences on the basis of our knowledge of children elsewhere and in regard to the town of Montpellier itself. Martha as a young child may have played in the streets of Montpellier. She may have traveled outside the town with her father or grandfather to visit their landholdings.[36] She would have heard her father and grandfather speak of foreign places connected to their trades. She may have overheard discussion of urban politics. She may have had a nurse who sang rhymes to her and taught her to talk. Perhaps it was Jacoba herself who was Martha's primary caregiver.[37] Girl children were often taught letters within the home. Martha may have attended a convent school, but more likely she was schooled at home in the vernacular Occitan dialect of Languedoc. Whether she acquired Latin is unknown, but she may have picked up some useful vocabulary in the artisanal and mercantile milieu in which she was raised. Later in her life, notaries would write business contracts for her in Latin. As the daughter of a skilled artisan, Martha may have acquired mathematical background as well.

Martha's unbringing was undoubtedly a mixture of instruction and play. Martha would have had toys. She may have had dolls and little cups and perhaps a cupboard. Dolls could be made of earthenware, wood, wax, or cloth.[38] They might be painted and clothed. As Martha grew older, she was probably taught to sew, to do needlework, perhaps to spin. From her mother she undoubtedly learned about household management. One wonders whether her father or grandfather took her aside to explain the workings of their artisanal and mercantile occupations. As a child, Martha may have known the personnel associated with their trades and run in and out of their workshops.

The options open to Martha as a young woman embarking on life were several, but a woman's ability to take advantage of opportunities varied greatly with family origin and family fortune. Women's choices across social strata were thus often very different. Young woman of property usually married, as Martha did, though some elite women of Montpellier entered nunneries.[39] Family ties were expanded, and larger communities were created through marriage, with the economic foundation based on a dowry, the contribution of the bride's father to the marriage, and a contribution called an augment (*augmentum*) from the groom and his family.[40] The augment had replaced the northern European institution of dower in southern France by the twelfth century.[41]

The choice of a groom was important. Who made the advances? An appropriate marriage for Martha would have been a primary priority for her parents Jacoba and Petrus. Given the compactness of the town, one wonders whether Martha knew Guiraudus de Cabanis, her future husband, before the marriage. If there was an age difference between them, as argued in Chapter 3 below, did he as a young man know her as a child? If they were close in age, Martha and Guiraudus might have met each other in religious activities, in encounters in the streets of Montpellier, or in other activities involving young people. The Cabanis family was well established in Montpellier. Petrus de Cabanis, a relative of Guiraudus, was town consul in 1305 and would have known both Martha's father and grandfather. Martha would have been prepared from an early age for marriage, for the management of a household, for the duties of motherhood, and perhaps for the partnership in business with a future husband. One wonders if her mother Jacoba was involved in her husband's trade and imparted her expertise to Martha.

Marriage was a business transaction in the Middle Ages, even if the couple were in love. Martha's marriage was undoubtedly a contractual arrangement, with serious discussion of the financial details involved. A dotal contract would have been drawn up before the notary.[42] For a woman of Martha's station, her father would have been expected to provide a significant dowry. What comprised Martha's dowry? In Martha's era, the dowry was often constituted in real property or a mixture of money and real estate. Later in life, we learn that Martha had real estate of her own in her widowhood, houses in the Coirataria area of the tanners, which she rented out. Perhaps these were part of her dowry. It would have been logical that her father had real property holdings in this quarter of town. Martha also had vineyards that she managed as a widow.[43] These too could have figured in her dowry, as they may have been part of her father's investments that he transferred to her on her marriage. Most self-respecting members of the commercial elite of Montpellier had investments in vineyards in the suburbs and surrounding region. The expectation would have been that Martha would bring a substantial dowry to Guiraudus, a successful mercer and merchant and member of an important extended mercantile family of Montpellier's elite. Martha would have benefitted from her grandfather the grain merchant's status and from the prominence of her tawer father. Guiraudus would have been expected to provide some resources as well; the augment may have included lands and cash. His father may have assisted in that contribution if he were still living.

In Martha's case, we have no information about her dowry or augment or about Guiraudus's will. In his will, a husband could make arrangements for the return of the dowry. A wife could expect the return of her dowry if the marriage was dissolved through death or other means. There was the expectation in southern Europe of the return of the dowry at the death of the husband, as Marie Kelleher noted.[44] Of the 160 Montpellier wills I have analyzed in the period before 1350, thirty-six made arrangement for the return of dowry to a wife who was widowed.[45] In the case of remarriage, additional arrangements might come into play. There is no indication that Martha ever remarried, and it is possible that Guiraudus in his will required Martha to refrain from remarriage in order to benefit from her status as wealthy widow and guardian of their sons.[46] There were only seven cases of remarriage noted in the wills. In the 132 marriage contracts before 1350 that I have studied, there was the occasional stipulation that a widow would lose the benefits of testamentary bequests and dowry if she remarried.[47]

A woman's right to inherit also reinforced the family finances and her own personal fortune and economic livelihood. She might inherit from her parents, her grandparents, her godparents, and other relations, and from her husband at his death. She might also inherit from her children. As noted earlier, Martha received a *donatio inter vivos*, a gift of land in the Montpellier suburb of Boutonnet from her mother while she was still alive.[48] Whatever the source of wealth, once widowed, it was necessary for a woman to manage her property herself or to designate some manager in her stead. In addition to marriage contracts and wills, notarial registers contain information revealing women's access to the urban and rural economy of the region of Montpellier.[49]

Martha's family was of solid commercial and artisanal rank. Her father and maternal grandfather had served in the municipal government of Montpellier. Her upbringing undoubtedly gave her the skills to be a good wife to Guiraudus and later to participate on her own and on behalf of her fatherless sons in the urban economy.

Women of many economic and social backgrounds participated in financial transactions, in sales of luxury products and agricultural commodities, in real estate transactions, in partnerships, in apprenticeships, making distinctions with men's activities more a matter of numbers and scale than of type.[50] Men tended to engage in larger transactions and investments. Martha de Cabanis, however, was a major player. To understand the foundation of her actions, we can begin with an examination of her marriage, Martha's husband Guiraudus, and her Cabanis in-laws.

CHAPTER 3

Marriage, the Groom, and the In-Laws

I, indeed, the said Bertranda, giving myself in the said legitimate
marriage with the said dowry to you, the said Guillelmus Audemarii,
and handing myself over to you as your legitimate wife, and receiving
you as my legitimate husband, promise and convey to you, receiving,
that I will always be good and legal [*sic*] to you and yours, and I will
never deceive you or yours in anything. On the contrary I will always
bring you and yours good faith.

> —A woman's perspective on marriage in Montpellier
> on 19 January 1328

There are no documents like the above surviving to inform us of the particular circumstances in which Martha married the merchant and mercer Guiraudus de Cabanis sometime before 1315, the date of the birth of her oldest living
son, called Guiraudus after his father.[1] As noted in the previous chapter, we
have no information about the nature of Martha's dowry or whether she
received an inheritance on the death of her father. According to statutes of
Montpellier and of many other southern French towns, dowried daughters
were not expected to participate after marriage in further paternal inheritance, at least in intestate situations.[2] However, Montpellier testamentary
practice permitted the testator to decide about bequests. Dowries in Martha's
era were often in both real property and cash, though the cash dowry was
growing in frequency in the fourteenth century.[3] Marriage with community
of property was also a trend from the late thirteenth century, though, again,
no information exists for the union of Martha and Guiraudus.[4]

Demographers distinguish two marriage models for late medieval and
early modern Europe: a European marriage pattern involving an age of

marriage in the mid-twenties, the woman twenty-three, the man twenty-six. The European model includes a significant number of people who remained unmarried. The Mediterranean marriage model sees women marrying in their mid-teens (fifteen or sixteen) and men marrying for the first time at twenty-five to thirty or even older.[5] Works by Claude Carrère regarding Barcelona, Rebecca Winer on Perpignan, and Christiane Klapisch-Zuber and David Herlihy on Tuscany, among others, have identified a pattern of marriage for merchants of the western Mediterranean world coming after an initial period of travel for the purpose of establishing or expanding the family fortune.[6] Returning home, these older men then married young women. In cities such as Florence, the remarriage of widowed men could extend the age gap even more. Though these marriage models have now been called into question in detail and applicability to all social strata, the Mediterranean model remains the likely marriage pattern for Martha and most women of the southern French urban elite.[7]

The 132 surviving marriage-related contracts of the Montpellier notarial documents and charters before 1350 took a variety of forms: actual marriage contracts, dowry contracts, dowry acquittals, and donations on behalf of marriage (*propter nuptias*) or augments (*augmenta*), the southern French version of dower that were the contributions of the grooms and their families at marriage. In contrast Rebecca Winer found seventy-nine marriage contracts in thirteenth-century Perpignan with two types of contracts.[8] The majority recorded the creation of the marriage with the consent of bride and groom, and the approval of the families. The second type dealt with financial arrangements for an already constituted marriage, generally without a record of consent. Relatives were present in sixty-six of the Perpignan contracts.

In the majority of the Montpellier marriage contracts, the groom acted alone on his own behalf across all levels of society in this urban environment, a fact suggesting that he was at least eighteen and probably twenty-five years.[9] Women, regardless of age, were always accompanied by family members on the occasion of their marriage, if such relations survived. The long widowhood of Martha suggests that she married young. Women of the elite married early and were often widowed at a young age.[10] The youth of their sons at the death of Guiraudus in 1326, (four, eight, and eleven) is consistent with the Mediterranean marriage model, though we do not know how old Guiraudus was at his death.

For Guiraudus, the situation is much less clear. Given the absence of age data in marriage contracts, the custom of men marrying late in life cannot be demonstrated conclusively, but it is likely that Montpellier followed the pattern of late marriage for elite men of mercantile status common in the Mediterranean world. It can be argued that Guiraudus was considerably older at marriage than Martha was. According to the historian Jan Rogozinski, who based his reasoning on the complex electoral procedure for the selection of the town government of consuls in Montpellier, it was unlikely that anyone under age forty held consular office.[11] While not elected as one of the twelve town consuls, selected annually, Guiraudus served on a commission (Quatorze de la Chapelle) to investigate consular accounting issues as late as October 1326 and was dead by December 1326.[12] Since there is no record of his having been a consul, this fact would provide an argument in favor of his being no more than forty at death.[13] This appointment for Guiraudus was likely a reflection of maturity and position, but the question remains open as to whether the political situation would have demanded younger men who were not cronies of the consuls. Given the succession of members of the same family (at least individuals with similar surnames) in the consulate, it is probable that even young men were allied to former or current consuls in their own families or in colleagues' families. That said, it seems likely that Guiraudus was a mature man when he served on the commission. Guiraudus can be traced as early as 1317 at Perpignan and again in 1317 in connection with debts from the Champagne Fairs, at Perpignan in 1324, and at Marseille in 1325.[14] His Champagne Fair debts suggest an experienced businessman in 1317. We have no clues to Guiraudus's age at his marriage, but it is possible to provide a range of possibilities. Guiraudus's death when his youngest son was four would be consistent with the Mediterranean pattern of older marriage for men of mercantile status, though we do not know the cause of his death and there is nothing that rules out his having been a young father, seventeen or eighteen at the birth of his first son, perhaps dying of accident, disease, or foul play in his late twenties. He may thus have been anywhere from his late twenties to early fifties when he died in 1326 but was more likely older than younger. Martha and Guiraudus's sons Guiraudus and Jacobus would marry in their early twenties, as we will see. If they were following in a family tradition of their father, then the Mediterranean model would need revision here, but their early marriages may have been a result of the loss of their father in childhood.

The marriage of Martha and Guiraudus was fruitful. The age separation of their three sons (Guiraudus, born in 1315, Jacobus, born in 1318, and Johannes, born in 1322) makes it possible that Martha lost children in between these births. The nursing of boys, sometimes extending over two years, limited, though did not prevent, the rhythm of childbearing. Childcare was one of Martha's primary responsibilities. The use of wet nurses was common in Montpellier, and Martha may have employed them when the children were under two.[15] Women of modest status participated in wet-nursing and in domestic service. We have evidence for this from Montpellier and from elsewhere such as Florence and Perpignan. The work was attractive, as a wet nurse usually had just one child at a time.[16] The Cabanis had the resources to fund this type of childcare. By the same token, wet nurses were certainly an option for wealthy merchant families, and their employment, with the mother no longer nursing, removed the obstacle to frequent pregnancies.[17] The large Cabanis household would also have had domestics to assist with the care of the boys.

That Martha produced sons and not daughters would have played well with the mercantile family into which she married. In the extended Cabanis family, there were mostly boys. In the Petrus senior line, there was only one daughter and five sons (see Table 2). Sons were needed for business, and the fact of having sons would have positioned Martha well, as it did many medieval women, including queens.[18]

Though Martha's mother Jacoba will appear in one act in the Nogareti notarial register to make her a gift, the vast documentation available in the Nogareti register and to a lesser degree in the registers of the notary Holanie concerns Martha and her sons, not Martha's maternal and paternal relatives, the Franc and Tornamira families, for whom we have little information. More information survives for the Cabanis family, her husband Guiraudus's relations. Consideration of in-laws is particularly important in Martha's case. Martha gravitated in her business operations toward the Cabanis side of the family where links with collateral branches of the family were many. It is likely that she would have left her dowry and her dower/augment in the estate.[19] The remaining sources reveal several Cabanis branches, and the relationships among them are not at all straightforward.

The patrilineal line of Martha's husband Guiraudus's family invites numerous hypotheses. This side of the family is worth exploring in detail, as Martha, once widowed, and her sons were intimately connected with the Cabanis business enterprise and with extended family members. Before the end of the thirteenth century traces of direct family ancestry for the Cabanis family are difficult to reconstruct.[20] We begin to find mentions of the Cabanis family at the end of the thirteenth century.

Table 2. Cabanis Family Branches

Progenitor: Petrus de Cabana[s] the old (*vetus*), mercer 1293

Martha + Guiraudus de Cabanis, mercer (dead in 1326)
  Children:
        Guiraudus born 1315 + to a daughter of the changer Salellis
        Jacobus born 1318 + married
        Johannes born 1322

Petrus de Cabanis *maior diebus* (senior), mercer (dead before 1336) + sister of
Nicholas Escuderii, mercer
  Children:
        Petrus, mercer, + Ermessendis, daughter of Petrus Masse, *jurisperitus,*
          emancipated before his father's death
          Children:
                Petrus, 14 in 1343
        Jacobus, linen merchant (*canabasserius*), emancipated before his father's
          death
        Maria + Johannes Naturalis, pepperer (will recorded in August 1325,
          died sometime thereafter)
          Children:
                Johannes Naturalis
                Flors + Jacobus Oliverii, merchant
                Guiraudus, over 20 in 1336
                Sibiunda, over 14 in 1336
        Johannes (dead by 1336) + Causida
        Stephanus, *legum professor*, emancipated before 1336, *miles* by 1342
        Guillelmus, merchant in Châlons sur Sâone, emancipated before 1336

Jacobus, draper + Bernarda mercer
  Children:
        Jacobus, *jurisperitus* in 1343
        Guillelmus, canon of Maguelone in 1343

The Cabanis name is very common. Numerous individuals named
Cabanis appeared in the surviving evidence. Thus, attempts to establish family relationships must in some cases remain speculative. It is possible that the
family came from the region of Ganges or closer to Montpellier from the
region of Aubagne where they later held property.[21] Regardless of the origins
of the family, the links among the three Cabanis branches in Table 2 (those
of Petrus, Guiraudus, and Jacobus) are indicative of close ties. A witness by
the name of Petrus de Cabana[s], the old, mercer, appeared in 1293.[22] Given

a similarity of last name and profession, he is perhaps the father, grandfather, or great uncle of Martha's husband Guiraudus. Petrus de Cabanis, senior (*maior diebus*), likely the son of Petrus the old, was mentioned as the owner of a house near Arc Saint-Nicolas in central Montpellier, along with an associate in 1301.[23] This Petrus was a municipal consul in 1305.[24] Petrus senior can be identified with the late Petrus, mercer, whose intestate succession occasioned a family compromise in 1336.[25] In that succession compromise, there was mention of a house of the late Petrus near Arc Saint-Nicolas.[26] Martha's late husband Guiraudus, tentatively identified as a relation of Petrus, also had a house near Arc Saint-Nicolas that was Martha and her sons' family home where most of her notarial acts were drafted.[27] That they were all members of the same extended family is reinforced by their shared trades and the topographic proximity of their real estate holdings.

At the time of the succession compromise, there were four living sons of the late Petrus: Petrus junior, Jacobus, Stephanus, and Guillelmus. There were also a widowed daughter named Maria, who was known by her married name of Maria Naturale from her marriage to the late Johannes Naturalis, pepperer, and a daughter-in-law, Causida, the widow of a deceased son Johannes. Petrus junior was a merchant, married to Johanna. Jacobus was a linen merchant (*canabasserius*), with a wife named Ermessendis. The emancipation of two of the sons of Petrus, Guillelmus and Stephanus, and their adult professions, along with the adulthood in 1336 of Petrus's grandchildren, offspring of his daughter Maria and her late husband Johannes Naturalis, suggests that Petrus senior may have been of an older generation than Martha's husband, Guiraudus, though the latter predeceased him.[28] Then, too, Petrus may have been a much older brother of Guiraudus. Emancipation was a common practice in the Middle Ages, often involving the freeing of serfs. In the urban context of the Cabanis family, it signified the freeing of children from paternal power, *patria potestas*, discussed in Chapter 6 below.

Maria and Johannes had four children: two sons, Johannes and Guiraudus, and two daughters, Sibiunda who was not yet married in 1336, and Flos who married Jacobus Oliverii, a business associate of Martha's sons.[29] The younger Johannes Naturalis also had business contacts with Martha's sons. The sons of Martha and Guiraudus would appear to be contemporaries in age of the grandchildren of Petrus senior. In large families today, it is not uncommon for young uncles and aunts and the oldest children of the next generation to be close in age. Whatever the precise blood relationship among these three branches, at a minimum the lives of specific individuals of these three Cabanis branches were intertwined. It is worth recalling that, in the Middle Ages, in large, extended families, ties among distant cousins, fourth or fifth cousins, could be as close as or closer than those among siblings.[30]

Though limited data regarding the real estate of Petrus's branch's outside Montpellier have survived, there is some evidence for coincidence of land-holding between the families of Petrus and Guiraudus, reinforcing their ties. In regard to the third Cabanis branch, nothing is known of the draper Jacobus's landholdings, though I am speculating that he too was a relative of Martha's sons on the basis of occupation and business ties. The families of Petrus and Guiraudus held vineyards at Montaubérou, a prized grape-growing location, as did many other Montpelliérains.[31] Both the Petrus and Guiraudus branches had houses near Arc Saint-Nicolas; their holdings of houses were numerous and widely dispersed in the town.[32] As noted earlier, there is no evidence of pronounced neighborhood groupings similar to Genoese *alberghi* or Tuscan tower societies, *consorterie*, or clans.[33] However, Montpellier streets frequently housed specific trades, carrying the name of the occupation, and one of four groups of mercers clustered near the Arc Saint-Nicolas, along the rue de l'Aiguillerie, where Martha and her sons lived.[34]

The first names in the Cabanis genealogy, even that of Guiraudus, are common in the south of France in this time period.[35] Martha's sons have names from this *Namengut*, rather than the names of her father Petrus and her grandfather Raymundus, though the name Petrus occurs in both Martha's and the Cabanis families. In each of the three Cabanis branches, the oldest son was named after the father. Martha's oldest surviving son Guiraudus was named after her husband Guiraudus.

Professional orientation can be used to distinguish among homonyms, but difference of occupation and even distance of status did not necessarily preclude family relationship. Similar occupations served to cement ties, however, when found in conjunction with other factors. Recurring family professions of mercer, merchant, draper, linen merchant, and jurist reinforced the links among the three Cabanis family branches. As late as the mid-fourteenth century, occupational designations were not rigid in Montpellier; persons could hold more than one occupational title, and the title "merchant," in particular, covered a great diversity of activity and was freely applied by the notaries.[36] The Cabanis younger generations reflected the professional specializations of older relatives. Beyond that there were more tenuous ties that also reflected connections. To take one occupation as an example, the linen/canvas merchant (*canabasserius*) orientation of the extended family was noted in the occupational title of Jacobus, son of Petrus, but not in those of Martha's sons although their business associations with *canabasserii* and with the linen industry of the region of Saint-Clément la Rivière and Aubagne, north of Montpellier, can nonetheless be amply demonstrated.[37]

The formalized business ties of procuration and partnership further reinforced links between the families of Petrus and Guiraudus. Among brothers, such connections were very common; most business affairs of the Cabanis in the Nogareti register showed Martha's sons Jacobus and Guiraudus as *socii*, that is, partners.[38] There were many forms of partnership in the Middle Ages for commercial, financial, and industrial purposes. The *commenda* partnership was short-term, for one venture. The *societas* was a more enduring partnership whose participants were *socii*. The division of profits at the end of the partnership differed according to the original investments in capital and labor. Often the original partnership contract has not survived, but the relationship frequently lasted several years and could be renewed. Partners often hired each other as legal representatives or procurators in business matters, recovery of debts, and litigation.[39] Multiple partnership and legal ties between the families of Petrus and Guiraudus can be documented. For example, Jacobus Oliverii was the procurator for Martha's son Jacobus.[40] The younger Johannes Naturalis, son of Maria, was also procurator for Martha's sons.[41] Martha's son Jacobus and Jacobus Oliverii, Maria's son-in-law, described as draper, were *socii* as early as 1333, putting Martha's son at age fifteen in this partnership.[42] They would remain *socii* in the Nogareti evidence of the years 1336–42.[43] The *socius* tie had no exclusivity attached to it, and Oliverii may well have had numerous such business associations. Martha's relative by marriage Guillelmus, the son of Petrus senior, was also procurator for her sons.[44] Emerging from the data is an interlace of business and family ties, linking, in particular, a younger generation, the grandchildren of Petrus, with the business operations of Martha and her sons. On the basis of the coincidence of houses near Arc Saint-Nicolas on the rue de l'Aiguillerie, common naming patterns (*Namengut*), similar occupations, and the existence of business ties, it is possible to demonstrate close relations between the family branches of Petrus and Guiraudus.[45]

There are fewer direct connections between Jacobus de Cabanis's branch and members of the families of Petrus and Guiraudus, making his family the weakest link in an argument for blood relationship. Jacobus's sons had adult professions by 1343, that of legal specialist (*jurisperitus*) for Jacobus, and canon of Maguelone for Guillelmus.[46] A *jurisperitus* in Montpellier was a university-trained professional, to be distinguished from a doctor of law, but someone who was learned in the law.[47] Established in the law and the church, Jacobus and Guillelmus were thus older than Martha's sons; her son Jacobus was still under her curatorship in 1339 at age twenty-one.[48] But there were ties. The draper Jacobus was associated with Jacobus Oliverii, a grandson-in-law of Petrus senior.[49] Jacobus's name and the names of his sons, Jacobus and Guillelmus, are compatible with the Cabanis *Namengut*, as is his profession of draper. The strongest tie of this Cabanis branch to Martha's and Petrus's families is through the occupational orientation of Jacobus's wife Bernarda, who sold silks and apprenticed young women in the mercery trade, the specialty of Martha's sons.[50]

Marriage strategies of elite families often served to expand the circle of economic ties. Guiraudus and Martha's marriage linked tawer and grain merchants with mercers and merchants. Marital strategies of the extended Cabanis family followed a similar pattern, reaching into the legal and commercial elite, some of whom held the status of urban nobility (*burgensis*).[51] No actual marriage contracts have survived for the three branches of the Cabanis family under study, but there remains some information. Marriages of the younger generation of Cabanis brought women from a range of backgrounds into the extended family: the daughter of a bourgeois (*burgensis*), Raymundus de Latis; the daughter of a jurist named Mass (*jurisperitus*); women associated with the *jurisperitus* families of Tornamira (perhaps because of Martha's connection) and of Affriano, a sister of the mercer Escuderii, and the daughter of the changer Salellis.[52] The latter was Martha's daughter-in-law, married to her son Guiraudus. Though the wife of Martha's son Jacobus was mentioned in relation to a house rental of 9 May 1341, she was not named.[53]

Granddaughters of Petrus's family for whom there remains more information married a pepperer Naturalis and a merchant Oliverii with mercer family contacts; the in-laws of these marriages were the close colleagues of Martha's sons.[54] Over time, marriage strategies seem to have enlarged the extended Cabanis family's economic activities, sustaining the Cabanis social status and perhaps even reflecting upward social mobility.[55] And marriage alliances reinforced the Cabanis's connections to the urban elite of Montpellier: bourgeois (*burgenses*), changers, jurists, pepperers, linen merchants, and mercers. These occupations reflect the urban identity of Montpellier in the Middle Ages: legal and intellectual with the presence of an important law school and university; commercial as an entrepôt of trade and a center of re-exportation of luxury goods, especially textiles, in the Mediterranean world;

and financial as a site of medieval banking operations such as foreign exchange.

Through marriage, Martha became part of the tight web of Cabanis family connections. She and other Cabanis women lived in the same part of town. They probably saw each other multiple times a week in the course of business- and family-related chores. Bernarda de Cabanis, wife of Jacobus, was a business-woman like Martha. Maria Naturale, daughter of Petrus de Cabanis, senior, and widow of Johannes Naturalis, pepperer, was less directly engaged in the business world, working through representatives and intermediaries to manage her real property estate.[56] Much of the informal interaction escapes the historian's grasp, but it was surely there. The male family members of the Cabanis family were intimately involved in business collaboration with Martha and her sons. The Cabanis branches likely lived in close proximity in the elite mercantile quarter of Montpellier, centered on the area surrounding Notre-Dame des Tables and the first town hall. Widows were not uncommon in the family, and, though Martha lost her husband when her sons were young, her family would have been sustained by extended Cabanis connections.

Martha would seem to represent an example of the exiting of women from their paternal family group to join the family of their husband. Anthony Molho and his collaborators described this pattern in studies of late medieval Florence. They focused on the fifteenth-century *Ziballdone* of Giovanni Rucellai, remarking on the particular place women occupied in Giovanni's complex and seemingly malleable memory of his past: "Women do not emerge from our study as figures relegated to the margins of Giovanni's consciousness, as a recent historian rather dramatically suggested, at the same time exiles from their familial environments and temporary, fleeting presences in their married homes. Rather, what emerges from our study is Giovanni's difficulty in conceptualizing his past without assigning a privileged role to women of other families who, married to men of his own family, gave life to the successive generations of the Rucellai."[57]

By the same token, Anita Guerreau-Jalabert described the da Besate family where the women linked by birth/blood ties were essentially ignored, whereas the ties by marriage were highlighted because they offered the opportunity to make alliances furthering social ascension.[58] Though widowed young, Martha had the support of a large, extended Cabanis family, deeply involved in business affairs. She could cultivate these relationships for the benefit of her sons' business. Before Guiraudus's death, Martha enjoyed married life, the topic of the next chapter.

CHAPTER 4

The Cabanis House:
Domestic Space and Possessions

> These acts were done in Montpellier in the house of habitation of
> the said lady Martha.
>> —A notary's comment on 26 January 1338, indicating that
>> Martha's site of business was often her home

Medieval domestic housing has left some trace in the archeology of Montpellier. The Cabanis home would have easily accommodated a variety of family affairs. Business was certainly done there, and the home was likely the site of the Cabanis shop.[1] The remaining evidence permits some speculation about the housing Martha and her family enjoyed. Insights into her role as the head of a large urban household can be gleaned, not through personal evidence left by Martha but from the information we have regarding household management in prescriptive literature and in merchant letters that have survived for this time period. The three-dimensional environment in which Martha and Guiraudus lived and worked, and which Martha continued to inhabit as a widow, is worth reconstruction as it affected the way she operated. This chapter will discuss elite urban housing and the personal effects that mercantile women such as Martha enjoyed.

Martha and Guiraudus's house, the Cabanis family home that was also the home of her sons, was, as noted earlier, located at Arc Saint-Nicolas, close to the Place Pétrarque in Montpellier today.[2] The Arc Saint-Nicolas was on a branch of the Via Francigena; it was a large arch across the rue de l'Aiguillerie between the rue En Embouque d'Or (En Bocador) and another smaller lane, resting on buildings on each side of these streets.[3] The Cabanis family business was mercery. There were four groups of mercers in the town from an early date, distinguished by the topographic sites near which they lived: those of Saint-Nicolas, including the Cabanis; those of the Sen Gros (the large bell), near Notre-Dame des Tables; those of Saint-Firmin; and those of Castel Moton.[4] Those mercers designated mercers of Saint-Nicolas clustered near the Arc. The distance between these clusters was a matter of a couple of blocks.

Martha's house is termed *hospitium* in the documents; it was a significant urban dwelling or mansion, very likely a quadrilateral building of two or more stories, situated around a central courtyard, a style that was favored in the late thirteenth and early fourteenth centuries by the mercantile and financial elites of Montpellier.[5] Whether Martha's house was as grand as the draper's house of the late thirteenth century that still stands today at 3, rue de la Vieille is unknown, but it was undoubtedly a solid structure.[6]

It is difficult to reconstruct medieval housing in detail, as most of historic Montpellier today dates from the seventeenth and eighteenth centuries when the town was an administrative center, a *ville d'intendance* of the Ancien Régime. The sixteenth-century Wars of Religion destroyed much of the earlier medieval constructions, though something remains of the late medieval era (ca. 1400 and after) when a second medieval building phase can be traced, the first coming in the twelfth and thirteenth centuries. Existing buildings in the old quarters of town sometimes preserve arches at street level that began to be uncovered in the twentieth century, as enthusiasm for ancient structures proliferated. Moreover, in the last two decades, dramatic new discoveries, such as painted ceilings at 3, rue de la Vieille and elsewhere in the central historic district of Montpellier, have greatly enhanced our knowledge of the material habitat of Montpellier merchants and revealed their artistic tastes in some detail.

Martha's house of the second quarter of the fourteenth century more likely than not represented the first phase of elite urban housing. The second and latter phase would include the house of Jacques Coeur in Montpellier that dates from the mid-fifteenth century, as does his *Grande Loge* (commercial exchange). Parts of these later structures survive, albeit altered or embedded in later buildings.[7] The draper's house, 3, rue de la Vieille, in Montpellier, recently studied by Jean-Louis Vayssettes and Bernard Sournia, reflects housing similar to what Martha and other townswomen of the mercantile elite would have inhabited.[8]

The design of the draper's house can be reconstructed from an official description of the state of the property (an *expertise*) in 1660 when it was

FIGURE 2. Façade of house today, 3, rue de la Vieille. Note the trace of the medieval windows. © cliché Jean-Louis Vayssettes, SRA, Drac Occitanie.

purchased; the building underwent a classical restoration following its sale. Classical-style windows altered the multilobed medieval fashion, while an interior spiral staircase ascending all stories replaced the *degré* or exterior stairs leading to the second floor and smaller staircases to the third and fourth stories. The *expertise* described the elements in need of being updated for early modern taste.[9] The expertise permits the recovery of what the house looked like.

The typical medieval *hôtel* or *hospitium* had an exterior staircase (*degré*) in the courtyard to service the second story, leading to a large hall, with windows, measuring perhaps 35 feet by 15 feet. Other less visible stairs gave access to upper stories. There may have been a loggia on the second story over the stairs. The ground floor could have accommodated a commercial enterprise with storage. If there were a basement, the *cave* was also a storage entrepôt or warehouse. Contracts in the personal register of the Cabanis, written by the notary Guillelmus Nogareti, suggest that a lot of business was done in their house.

The Cabanis mercery shop that we learn of in 1338 was very likely part of the family house.[10] It may have had street frontage with windows or shelves opening to the street.[11] Most medieval urban shops were associated with the homes of merchants and artisans, though there are cases where shops were located elsewhere than in the family home. We do not know whether, in the draper's house with its multiple entries or in Martha's house, there would have been a window or opening to the street for public access or retail sales, perhaps with a shutter that could be closed at night. During daylight hours, merchandise would have been displayed on a kind of shelf created by the shutter, akin to the shops that are visible in Ambrosio Lorenzetti's painting of "Good Government" in the town hall of Siena.[12] Important clients could have been invited into the courtyard area that was partially shielded from the weather by arched areas under the stairs leading to the upper private quarters, large hall, and kitchen. The Cabanis brothers had a specialty in mercery of Lucca, the brocades and damasks that were a specialty of Lucchese artisans. They were also merchants of silks of various origins.[13] They dealt in woolen and linen cloth and in spices. Some of their merchandise would have been displayed in the mercery shop managed by their factor. Their business associated with mercery and silk was sometimes contracted at the notary's atelier and sometimes in their home with the notary present to record contracts.[14]

FIGURE 3. Design of exterior of the medieval house, 3, rue de la Vieille. © Dessin Michel Antonpietri, extrait de SOURNIA (Bernard), VAYSSETTES (Jean-Louis).—*Montpellier: la demeure médiévale.* (Paris: Imprimerie Nationale, 1991), 86.

A tower or crenellation might have been incorporated in the structure. This was the case with the draper's house. We know that towers of the town walls were part of some urban housing.[15] There is speculation among architectural historians of medieval Montpellier as to how widespread towers were, as they have only fragments of structures to work with in

FIGURE 4. Design of interior of the medieval house, 3, rue de la Vieille. © Dessin Michel Antonpietri, extrait de SOURNIA (Bernard), VAYSSETTES (Jean-Louis).—*Montpellier: la demeure médiévale*. (Paris: Imprimerie Nationale, 1991), 76.

attempting to reconstitute the patrician home of the Aragonese-Majorcan era (1204–1349).[16]

Patrician domestic housing in medieval Montpellier reflects a consistency that echoes Mediterranean urban elite design. There was a formula of composition and disposition of rooms with modifications to fit specific sites and variation in construction materials, whether stone or brick or other. In central Montpellier, the habitat was dense; space was tight, causing the design to be altered to accommodate the restrictions of the site.[17]

Bernard Sournia and Jean-Louis Vayssettes describe the Montpellier formula. The ground floor of the draper's house contained an open courtyard, a loggia or covered porch that opened onto the courtyard, and a capacious storage area that ran along the street and had several entrances that led directly into the warehouse/shop area. There was an arched entryway from the street that led to the courtyard. The house sits on a corner with the main entrance to the courtyard in front and doors on the side to the storage area. The exterior staircase in the draper's house led from the courtyard to the second floor where a large reception hall with a ceiling height of 16 and a half feet measured 36 feet by 16 and a half feet. This was a room of impressive dimensions that suggests the nature of the urban elite's lifestyle. There were also two main chambers on the second floor used by the owners for social and familial activities. Windows illuminated this space. The kitchen was in proximity to serve their needs. In the draper's house, one of the chambers had an elaborately painted ceiling and walls.

The upper stories had smaller rooms reached by narrow stairs and distributed along a corridor with separate entrances. This space would have housed domestic servants, maybe apprentices and assistants. Whether families with a large number of children accommodated some of them in the upper story rooms is unknown. Often, families would have slept together in the main second-floor chambers, perhaps sharing beds.[18]

Montpellier's housing was echoed in Barcelona, where Stephen Bensch described the patrician residences as "an ample, solid stone structures" with slight variations in the disposition of rooms:

> As elsewhere in the Mediterranean, the principal residence provided at the same time a living space, storage area, bureau, and economic center. The main building consisted of two or, for the wealthiest families, even three stories. The ground floor of a substantial patrician house usually contained a storage area (*cellarium*) for wine and grain, workshops, and rooms for servants or slaves, while the top floor was divided into a large central living space (*solarium*), a kitchen, and smaller individual chambers. The ample home of Berenguer Durfort had twelve rooms and a kitchen on the second

floor and the *solarium* on the third. A squat attached tower (*pignaculum, turris*), rare in the twelfth century, enjoyed a vogue in the substantial new houses built in the thirteenth, probably in imitation of the old houses attached to the Roman wall-towers rather than for any military value.[19]

This type of housing was characteristic of the Montpellier and the Mediterranean mercantile elite of southern Europe and very likely the setting in which Martha and her sons lived. There were public spaces, domestic spaces, and storage in the elite mercantile house. There was an interior courtyard that one accessed through an arched doorway from the street. It probably permitted the entry of carts and horses, as well as people. Within the courtyard, visitors could have gathered, business was undoubtedly conducted, and goods may have been strewn about.

The climate in Montpellier was mild, typically Mediterranean, and sunlight was probably a common sight. Today the town of Montpellier proudly advertises three hundred days of sun a year. The courtyard of Martha's house would have provided congenial outdoor living for her sons when young and for the many Cabanis relatives. Shirtsleeves are possible today in December, though the months of January through March tend to be rainy, often torrentially so, with serious winds whipping through the narrow streets. Martha's brood could have huddled around a chimney in the reception hall or in the second floor chambers in bad weather.

The houses of the urban elite contained elaborate decorations. Painted ceilings and walls graced houses dating from the later thirteenth century. Knights jousting, musicians courting a lady, and more abstract décor are among the images that remain from the draper's house.[20] Inspiration for these ceilings seems to have come from *The Golden Legend* (ca. 1260) of Jacobus de Voragine.[21] Elite inhabitants commissioned paintings from a local artistic community of some prominence, as described below.

In the second quarter of the fourteenth century, the artistic trades of Montpellier were in full expansion. There was an abundance of local and immigrant Italian talent in Montpellier that would have staffed painting ateliers. The artistic patronage of the period was shared between religious establishments on the one hand and prominent citizens of Montpellier on the other. Painting was in considerable demand.[22] Religious commissions included those by the hospital of Saint-Lazare, which ordered two altar paintings in 1333, one of Saint Lazare beside the Virgin and Saint John the Baptist and the second a representation of Saint Didier with the eleven thousand virgins.[23] Lay patrons of Montpellier before 1350 included a grain merchant Petrus Corberii, a merchant Petrus de Panato, and Raymundus Aymundi who, in his will, left 20 *l.* for a painting for the high altar of the Dominican house where he requested burial.[24] Unfortunately, none of the freestanding paintings of the period prior to 1350 survives in Montpellier because of the terrible devastation of churches and houses in the region and town during the Wars of Religion, referred to earlier.

There is no record of a painting commission from Martha and Guiraudus, but there is no reason to suppose they did not do as their compatriots did. Painted ceilings, including that in the draper's house, have been found in ten houses in the historic center of Montpellier.[25] Analysis with dendrochronology of the wood of the draper's ceiling suggests it may have been cut in the last third of the thirteenth century.[26] Similar dendrochronological results were found for a house at 22, rue de l'Aiguillerie, not far from the Place Pétrarque and the Arc Saint-Nicolas. A house on the Place Pétrarque has the trace of a painted ceiling.

The draper's house had other decorations as well. Scenes of the life of Saint Eustache were included in the themes of the draper's house ceiling. Unidentified coats of arms grace 3, rue de la Vieille. Archeologists Sournia and Vayssettes determined that the wood was painted in an atelier before being installed. The fragments and remains of the other ceilings that have been located suggest similar techniques of painting, resulting in considerable consistency of style in patrician houses and an established network of ateliers of painters catering to their clients.

In the first half of the fourteenth century, the links between painters of Avignon, often of Tuscan origin, and the small school of immigrant Tuscan painters in Montpellier had ramifications for the local artistic community. Avignon was a large market for artists, beginning in the first decades of the Avignon papacy (1309–77). The explosion of artistic production stimulated by the Avignon market spilled over into Languedoc, and the elite mercantile population of Montpellier would benefit in its domestic interiors from this immigrant talent.

Art historian Dominique Thiébaut has argued that, beginning in the reign of Pope John XXII (1316–34), the papal capital in Avignon was exercising a role of artistic leadership within Europe.[27] Tuscan painters came to Avignon and established themselves.[28] Among the Sienese artists based in

Avignon were Simone Martini, Matteo Giovannetti, Memmi family members, and the master of the Codex de Saint-Georges who was tied to Cardinal Jacopo Stefaneschi.[29] The arrival of Simone Martini in Avignon in 1336 or, perhaps as late as 1340, acted as a magnet for other Italian painters. Matteo Giovanetti, a student of Martini, called *pictor pape*, painter of the pope, was a priest who directed painting at the papal court from 1342 to 1368. Martini probably introduced Giovanetti into the papal and curial circles. Under the supervision of Giovanetti, more Italian artists came to Avignon.[30] Italian painters who appeared in Montpellier were part of a larger diaspora. They had Avignon contacts and may have been attracted initially to the south of France by one or the other of these great painters, Martini and Giovanetti. When in Montpellier, these immigrant painters were employed in the decoration of patrician houses or in commissions for altarpieces in local churches that were an offshoot of patrician piety and patronage.

Whether Martha decorated her home with paintings from the local Montpellier workshop or from that of immigrant painters is unknown, but the possibility exists given the dynamism of the local artistic scene. If she herself did not invest in art, she likely knew members of the urban elite who did and may have admired their homes. Her sons could have encouraged her to decorate, as they grew older. Martha's sons Jacobus and Guiraudus had major business contacts with Avignon where hundreds of florins changed hands. Their mercery of Lucca business was the basis of this connection, and some of their major mercery clients, such as Petrus Cotelli of Toulouse, were also involved.[31] Martha may not have had time as a businesswoman to be an artistic patron, but she would have been exposed to the work of these artists in Montpellier in the housing of the mercantile elite and more broadly through the commercial and financial interests of her sons in Avignon in the 1340s.[32]

Martha and Guiraudus's house would have been furnished according to the fashion of the time. Among the few surviving inventories of estates before 1350, one inventory done by a notary in 1345 describes the interior furnishings of a leather merchant and his wife.[33] In a large hall, one discerned a table and benches, a chair, a buffet, chests, and a washing station. Nine candelabras were mentioned, eight in iron. A story above, there was a chamber with a furnished bed, the clothing of the couple, and the jewelry of the wife, some in gold and silver. An armoire and a small chest, elaborately decorated, were also present in this room. A second chamber had a bed, a chair and a table for writing. On this level there was also the kitchen with much tableware and kitchen equipment, including eleven pots, thirteen chopping boards, and ten bowls. There was also a wine cellar that was well stocked. This family household occupied two stories of a house; it would have been more modest than that of Martha and Guiraudus or the draper's house at 3, rue de la Vieille.

Comparison with Italy shows similarities in design and furnishings with the fourteenth-century houses of Montpellier. The house of the patrician Francesco Datini da Prato, a successful Italian businessman whose surviving ample correspondence has permitted unusual scrutiny of his affairs, in late fourteenth-century Prato, or the house of Lapo di Giovanni, a wealthy Florentine wool merchant, about 1400 in Florence, shared certain features that belong to the Mediterranean urban elite home. As Frances Gies and Joseph Gies described it,

> Lapo's house was "tall and square, with a narrow street frontage, its façade perhaps ornamented with a religious fresco. The ground floor contained loggia or parlor, kitchen, perhaps a guest room, and the business offices. The second floor probably contained a "great room" or salon in front, a master bedroom, and other family bedrooms. The upper floor or floors contained servants' quarters and perhaps a summer loggia or penthouse for retreat in hot weather. Every important room had a fireplace. Lighting was by tallow candles, horn lanterns, and brass oil lamps. Furniture included trestle tables, wooden chairs as well as benches, curtained beds, and chests, similar to the comforts of Caister Castle. Whether Lapo indulged in paintings and sculpture by way of interior decorations he does not say, but Renaissance art was already moving out of churches and cathedrals into private residences. In the rear of the house a kitchen garden probably grew, and perhaps a flower garden as well.[34]

Coffers, chests, clothing, jewels, and enamels show up in the notarial contracts and would have been available for purchase by the members of the elite such as Martha and others.[35] In the 1320s through the 1340s, the Montpellier notaries recorded sales of chests. In 1342, a chest or wardrobe (*gardacossa*) and a tunic were sold by an auctioneer to a woman, probably a prostitute.[36] The auctioneer had other clients among prostitutes in 1342 for chests and for clothing: in one case for two chests, in another for one.[37] Prostitutes were often in transit. They would have traveled with their worldly goods in chests if they could afford them. The cost of the chests ranged from a little over 5 *l.* in current money to 15 *l.* current money.[38] These were luxurious chests, described in one case as painted and lined with green silk and in two other cases as lined with murrey cloth and feathers. The purchase sums were on a par with the cost of a year's rental of a modest house in the prostitutes' quarter. The wardrobe chest was useful for prostitutes and was an indispensible storage item for the urban household. Martha and Guiraudus's house undoubtedly had several at least as elaborate as those purchased by the prostitutes.

Though the formulaic business contracts drawn up by the notaries do not evoke the range of household furnishings and personal possessions Martha might have enjoyed, it is worth surveying the local evidence for a sense of what was available for elite women like her to acquire. Wooden bowls, plates, and utensils have been excavated. There was a local ceramics industry, some artifacts of which may have made their way into the household of an elite mercantile woman. In the museum collections of the south of France are examples of glasses, bowls, beakers, large cooking pots, among other objects of material culture that survive from the first half of the fourteenth century.[39]

The Cabanis business connections to the Montpellier market brought them into contact with all aspects of the trade in fabrics, silks, brocades and embroideries of Lucca, local gold thread production, and woolen cloth dyed in the signature scarlet of Montpellier (from the scrub oak, *chêne kermes*).[40] Enamels and precious gems flowed through the town. The possibilities tantalize.

Montpellier had a significant role in the medieval luxury trade. The material goods available to women like Martha suggest they could have indulged themselves in any number of ways in their personal possessions. The market of Montpellier was a major supplier of luxury goods. In the Montpellier markets and at the fairs of Pézenas and Montagnac, the famous white cloth of Narbonne, as well as more ordinary cloths, were for sale.[41] Martha could have obtained luxury brocades and damasks of Lucca from her own family business.[42] Through her business ties, through her sons Guiraudus and Jacobus, and undoubtedly through her late husband before them, Martha would have been exposed to a wide range of silk products. Guiraudus and Jacobus sold raw silk, China silk, and dyed silk of Lucca, as well as mercery of Lucca.[43] Silks reached the Cabanis from China via intermediaries such as Lucchese immigrants. Talich on the eastern shore of the Caspian Sea was another source of silk. In all likelihood, Genoa was a purveyor of silk that

was transshipped to Montpellier, as it was the major market in Western
Europe for silk. A merchant of Genoa recorded the sale of China silk worth
thousands of pounds in the 1330s in Lucca.[44] In wills wealthy women commissioned religious vestments such as chasubles of rich fabric for churches.[45]
Mercers (*mercerii*), silk merchants (*sederii*), and changers of Montpellier dealt
in silks, the latter probably because of the spun gold that was used in silk
embroidery.

Montpellier was the site of a silk finishing industry as early as the late
thirteenth century when dyeing in green, black, and red hues can be documented.[46] Present on the Montpellier market were a variety of finished silks,
including garments such as shirts of silk and gold, black silk cloths, red silks
of Novara, and silks of various other colors. There is also evidence of the
embroidery of silk with gold stripes in Montpellier.[47] Thanks to the presence
of the papal court, there was a growing market in Avignon for silks coming
through Montpellier.[48] Already in the 1310s and 1320s, papal accounts reveal
this traffic.[49]

Sumptuary laws throughout medieval Europe regulated the use of luxury
fabrics, particularly silks, to limit the personal display by individuals. Montpellier was no exception.[50] Montpellier women were theoretically prohibited
from wearing silks and other luxury fabrics. Sumptuary legislation in Montpellier through a consular regulation of 1273 prohibited the use of silk and
some gems by Montpellier women, allowing only taffeta (*cendal*) as a kind of
lining. But the fashion of silks was so ingrained and widespread by the later
thirteenth century that it is unlikely such rules were followed. It is well
known how difficult enforcement of any sumptuary legislation was, and it is
hard to imagine that the ladies of Montpellier denied themselves some sam-
ples from the products that made the fortune of their families and their fellow
townsmen.[51] The Montpellier market was overflowing with such goods.

Although scholars note specific sumptuary regulations and dress codes
for prostitutes, interestingly, information remaining for Montpellier regarding women's luxury clothing and personal effects comes from purchases of
dresses by prostitutes.[52] For example, one Montpellier prostitute bought a
woman's tunic embroidered in red and a cloth towel at the cost of 65 *s.*[53]
Dowry arrangements in some cases provide information on nuptial outfits. A
blacksmith's daughter in her marriage to a cultivator brought a dowry that
included 12 *l.*, along with the bride's nuptial clothing of red percet and a
coat with a silver-trimmed collar.[54] The tastes of ladies such as Martha were

undoubtedly equally if not more ambitious than those of a prostitute clientele. The chests and dresses documented suggest the inventory that was available on the Montpellier market. If prostitutes and a blacksmith's daughter could clothe themselves opulently, so too could Martha and on a larger scale.

At Guiraudus's death, Martha most likely had something made in a black silk suitable for a Mediterranean widow.[55] Mediterranean widows clothed themselves in black. In fact, black was the color of mourning since Roman times. Widows could wear black for an extended period, and some did so for life. If Martha wore black for years, it meant she was surrounded by gloriously colored fabrics and mercery and not able to indulge in them. However, black garments would have given her a certain presence, a kind of solemnity that could have made an impression on her business collaborators and clients and also on her sons.

Urban populations were keen on fashion. Self-representation in clothing was commonplace by the twelfth and thirteenth centuries. Clothing provided social markers for status.[56] The availability of worldly goods increased as the European economy matured, and conspicuous consumption abounded. Retail sales multiplied, and displays of wares were common, raising the awareness at all levels of urban society of luxury goods, even if they could be purchased by only a fortunate few. Merchants and their clients were keen on texture, touch, color, and sheen of fabrics. Satins, silk brocades, and cloth of gold were highly prized. Belts permitted particular display of wealth. Zonas belts from Ragusa were made of silver squares, latched together.[57] A long strap of these squares hung down from the waist and must have created its own whush as the wearer walked. The tactile processes in gold and silk industries, very much hand production by silk reelers and gold beaters, not mechanization, were echoed in the products themselves.

Precious metals furnished raw material for coinage and for metalwork. Silversmiths and goldsmiths of Montpellier of the first half of the fourteenth century had an international reputation, and there was a lengthy tradition of metalwork in the town. Montpellier was rich in personnel specialized in the production of metalwork.[58] A silversmiths' confraternity existed from 1292.[59] In a survey of the notarial registers, one finds mention of multiple members of the precious metal industry, including several *argenterii* (silversmiths), *deauratores* (goldsmiths), *batitores auri et argenti* (beaters of gold and silver), *affinatores argenti* (refiners of silver), and an *aurifaber* (goldsmith) in 1343, and an *orfevre*, the vernacular for goldsmith, in 1348.[60] There were, in addition, in

Montpellier jewelers, ringmakers, gold beaters, and silver refiners. The earliest specific mention of a goldsmith as *aurifaber* in Montpellier was in 1343, as noted, though there were numerous *deauratores* recorded in gold leaf production before.[61] In 1347, the workers in gold and silver leaf (*batitores foliorum auri et argenti*), Salvator Salini of Avignon and Andreas Christofori, inhabitant of Montpellier, appeared together in Montpellier before the notary.[62] The involvement of merchants of Montpellier in papal finance may have facilitated the acquisition of raw materials for metalwork.[63] These trades working in precious metals were, undoubtedly, closely associated with changers and moneyers and with the long-distance commerce of Montpellier in which Martha's sons engaged. They created an impressive inventory from which Martha and other elite women could have shopped.

Quality control of precious metal products was already an issue in 1190 when the lord of Montpellier, Guilhem VIII, promulgated a series of statutes later to be incorporated into the 1204 urban charter in which statute 27 stated that no vases of gold or silver should be made unless they were of fine alloy.[64] The mark of the town of Montpellier ("MOP"), preserved in surviving objects, dates from some time after the conquest of Majorca by the king of Aragon in the years 1229–33 and, in all likelihood, after 1276 when Montpellier became part of the kingdom of Majorca, a status that lasted until the town was sold to the king of France in 1349.[65] Those who worked in gold and silver in Montpellier took an oath to the king of Majorca, lord of Montpellier, mentioning this mark.[66] Statutes of 1355 for the Montpellier silversmiths inaugurated an individual silversmith's mark (*signetum*).[67] Thus, 1355 represents a kind of watershed in the identification of objects of Montpellier production. Before 1355, in Martha's era, one finds only the mark "MOP", not the artist's mark, permitting the identification of a corpus of surviving objects directly attributable to Montpellier before that date.[68]

The local silver plate production of Montpellier suggests the kind of serving dishes a wealthy family might own. Among silver objects that can be identified with the Montpellier corpus through the existence of the MOP mark are examples of secular silver plate. Items such as these might have been fancied by members of the mercantile elite for use in their homes. Documentary evidence suggests a substantial Montpellier production. In the inventory of holdings of Humbert, dauphin of Vienne, for the period 1276–1344, especially May 27, 1344, there are forty-two examples of secular plate, from goblets to bowls, platters, and basins that are said to have the Montpellier mark, some of the objects carrying more than one imposition of the mark. Further, an inventory of the holdings of the duke of Anjou, dated about 1365, mentions fifty-two objects as "of the manner and silver of Montpellier."[69] These include silver beakers, liquid containers, some of parcel-gilt, as well as bowls of several sorts. Members of the urban elite like Martha had the financial means to acquire several such objects. Martha may have used silver objects such as these in her role as the head of an elite mercantile household.

If Martha fancied jewelry, she would have been well served by local production. The prime site of production of translucent enamels was Limoges. However, Montpellier artists also worked in enamel. Translucent enamels were frequently traded and easy to transport, given their light weight.[70] Medieval jewelry incorporated champlevé and translucent enamels, as did religious objects.[71] For Montpellier, there remains some information regarding the use of enamels, and there survive some examples of Montpellier work.

The *pièce de résistance* of Montpellier enameled metalwork is a picture-reliquary called the Chessboard of Charlemagne, preserved at the treasury of the collegiate church in Roncevaux.[72] In a rich and complex design, the reliquary consists of bassetaille enameled plaques entirely constituting the frame and forming a checkerboard pattern in alternation with rock crystals that have been labeled and wrapped in gold cloth of a chevron design. Blue, yellow, and green translucent enamels are present with violets and opaque reds, in the spandrels of the arches and in the centers of rosettes. These vivid colors may reflect influence on Montpellier artists of the work of Avignon metalworkers.[73]

Occupying the center of the field of the Roncevaux reliquary is the enthroned Christ. He is surrounded, above and below, by angels who hold instruments of the Passion and sound trumpets for the Last Judgment over which He presides. Below, responding to the judgment call are various persons, including kings and bishops, who leave their open tombs. Around the frame are plaques with prophets and patriarchs and, below, the Martyrdom of Stephen. Underneath trefoil arches, the figures are reserved against a blue background spangled with yellow and green rosettes. Along with the blue, yellow, and green translucent enamels are clear violets and opaque red enamels, the red appearing in the spandrels of the arches and in the centers of the rosettes.

This ambitious piece indicates that metalworkers in Montpellier were well acquainted with recent achievements in enameling. Martha lived not far

FIGURE 5. The Chessboard of Charlemagne, Iglesia de la Real Colegiata de Santa María, Galicia. Photograph by the author.

from the rue de l'Argenterie (the Street of Silvermithery) and could have witnessed the production of silver objects, perhaps even the Roncevaux chessboard. The objects of Montpellier metalwork were surely of interest to Montpellier inhabitants.

Montpellier objects such as the reliquary cross of the church of Récoules-Prévinquières were decorated with champlevé enamels.[74] We do not know whether the champlevé enamels on the cross were the work of a Limoges enameller in Montpellier or that of a local artist or some other immigrant. Further Montpellier objects reveal the presence of the technique of bassetaille enamels, that is, using "translucent enamels on a chased silver ground."[75] The Taft Museum of Cincinnati has a monstrance-reliquary from the Montpellier corpus with translucent enamels of blue, green, yellow, and violet, high-lighted by opaque red.[76] The presence in Montpellier of inhabitants and merchants of Limoges can be traced in the thirteenth and fourteenth centu-ries.[77] Martha would have been exposed to this vibrant metal industry.

Tradespeople in Montpellier produced other items that could have formed part of the Cabanis household goods. Martha's interest may have been attracted by glassware. The glass industry in Montpellier was well devel-oped, perhaps given the proximity of the town to sand and the sea. It is possible that enamel production for local and foreign markets was one off-shoot of this industry. There is evidence of export of glass and of local glass-makers.[78] Glassblowers with Venetian ties were present in small numbers in the Montpellier notarial registers, bringing with them skills from the renowned glassware production of Venice. Mirror makers and crystal makers were occasionally noted. Glassware and mirrors would likely have been part of the elite urban household. Candle makers were relatively numerous in Montpellier, as candles served both practical and liturgical purposes. The candle makers of Montpellier had a large clientele in Avignon.[79] Illustrators and bookmakers were also present, and the Cabanis family through Martha's father the tawer may have had connections here. Some of the Cabanis family relatives were university-trained in the law and in the church, and books would have been familiar possessions.

Every well-stocked household of the urban elite would have had silver plate of some sort, glassware, ceramics, and candles. Martha was in all likeli-hood an avid consumer of the material goods available on the Montpellier market, particularly those she was exposed to through her business dealings and those of her extended family. The wealth of material culture that can be documented in Montpellier during Martha's lifetime is truly remarkable, and elite women were undoubtedly beneficiaries of its abundance. All this mate-rial wealth came with the burden of management.

Martha had responsibilities that were those of an urban elite woman managing a large house, domestic personnel, children, and menfolk, along with members of the family business entourage. The Middle Ages has left us several windows on this urban world. The letters exchanged between Tuscan merchant Francesco Datini da Prato and his wife Margherita frequently fea-tured household management as their topic. The Goodman of Paris (*Le Ména-gier de Paris*) offered unceasing advice for his young wife on how to manage their household.[80] For the fifteenth century, Leon Battista Alberti offered

further advice in his *I libri della famiglia*.[81] Modern scholars such as Christiane Klapisch-Zuber have studied revealing cases from late medieval
Florence.[82]

The responsibilities and skills needed in managing a large household in
a patrician home with much material wealth should not be underestimated.
In many respects, such an enterprise was a full-time job. Certainly, the management of a patrician household occupied women of the mercantile elite.
But the example of Martha makes clear that this was only the beginning of
some women's activities.

Household management for Martha and other members of the urban
elite was complex.[83] The lady of the house had a set of keys at her waist to
open cupboards and storage chests. Locking things up and organizing important storage areas for household goods were encouraged. Leon Battista Alberti
offered specific advice on safety:

> everything should be set where it is absolutely safe, yet accessible
> and ready to hand, while encumbering the house as little as possible.
> . . . If you think something would be better placed elsewhere, more
> convenient and securely locked, think it over carefully and arrange
> things better. And so that nothing gets lost, just be sure that when
> something has been used it is immediately put back in its place,
> where it can be found again.[84]

There were storerooms, pantries, chests, the keys of which were either hung
around the waist of the mistress or perhaps confided to trusted servants. The
valuables, plate, spices, silverware, and glassware were probably secured in
some sort of storage container or area. Care would have been taken with the
organization of household equipment.

Large households had to maintain domestic personnel to perform all
the tasks that were daily necessities. Servants were sent out to shop, or, in the
case of Alberti's advice, the husband procured the necessary goods.[85] Training
servants was the responsibility of the lady of the house. Martha mentioned
no servants in any of her contracts. Are we then to believe that she lived
without domestic assistance? It would be unlikely that she had no servants.
A lady had to have domestic personnel, both male and female, and she had
to supervise them.

In fact, the Cabanis business structure had many lesser personnel who
always surrounded Martha and her sons at the drafting of contracts in the

Cabanis home and at the notary's, witnessing acts, receiving nominations as procurators, and acting in general on their behalf.[86] Did this personnel manage the horses, the carriage if there was one, the carts, and the mules? Were these animals housed in the courtyard of the house or at a site in the suburbs?

It is possible that the lesser personnel, such as the factors, of the Cabanis entourage lived in the Cabanis house if they were unmarried. The Cabanis had apprentices who likely lived with the family.[87] Domestic help often lived in, perhaps sleeping on mats in the kitchen or upper-story rooms. The household may have housed three generations of family members, with Martha, her sons and their wives and lively offspring. Martha's mother, Jacoba, as noted earlier, did not live with Martha.

The day began early in all likelihood. Someone had to open up the house in the morning—a trusted servant or the lady of the house; Margherita Datini assumed this responsibility herself, due the servant problem she coped with. There were always personnel problems, if Margherita can be believed.[88] The bedchambers would have been straightened, and the public spaces swept. In the morning, beds may have been made up for the day; in some rooms, they may have been taken apart and stored until needed so that other use could be made of the space. Mending of sheets, sewing tasks for clothing, and needlework would have occupied servants. Water had to be carried in from town fountains. Privies needed cleaning. Some households such as that of the Datini contained slaves as well as domestic personnel to carry out these tasks.

Food would have to be made available to Martha's family and other household inhabitants. Martha undoubtedly had one or more maids who would have assisted her with the marketing and a cook to prepare the meal. We do not know whether elite women met each other in daily marketing. But they or their maids undoubtedly had a favorite butcher they frequented, a fish market stall they patronized, and a vegetable seller's stall they visited daily. Martha would have planned the menus for the day and likely sent her maids to the market, up near the Town Hall where the Herbaria or vegetable market, meat markets, and the fish market were located. She would have supervised the kitchen personnel as they awaited the arrival of fresh foodstuffs. Maids may have taken goods to be baked in the municipal ovens on a daily basis.[89] Bakers also would have provided bread and other pastries.

Household accounts had to be maintained. Did a woman like Martha keep track of household expenditures in an account book? Did Martha pay cash, or did she have a running account with local merchants? She would have tracked the prices of bread and foodstuffs that were regulated in some cases by municipal ordinance.[90] Price data have survived for the Middle Ages.[91] In the pre-plague period, inflation was a problem compounded by bad harvests, deteriorating climate, and piracy on the seas that threatened food imports, especially grain.[92] The large population pre-plague meant that there were fewer resources per person.

Though set back from the sea, Montpellier was a Mediterranean site. There were several fish markets in town, and the Mediterranean supported multiple fishermen who lived in Montpellier or in the small towns on the coast. Martha and her family would have had easy access to the fruits of the sea. In fact, foodstuffs abounded in local markets. Fish, especially tuna, would have been purchased for days of abstinence. Fruits, nuts, meat, and wine from the region around Montpellier were also plentiful. The central Herbaria Square resellers sold chickens and vegetables, perhaps also herbs and garlic (much as resellers do today with long braids of garlic available for purchase).[93]

The medieval elite had sophisticated palettes, documented in surviving medieval cookbooks.[94] Spices were much sought after and a specialty of medieval Montpellier. The argument that medieval inhabitants employed spices to make tainted meat and poorly preserved produce more appealing is no longer accepted. In fact, medieval inhabitants favored a variety of spices in their food, according to their budgets, for spices were costly purchases. Pepper, cinnamon, cumin, saffron, and the like, imported from markets in the western Mediterranean and in the Levant, fetched high prices on European markets.[95] The spice sellers, pepperers, and apothecaries of Montpellier had a large clientele locally. Montpellier had a distinct reputation for specialties such as spiced wines that sold well in distant markets such as England, where royal accounts detail the purchases of Montpellier products such as the coveted spiced wines.[96] The tables set by women of the urban elite could cater to diverse tastes with a panoply of available delicacies.

Records of the Avignon papacy and notarial contracts of Montpellier note much market activity in spices and other goods.[97] Martha would have had access on the Montpellier market to a variety of spices and other products, including cloves, several sorts of ginger, pepper, cinnamon, anise, basket sugar, sugar of Babylon, and saffron.[98] Martha and her sons as merchants were engaged in a wide variety of trade, including the very lucrative spice trade. There is no evidence that she participated directly in this trade, but, as we will see in following chapters, she was instrumental in setting up financing for the luxury trade of her sons. She may have benefitted from wholesale

prices, greatly discounted, in access to these luxury products. Merchants of
Paris and Aurillac were clients of her sons in Montpellier for sugar, pepper,
and saffron from Catalonia.[99] In 1341, Martha's sons sold 1,376 pounds tournois of pepper and sugar to an agent for these Aurillac merchants, the largest
local sale of spices surviving in the notarial evidence before 1350.[100] The same
Aurillac and Parisian merchants acquired saffron in the local market from
merchants of Montblanch and Puigcerda.[101] The Cabanis brothers shipped
saffron from Catalonia to the markets of Paris. In Valencia, the Cabanis had
a partner, Petrus de Calvo, who shipped them saffron and leather and marketed silks and mercery on their behalf in Spain.[102] Would Martha not have
sampled some saffron and perhaps cooked with it? Her sugar and her pepper
would have come from her sons' affairs. The urban elite to which Martha
belonged ate well. The intense involvement of Martha's sons in the spice
trade again leads to the speculation that she would have set a very sophisticated table at the mansion near Arc Saint-Nicolas. The standard of living of
the Cabanis household would have been high.

Five banquet menus of Montpellier town consuls have survived in a
manuscript of the municipal accountant of 1357–58.[103] The pretexts for these
festive feasts included charity, the welcoming of a new bailiff, the celebration
of the feast of Notre Dame, the election of new consuls, and the concession
of hospitality fees for the bishop of Maguelone. On the menus were hors
d'oeuvres including an aperitif (often sweet wine), fresh fruit and salty cakes,
a first course of something boiled, a soup with pieces of meat or fish and
maybe eggs, roasts of meat or fish, desserts of dried fruit, cheese, and cakes
with sweet wine, and a digestif. Also on the shopping lists were multiple
spices, a specialty of Montpellier trade, and herbs. While Martha's daily fare
for her family would not have included this array of elaborate dishes, these
menus provide an idea of what was available on the Montpellier market and
what appealed to local tastes.

In her survey of medieval women, Shulamuth Shahar argued that the
energies of elite urban women were concentrated in household management
and family matters: "The wife of a great merchant was more closely confined
to the home, there was no economic need for her to work and her husband
did not require her help."[104] Prescriptive literature such as *The Goodman of
Paris* or the letters of Francesco Datini da Prato to his young wife encouraged
a domestic focus for the married women of the elite, but prescriptive literature and male opinions did not always dictate reality.[105] Household management was a major responsibility of most elite women, but it was just the

beginning. The lives of women like Martha reflect the activities of the *maî-tresse de maison*, who ran a large urban household.[106] The role of women must be adjusted to permit the combination of this role with that of business-woman. The case of Martha reinforces that of other urban elite women of the Low Countries, Roussillon, and Aragon-Catalonia. The generalizations of Pernoud and Shahar must be set aside in light of the complexities of the experiences of medieval women that have been studied in recent years. Shen-nan Hutton in her study of Mergriete Scettorf, the daughter of a wealthy Ghent burgher and the wife of a prosperous baker, Frank van der Hamme, paints a picture of Mergriete's economic career.[107] She and her husband were real property landlords and moneylenders, as well as artisans. Mergriete began her economic career as a married woman, much as Martha undoubtedly did, but she can also be traced as a widow, litigating successfully. She seems to have gravitated, as Martha did, to her husband's side of the family, having had some financial difficulties with her brother. When she remarried, she continued to defend her economic interests. She was undoubtedly in charge of the household associated with her marriage but had activities outside the household.

Clearly, the level of economic engagement would have depended on the woman, and personality played a significant role.[108] There is no one formula that fits all. Still, we can be certain that blanket statements such as Shahar's have to be revised. In Martha's case, she may have collaborated with Guirau-dus during his lifetime, and we know, on the basis of surviving documents, that, after his death, she ran the family business and, as her sons grew up, she collaborated with them. Regardless of whether Martha was already involved in the family business before the death of Guiraudus, for a woman with the responsibilities of young children and a large household, the loss of her hus-band would have been a tremendous blow, the topic of the next chapter.

CHAPTER 5

Guiraudus's Death and the Beginnings
of Guardianship

> I, Martha, wife of the said late Guiraudus de Cabanis, and *tutrix* and
> in the name of *tutor* of the said Jacobus de Cabanis, my son, the
> aforesaid heir, having certified fully concerning the aforesaid.
>
> —Martha's first appearance in the extant notarial record,
> 18 March 1328

Martha was widowed in a time of crisis. Guiraudus died sometime in late
November or December of 1326, in the middle of a fiscal crisis that shook
the town and its municipal government and would persist into the early
1330s. The year 1323 saw the beginning of a period of challenge to consular
government and the urban patriciate. A group calling themselves *populares*
(the popular party) criticized the legitimacy of the consular regime and its
fashion of governance.[1] Guiraudus was deeply involved in this *populares* crisis
over municipal finance. He was part of the "Fourteen of the Chapel" who
had been charged in 1323 with investigating consular mismanagement. The
town consuls were accused of excessive spending, and the accusations, along
with a consular attempt to levy new taxes, had caused multiple protests.

The pretext for revolt was the imposition of a tax (*taille*) by the consuls
that the *populares* viewed as unnecessary, coming on the heels of significant
fiscal exaction over several decades. Taxation was distributed proportionately
ad solidum et ad libram, that is, according to the resources of the taxpayer.
The *populares* refused to declare their wealth in order to be taxed. They
demanded that the books and registers of consular accounts stretching back

over twenty years be examined to determine whether the accounting practices were just and if the proposed tax was necessary.[2]

The dispute led the consuls to name a commission—the "Fourteen of the Chapel"—on 20 November 1323 upon the advice of the judge (*juge mage*) of the *Sénéchaussée* of Beaucaire and the archdeacon of Autun.[3] In a tradition that went back to 1204, the Fourteen were charged with estimating the level of resources of Montpellier inhabitants and setting the level of taxation according to the wealth of individuals.[4] In this case, as the urban financial commission, they were to review the consular accounts. The Fourteen included Guiraudus de Cabanis, Martha's husband, and Johannes Naturalis, a business partner of the Cabanis. In the current crisis, added to this list of the Fourteen were six more inhabitants including Petrus de Cabanis and the Pontius Alamandini the younger, of an illustrious Montpellier family of spice merchants and changers. Petrus de Cabanis was likely a blood relative of Guiraudus, perhaps his brother or uncle. Sociologically, these commissioners were similar to the consuls themselves.

Martha witnessed the subsequent events firsthand and would have heard specific details through Guiraudus. Arbitration by the seneschal of Beaucaire and the lieutenant of the king of Majorca led on 8 January 1324 to the creation of a another commission of twenty citizens, half chosen by the *populares*, charged with reviewing the consular accounts in a period of thirty days.[5] No audit had been produced by November 1324, something acknowledged by King Charles IV of France.[6] The *populares* were permitted by French administrative district (*Sénéchaussée*) authorities to choose an official called a *syndic* to represent them. They wanted to use the large bell at Notre-Dame des Tables in the center of town to call their members to assemble. The jurist Guilhem Servier, prosecutor (*procureur*) of the king of France, was against their use of the bell, so he placed three sergeants in the Notre-Dame bell tower to prevent access. Servier wanted to restrict the *populares* to assembling where they were accustomed, in the churches of the Franciscans, of Saint-Thomas, and of Saint-Guilhem and at the palace of the king of Majorca, not in the center of town at the call of the large bell.[7]

The significance of the bell resides in the fact that news in town was often reported at the sound of a bell, as noted earlier. Great care was taken of bells, such as those at Notre-Dame des Tables around which changers clustered, not far from Martha's neighborhood. In 1309 on Christmas Eve, the town chronicle reports that a large bell made by M. Anthony was placed in the bell tower of Notre-Dame.[8] In 1325, the chronicle noted that a middle-sized bell was made for Notre-Dame and that it broke on All Saints' Day in 1337.[9] Bells functioned as a means of summons for the town inhabitants. In the period of social and political crisis that was the 1320s, Montpellier inhabitants were called on numerous occasions to assemble at the sound of the large bell of Notre-Dame des Tables, though the *populares* were not given permission to do so.[10]

The crisis continued to escalate. In fact, by December 1325, thousands of protesters were in the streets, vocal in their complaints against the consuls. A big demonstration occurred during a welcoming ceremony for the archbishop of Narbonne. The large student body in the town—five hundred to a thousand—plus criminals, prostitutes, vagabonds, and other marginals or marginally employed, along with thousands of urban agricultural workers, swelled the crowd.[11] Finally, in October 1326, the audit of consular accounts took place under the supervision of yet another set of royal commissioners designated in June 1326.[12] The investigation was recorded on a large parchment roll, containing fifteen parchment skins sown together.[13] Guiraudus de Cabanis was mentioned as a commissioner several times in this roll.

The result of the audit, informed by the assiduous accounting expertise of the *populares*, revealed irregularities of consular accounting, particularly in expenditures during their diplomatic missions and in gifts for their families. The dishonest management of the consular forest, the Bois de Valène, was also discovered. However, the upshot of the investigation and the audit was a resolution of 5 October 1331 that favored the king of France and represented the *populares*' defeat along with increased French royal influence over the consuls.[14] But there were echoes of these incidents well into the 1330s.[15]

The *populares* viewed themselves as representing the community as a whole. They were by no means have-nots, though they sought to represent the less favored among the urban population. Their protest occurred in a period of subsistence crisis that climaxed in the early 1330s. The south of France had not suffered gravely from the famine of 1315–22, but bad harvests would come at the end of the 1320s and in the early 1330s. The disruptive financial crisis would extend through 1333 and beyond.[16] For Martha, these were worrisome times.

In the midst of this turmoil Guiraudus's death was likely a shock. He was dead by 22 December 1326. Did he have an accident, or did he fall ill? Did he die while on a business trip? Was his death connected to the *populares* unrest? We have no information about the cause of his death. The young age of his sons at his death and the fact that he can be traced in the late fall of 1326 suggest serious illness leading to a rapid demise, an accident, or foul play.[17]

The boys at four, eight, and eleven were still of school age at their father's death. We know nothing of the schools or basic instruction available in Montpellier in the fourteenth century. Martha and Guiraudus may have had private tutors for their sons. Montpellier, as a university town, had lots of needy scholars who could have lived from tutoring children. They might have been hired in informal arrangements or in work contracts.[18] The boys would have needed basic arithmetic and reading skills as future merchants. It is possible that Berengarius Gombergua, the priest who witnessed many of Martha's contracts and others of her sons, could have taught the Cabanis boys in earlier years. Such activity could explain his frequent presence in the Cabanis home, along with that of other close members of the Cabanis entourage such as the cleric Petrus de Albinhaco, who may also have offered lessons. Geographic knowledge would have been necessary, as the Cabanis boys acquired an understanding of the Western European and Mediterranean world in which they would operate and in which their father did business before them. Did they learn foreign languages? Perhaps they acquired some basic vocabulary useful in the Mediterranean world from their father's colleagues.

The boys would have been of an age where play was still important. Where in the confined urban center of Montpellier would they have played?[19] There were not many open spaces, except on the town squares, and those would have been filled with resellers and merchandise. The boys would have played in the streets near their home. In the suburbs where the family possessed property or on the banks of the Lez River, the boys may have played more ambitious games, ball games, sports involving acrobatics or wrestling, throwing games such as quoits and kayles. Common childhood games such as follow the leader and hide and seek would have figured as well.[20] The boys would have learned to ride. The horse was the common means of transport for the medieval merchant who traveled extensively.[21] Martha would have attempted to maintain a normal childhood for her boys in the face of the loss of their father.

However, Guiraudus's death would have irreparably altered Martha's life and the life of her boys. The boys would have sought male role models within the extended Cabanis family.[22] They could have sought role models within the business entourage of the late Guiraudus.[23] Close contact with the late

Guiraudus's colleagues, with members of the business entourage, and with Martha could have assisted in imparting the skills and expertise necessary to them as future merchants.

Specific training was necessary to produce a successful merchant. Merchants needed to cultivate a whole range of subtle responses via the senses to make informed judgments about products. The ability to evaluate products via taste, touch, smell, and sight was essential to determining product quality and, hence, value. Merchant manuals were explicit regarding what made high-quality merchandise. Francesco di Balduccio Pegolotti of Florence provided long lists of merchandise that could be acquired in various parts of the known world (1310–40).[24] The detailed description of merchandise in Pegolotti and in the fifteenth-century manual of undetermined authorship, *The Book of the Wares and Usages of Divers Countries*, suggests the level of skill of observation and acquaintance with products that were necessary for the medieval merchant.[25] Only experience in the end could produce that level of expertise.

Martha and members of the extended Cabanis family, as well as colleagues of the Cabanis entourage, would have stepped up in the absence of Guiraudus to instruct the boys. Beyond the evaluation of quality, the medieval merchant needed an understanding of consumer tastes and current fashion. There is no record that Jacobus and Guiraudus went through the formal apprenticeship phase of merchant training, though their younger brother Johannes was an apprentice mercer in 1342. In these circumstances, the Cabanis mercery shop in the family home, under the guidance of their father's entourage, would have provided much necessary hands-on exposure for the boys, who could have wandered in and out or spent days among the silks and mercery.

We do not know whether Martha was Guiraudus's business partner before his death. The fact that they had young children might have played a role in limiting the extent of her engagement. But we have evidence of the involvement of wives in the Crown of Aragon, in Italy, and in Montpellier where the mercer Bernarda de Cabanis, a likely in-law of Martha, had a career separate from that of her draper husband, Jacobus, in which she sold mercery to mercers in Montpellier, apprenticed young women from the Montpellier hinterland to learn the mercer's trade, and loaned money to rural women with the expectation of repayment in kind in mercery.[26]

Perhaps even more surprising is the fact that wives served as sureties for the husbands, exercising a significant form of legal agency.[27] A particularly striking instance occurs in the legal proceedings of the mid-1350s against the pepperer Johannes Andree, accused of saffron fraud, that is, of selling adulterated saffron. After a series of witness testimonies, all pointing to Andree's guilt, in 1357 he was released with sufficient guarantees for later sentencing. At this time, his wife Mirabella served as his *fideiutrix* (surety), as well as his principal defendant, debtor, and *paccatrix* (synonym for surety). She made a series of renunciations of legal protections to overcome her legal incapacity as a woman.[28] These renunciations cover more than one folio page of the legal dossier and include the *Senatusconsultum Velleianum* (a Roman law protection of women to be discussed in detail in Chapter 6 below). The surviving evidence does not reveal whether Martha ever served in the role of guarantor for Guiraudus before his death, and we do not find her in that role in regard to her sons when evidence is available. Elsewhere in Europe, women worked with their husbands and on their own. Shennan Hutton found that Mergriete Scettorf of Ghent collaborated with her husbands and functioned alone as a widow.[29] Rebecca Winer also found wives involved in financial transactions on their own in Perpignan, as they hired wet nurses to care for their children.[30]

There is evidence in mercantile correspondence here and there of women who were part of the business operations of families. A case in point is a letter of 29 November 1265, written in the Champagne Fair town of Troyes by a correspondent of the Sienese company of Tolomei.[31] After much detail regarding markets and monetary matters, the correspondent stated, "If you have not paid L 10 Sienese petty to the wife of Giacomino del Carnaiuolo, as I advised you from the past fair of Saint-Ayoul, pay them, for they are for the L 3 Provisine which I received from said Giacomino."[32] The wife of Giacomino was clearly directly part of the business dealings of her husband. A little further on, the correspondent mentioned cloth that was to be delivered to Giacomino's wife. The correspondent was questioning whether this had happened. This merchant wife handled the finances and merchandise for her husband in his absence. Women worked behind the scenes, escaping notice in the documents. Evidence fails us for Martha's married life, but we have significant details of her business involvement during her widowhood and as guardian of her sons.

The elaborate collaboration documented for Martha with her sons would suggest that they shared close family ties.[33] At least in recent times, it is quite clear that generational differences are profound. Just how dramatic such changes were from one generation to the next in the Middle Ages is difficult to establish. Generational differences might include greater or lesser involvement in business and real estate management, differing philanthropic and religious orientations, differing approaches to family and child care, greater or lesser partnership with spouses, differing strategies for the preservation of family fortune, to name but a few possible variations. In the one area where comparison is possible, Martha's approach to real estate investment is quite different from that of her sons, particularly Jacobus.[34] Martha's extensive interaction with her sons in business was likely underpinned by significant affective ties between mother and sons. She herself benefitted from a close affective relationship with her mother Jacoba.

Notarial documents rarely address familial emotions—the exception would be the *donatio inter vivos* of Jacoba, who proclaimed her maternal love for Martha.[35] The affective ties between Martha and her sons have left only a trace, as Jacobus stated on 18 March 1338 (n.s.) in a large partnership contract: "with the authority and consent of Lady Martha, revered mother and *curatrix*."[36] However, parents were committed to their children, and children undoubtedly had sincere feelings for their parents.[37] In this case, Martha was the one surviving parent. Though we are left with the boys' formal reverence for Martha, their continued involvement with her in business contracts suggests that theirs was a close collaboration reaching beyond the world of business.

Guiraudus designated his son Jacobus as his universal heir, and Jacobus will be identified in later notarial documents in this capacity.[38] There are 127 wills of the 160 extant in Montpellier that make explicit reference to heirs.[39] Testators in the remaining thirty-three wills, instead of naming people as heirs, often founded chantries, that is, endowments, sometimes in the form of chapels, for the chanting of masses, usually on behalf of the founder, as a means of disposing of an estate. Testators often made bequests of real estate and personal effects to individuals, but there is never any guarantee that all of a testator's property was noted in a will. The appointment, in particular, of a universal heir, made it unnecessary to enumerate property, since all property not included in burial ceremony, masses, charitable giving, and bequests, passed to the universal heir.[40] Universal heirs accepted the credits and debts of the estate, and it was possible to refuse the appointment. Of the 127 wills naming heirs, sons were the most popular universal heirs with thirty-seven mentions. Daughters figured as heirs in fifteen wills, and wives in fourteen. In two cases, there were daughter and son combinations, two with daughter and grandsons.[41] Siblings were heirs in another sixteen cases, relatives in five, mother or father in five, grandchildren in two; and eighteen additional cases included an heir whose relationship to the testator was not known and/or a variety of charities or religious figures. These latter categories were also the beneficiaries of bequests in wills where someone else was named heir. Jacobus as universal heir was the beneficiary of a large paternal estate of which we catch glimpses in the surviving documents.[42]

Martha performed her guardianship duties admirably, as the following chapters will demonstrate. The haunting question remains of why she did not remarry. It may have been that she was constrained from doing so by the terms of Guiraudus's will. Southern Europe presents considerable information on remarriage of widows. Some dotal contracts in Montpellier expressly guaranteed the return of the dowry, but the situation remains somewhat ambiguous.[43] The Montpellier statutes of 1205 stated, "Every woman, girl or widow, can give all her goods in dowry to her first or second husband, even if she has children."[44] This suggests the widow's right to recover her dowry, but a husband could put stipulations in his will to constrain the widow.

The lands of the Crown of Aragon in general discouraged remarriage of widows. Stephen Bensch argued that the independence of widows was a feature of patrician society that was vaunted and that widows had lots of leverage, as they were granted administrative power over the estate. He noted that the patrician Bernat Durfort, (the ample house of Berenguer Durfort was described in Chapter 4), "went so far as to deny his wife Berenguera custody of their children if she took another husband or entered a religious house."[45] Rebecca Winer noted that widowed mothers in a second marriage lost the usufruct of their first husbands' estate, which passed to the children of the first union. The *Furs* of Valencia were hostile to the remarriage of widows, fearing financial damage to the children.[46] In Perpignan, a widow risked losing her marriage gift. But some young widows were encouraged to remarry, and some widows who did so remained active in the lives of the children of their first marriage. In order to enjoy the rights of guardianship fully, women like Sança, widow of Duran de Pererar of Perpignan, had to perform a ritual renouncing Roman law protection of women (the *Senatus-consultum Velleianum*).[47] Marie Kelleher argued that, in Crown of Aragon territories and elsewhere in the Mediterranean, "a widow's right to enjoy the fruits of the entire estate of her late husband was contingent upon her remaining a part of the late husband's family, caring for the children, spurning remarriage, and (most importantly, perhaps) not diminishing the estate by demanding the return of her dowry."[48] Kelleher found that widows had to swear they would not remarry; they too needed to renounce the legal protection of the *Senatusconsultum Velleianum*.[49]

If we turn to Provence, Andrée Courtemanche found little testamentary constraint against remarriage of widows in Manosque; as widows, they were encouraged to maintain chastity in the face of some skepticism.[50] If widows did remarry, they abandoned their children and patrimonial goods, all the while requiring reimbursement of the dowry and thereby diminishing the estate.[51] There is general agreement in southern Europe about the legal support for the return of dowry, if the widow desired it.[52] There was even support for preemptive return of dowry on the part of wives who probably sought to protect their own dotal resources and perhaps the family patrimony in the face of their husbands' debts. There is some disagreement among scholars in this regard, Daniel Lord Smail and Thomas Kuehn along with Julius Kirshner seeing such strategy as likely, while Andrée Courtemanche and Francine Michaud are more skeptical.[53]

In Florence, the widow who remarried left her children and her dowry in the patrilineal line of her first husband.[54] Kelleher saw the widow in the Crown of Aragon remaining attached to her late husband's family, in charge of her children, foregoing remarriage, leaving her dowry in the estate. The *Fueros* of Aragon, according to Kelleher, were hostile to the widow, menacing loss of use of her late husband's property and also of her own dotal property were she to remarry or have sexual relations with someone as a widow.[55]

Kelleher took issue with Cécile Béghin's belief, on the basis of her study of towns in Languedoc, that giving up guardianship upon remarriage would be giving up "an economic role incomparable to that of the married woman, a place at the heart of the family and the urban community that would seem difficult to renounce."[56] In contrast, Kelleher argued for generalized gender inferiority for women, whether wives or widows. Somewhat inconsistently in light of the above, Béghin traced three cases of remarriage from the late fourteenth and fifteenth centuries in which the widows, having become wives again, seem to have come out quite well in remarriage.[57] But, as widows, they had exercised professional activities successfully, providing a useful parallel to Martha. Béghin also found in the late medieval wills she studied that one *textatrix* in six was a widow who had remarried at least once.[58] This led her to argue, unrealistically I fear, at least for the first half of the fourteenth century, that most masculine testators tried to preserve the material situation of their widow in facilitating their remarriage and a comfortable family life.[59]

At issue may, in fact, be the evolution of stricter practices toward the end of the Middle Ages. Bensch identified an earlier evolution in Barcelona with the dowry system having a negative effect on women and providing a deterrent to her integration into the inheritance strategies of her husband's family.[60] He stated for 1250 and later that "it became less common for male testators with children to designate their wives as administrators of the entire estate for their lifetimes provided they did not remarry, or, in the language of the charters, to make them *dominae et potentissimae*."[61] The point is that change and evolution may have occurred at different rates and toward different ends across the geography of southern Europe.

The question of age played a part in whether widows remarried, though it was not a handicap for young widows, as Martha probably was in 1326 at Guiraudus's death, and for at least one of Béghin's widows. Lucie Laumonier has argued that widows had little chance of remarriage if they were over age forty-five.[62] Courtemanche saw the competition from young women making remarriage of older widows difficult in Manosque.[63] On balance, societal practice did not favor remarriage of widows, and age made it difficult.

Martha did not remarry. Closely linked to her in-laws, Martha de Cabanis has the persona of a businesswoman engaged in managing the commercial fortune of her sons after their father's death and her own and their real property. Martha faced many challenges as a young widow, but she was not alone. The wider family networks she enjoyed were essential to the Cabanis business operations and to the childhood and young adulthood of her sons. Martha may have been widowed in her mid- to late twenties. Ten years later when we see her as a practicing businesswoman in the late 1330s, she was perhaps in her mid-to-late thirties. She had remained a widow for at least twenty years when we catch the last trace of her. She appeared repeatedly in the private Nogareti register devoted to the economic affairs of the Cabanis family that spans the years 1336–42, with internal references extending to the mid-1340s.[64] She entered into partnership arrangements, the basis of the Cabanis business structure, in the role of guardian of her sons.[65] She hired legal representation in the form of procurations to further her own and her family's business interests and to defend those interests in court. She managed real property transactions and restructured her real estate holdings. Most important, she groomed her sons, ceding more responsibility to them in the early 1340s.[66] It is time to examine more explicitly the legal position Martha enjoyed as widow and guardian of her children.

CHAPTER 6

The Widow's Legal Position as Guardian

> 1347: Likewise, confident in the legal status of the said Gaudiosa, my wife, I give and ordain her guardian [*tutrix*] of my said children and without that she be held by any person to render an explanation concerning her administration and that she not be held to render account or to give any caution concerning use and enjoyment.
>
> 1403: Likewise I wish and ordain expressly that Raymunda, my wife, be the mistress (*domina*), powerful usufructuary, and testamentary guardian (*tutrix testamentaria*) of all my children and my goods and that she not be held to make an inventory nor to render account or explanation to any court or person, ecclesiastical or secular, concerning the direction made by her.
>
> —Examples of testamentary guardianship for Montpellier women

What were Martha's first challenges when widowed? There would have been a funeral and a period of mourning. She had three young sons who needed her love and guidance. Then putting the estate in order according to the terms of Guiraudus's will had to be a priority. His last will and testament does not survive, but the size of a bequest for poor girls to marry, for which son Jacobus received an acquittal many years later, suggests a significant estate and a complex will.[1]

As noted earlier, it is likely Martha was named as a testamentary guardian (*tutrix testamentaria*). In her era, we have examples of elite women filling this role. In 1336, Auda de Conchis, widow of Guillelmus de Conchis, an urban noble (*domicellus*), was called *tutrix testamentaria* of her son Guillelmus, the heir of his late father, in a series of acts ceding usufruct of a house of the heir in Montpellier, acknowledging the receipt of rent for the property, certifying a land transfer for which the estate held eminent domain, and renting another house in Montpellier.[2] Auda undertook these transactions on her own as guardian.

There would have been executors for Guiraudus's will. Martha may have been one of these, though it was not very common for women to serve in that role. As noted earlier, Guiraudus very likely named her guardian in his will. She also would have needed to get herself recognized as such by the courts.[3] Was there any court intervention beyond validation of the will and Martha's role as guardian? Any challenge to the will?[4] Finally, after the funeral, Martha would have begun to involve herself again—or for the first time—in the family business. In Martha's case, we have no information about what happened immediately after Guiraudus's death, but it is useful to explore the legal situation of widows who were guardians of their children. In the following chapters, we can trace her actions as guardian and beyond.

In the Middle Ages, there were many strains of law that affected the south of France in addition to its Roman law legacy: Germanic Visigothic laws, local customs, codified municipal statutes in the growing towns of the twelfth and thirteenth centuries. Legal scholars developed another source of law, the *ius commune*, the learned law of the universities that was a combination of Roman and canon law.[5] Finally, notarial practice reflected a living law of contract.[6] The legal historian Pierre Tisset argued persuasively from a study of southern French customary collections that Roman law was known more or less in-depth but not held in reverence, since it was often set aside in favor of local private law.[7] Scholars tracing the rediscovery of Roman law and its "reception" in the High Middle Ages in the south of France, André Gouron and, earlier, Edmond Meynial, noted the appearance of Roman legal terminology in the twelfth or thirteenth century, without asserting its systematic imposition.[8] Scholars have maintained that, as of the end of the twelfth century, Roman law was recognized as a supplementary law in cases where local customs failed to cover a particular issue.[9] It would only be in the sixteenth century that the prescriptions of Roman law came to be more rigidly imposed.[10] Against this legal background, it is useful to describe the position of women before the law, specifically in regard to their ability to function independently.

The legal status of women in Montpellier owed much to the laws and customs of Mediterranean Europe, that is to say, to the influences of a written law culture and to the distant Roman past.[11] It is clear from the existing statutes of Montpellier and from the use of renunciations of Roman law protection in notarial contracts that the local law of practice must be distinguished from the *ius commune* in its treatment of women.[12] In practice, women were able to participate legally in financial operations, industry, and trade, contracting obligations on their own behalf and on behalf of others. In the more conservative realm of real estate, wives generally acted with their husbands' consent, but single women and widows might act independently. The question of married women's agency remains open, but the findings from Montpellier suggest they enjoyed considerable independence of action.[13]

Women like Martha who found themselves widowed with small children were frequent participants in contracts of the notarial registers. In a departure from the letter of Roman law that did not readily allow a mother to be the guardian of her children, in Montpellier such was often the practice. One of the most prominent capacities in which women appeared in business transactions was as guardians of their children.[14] In these roles and as executors of their husbands' estates, they were involved in the payment of debts, acquittals, real estate acts, and in the apprenticeship of their children. Martha's status as widow can be explored within the legal context of Mediterranean Europe and specifically within southern France.

Montpellier's statutes are not explicit in regard to the mother as guardian of her children. However, article 7 of the 1205 statutes stated: "If anyone having minor children in order of succession instituted some executors in his will, those executors are understood to be guardians of these minor children unless in the same testament, he will wish another to be guardian specially and expressly."[15] There was certainly a presumption of a mother holding such a position, as we will see below.

More generally, Rebecca Winer provided useful background on the situation in the Crown of Aragon within which Montpellier figured first under the king of Aragon and then from 1276 until 1349 under the king of Majorca. The *Furs* of Valencia stated in regard to the mother as guardian: "With the death of a father his children are in the power of their mother." The *Costums de Tortosa* declared in the case of the death of the father, the mother, if living, was considered the testamentary guardian. Winer commented: "In Catalan society, if a man's wife was alive, and he intended to appoint someone other than his wife as guardian for their children, that was considered exceptional. Throughout medieval Iberia, if a father preferred another guardian he was required to state this explicitly in his will; otherwise his wife would automatically assume the office."[16] As early as 1272, King James the Conqueror proclaimed on 15 November, "we consider that it is consonant with reason and the law that in the event of a father's death the mother raise her minor children."[17] Castilian towns held the same preference for the mother as guardian, determining that, if a father died intestate or without choosing a guardian, his widow and the children's mother filled that role.[18]

Winer noted the enduring influence of a mother who had served as guardian and commented that the *Costums* "recognized that a widowed mother's influence conceivably could last into her son's adulthood, especially if she had been *domina* of his father's estate and so had been appointed to lead the family."[19] Such practice could explain the continued presence of Martha in business after the formal Roman law majority (age twenty-five) of her oldest son Guiraudus and the near majority of her husband's universal heir, Jacobus.

Provence, specifically Manosque and Marseille, also reveals a preference for the mother as guardian. Andrée Courtemanche found that one-third of male testators in Manosque confided children to their mothers and 80 percent of these also added the mother's control over the administration of goods.[20] Francine Michaud found that numerous testators in Marseille confided both children and the patrimony to the widow, which in a third of the cases carried the additional requirement that the widow remain a widow.[21] Michaud argued that the interests of the children were the primary motive for a husband to discourage his widow from remarrying after his death. And she noted that husbands who did not have children failed to include an admonition against remarriage for their wives who were their only heirs.

The evidence for Martha's experience comes from notarial registers, as noted in the Introduction above. Notarial contracts of southern Europe were influenced by layers of law, oral custom as in oaths, written law of urban statutes, university treatises, and Roman law. In regard to Roman law, in particular, John Pryor, in his study of notarial practice in mid-thirteenth-century Marseille, commented, "Across the entire, wide field of obligation, notaries adopted with enthusiasm the formulas of Roman law, which they found served two purposes: to give precision to obligation where before there had existed only vagueness and at the same time to attach a veneer of learned mystery to their documents and thus to exalt their profession."[22]

The Roman law concept of *patria potestas*, paternal power, influenced the father's authority in the family in the south of France. The 1205 statutes of Montpellier endorsed extraordinary paternal power over a diverse house-hold of family members, servants, relatives, apprentices, and so on, termed the *familia*.[23] However, *patria potestas* did not extend for life in Montpellier in contrast to the Roman *patria potestas*. As long as a child continued to live under the paternal roof, the power was in effect, but, when the child departed to set up his/her own household, there was a tacit cessation of the power.[24] According to article 53 of the 1204 *coutumes* of Montpellier, sons and daugh-ters, married with the consent of their fathers (and for women that consent was necessary to enter into marriage), were considered emancipated.[25] There existed, in addition, the act of formal emancipation.[26] The private law special-ist Pierre Petot went so far as to state that the *coutumes* of Montpellier (1204) and Toulouse (1286) recorded dispositions on paternal power that were the complete opposite of Roman law.[27] Some of the Cabanis extended family members had enjoyed emancipation, as noted earlier. Martha's sons escaped *patria potestas* through the death of their father, but Martha had considerable authority, as we will see, and may have inherited that power.

In notarial practice in Montpellier, one finds situations that owed noth-ing to Roman law, where women were provided significant powers. For example, as early as the mid-thirteenth century, there is the stipulation in the will of a prominent Montpellier merchant, Petrus Vesiani, of his desire that his wife succeed to his authority: "wishing and instituting that she be the mistress and powerful one, as long as she lives, in my house."[28] Martha de Cabanis very likely enjoyed this kind of authority after Guiraudus's death.

The legal scholar Jean Hilaire noted that a father, in designating the mother as guardian in his will, applied terms to her such as *domina et potens* in his house and that such clauses in wills from the thirteenth to the fifteenth century characterized the mother as lifetime head of the familial community in the terms of "mistress and lord, power, judge" ("domina et senhoressa, poderosa, rectrix").[29] Martha would likely have held this position for her lifetime, if she was so appointed by Guiraudus's will. An interesting twist on this authority was also present in Provence, where, at the end of the Middle Ages, in spite of the evolution of stronger Roman law influence, legal special-ist Roger Aubenas spoke of a "veritable delegation of paternal power to the widow," when she succeeded by virtue of her husband's will to his position as head of the family and the estate, becoming "lady and administrator" ("dame et administraresse").[30] The widow in Provence was also called *seig-neuresse* and *dame du patrimoine*.[31] According to Aubenas, the widow could throw sons out of the family household. Widowhood throughout Europe was a privileged status, nowhere more so than in medieval southern France.[32] Scholars of the Crown of Aragon found some of the same terminology in documents relating to widows as guardians. Winer finds the formula "domina et potens" in wills where women were not officially named guardian just as in cases where they were. She found cases where the mother and grandmother would jointly be guardians. "On 20 July 1279, Bernat Marti of Peyrestortes, tailor and resident of Perpignan, directed that his wife Maria and mother Esclarmonda Marti be: '*dominae* and *potentes* of their children and my goods and *tutrices* and *gubernatores* of them.' "[33] The title of *tutrix* was often linked to that of *domina*. Bensch noted similar language in Barcelona, "dominae et potentissimae," but argued that there was a decline after 1250 in the tendency to grant widows broad administrative powers.[34]

Roman law sought to protect women from being defrauded or duped in obligations they might make. To this end, Roman law restricted their actions, with the result that they could not fully engage in business. The *Senatusconsultum Velleianum*, a first-century CE action the institution of which is the subject of some controversy among Roman legal historians, established an essential rule: "women are not to intervene on someone else's behalf" ("ne pro ullo feminae intercederent"). The *Senatusconsultum Velleianum* extended the original prohibition of a woman obligating herself in favor of her husband to all obligations for another.[35] This *senatusconsultum* applied only in those cases where the woman had no stake in what she was doing and ceased when she was acting for personal profit.[36] As Roman legal historian John Crook commented, the most common instance for such intervention, in the literal translation of the verb *intercedere*, was between debtor and creditor, that is, in the guaranteeing of someone else's debt, thus as a guarantor or a surety, in Crook's terms.[37] Crook pointed out that the dangers of suretyship went far beyond those of gifts, for which the amount was established, to include debts. The surety or guarantor might not be aware of the extent of her obligation. Crook saw the *Senatusconsultum Velleianum* as a measure of protection for women in an area of risk at a time, the first century, when agnatic guardianship (in the male line) no longer furnished such protection.[38] There is not a consensus about circumstances of its establishment, but what is important is how the *senatusconsultum* was used in the Middle Ages and, in particular, what basis it laid for women's legal agency, whether in business, in court cases, or in witness testimony.[39]

In Martha's case, these protections could have constrained the kinds of actions that a guardian might need to take, as they focused specifically on not undertaking obligations on behalf of others. Within Roman law, there were in the *Digest* of the *Corpus Iuris Civilis* several succinct prohibitions against a woman's legal capacity in the affairs of others.[40] Jean Hilaire viewed renunciations of these actions, in general, as a further basis beyond marital authorization for a woman to act.[41]

In this context, renunciation of the *Senatusconsultum Velleianum* offered a significant building block, along with other renunciations, in the construction of legal agency for women and is pertinent to the role of women as guardians.[42] Notarial contracts were filled with often-abbreviated renunciations of various protections or actions in Roman law stemming from decrees and orders of the Roman Senate, so-called *senatusconsulta* or certain defenses (*exceptiones*) available to the defendant to counter the plaintiff's claims. Women frequently renounced the *Senatusconsultum Velleianum*, as it restricted their ability to manage their own affairs and to make engagements on behalf of others.[43] The renunciation of a legal remedy or action was one of the options under Roman law and a very common formula in medieval notarial acts.[44] Martha in her notarial contracts renounced Roman law protections regularly.[45]

The Montpellier practice is echoed across the Crown of Aragon territories. Marie Kelleher found the interpretation of the *Senatusconsultum Velleianum* varied across the geography, but there are examples where its renunciation was required for a woman to assume guardianship. She noted that, as early as the Theodosian Code of 438, women had to renounce the *Senatusconsultum Velleianum* in order to assume guardianship. They also had to declare they would not remarry.[46]

The legal treatise *Practica aurea libellorum*, written in Martha's era, demonstrated how Roman law was put to the service of women's legal agency. Its author was Petrus Jacobi of Aurillac, a legal specialist of the late thirteenth and early fourteenth centuries, who was a doctor of laws and law professor in Montpellier, as well as a judge in Mende. He studied in Toulouse and with Montpellier masters. Jacobi's discussion of the institution of a mother's guardianship of minor children (*tutela*) can shed light on Martha's agency.[47]

Petrus Jacobi was very much concerned with the reconciliation of legal practice and Roman law in his book of legal procedure, *Practica aurea libellorum*, written about 1311, with several additions over the first half of the fourteenth century.[48] Jacobi offered a useful perspective on the matter of Roman law renunciations and the matter of women's legal agency that drew upon his actual experience in the law in fourteenth-century Montpellier.[49] In addition to students, his audience included legal practitioners for whom real life examples would have had resonance.[50] His discussion of guardianship reflects directly on its practice by widows such as Martha when they appeared before the notary.[51]

In the passage on *tutela* (guardianship) in the *Practica aurea*, Jacobi referred frequently to Roman law but also to the learned law of the Middle Ages, the *Glossa ordinaria* of the *Corpus Iuris Civilis*, and treatises by significant legal scholars, such as Placentinus, Azo, Odofredus, and Martinus, who themselves commented on a woman's role as guardian of her minor children. At the heart of the problem of a woman acting as guardian of her children was her incapacity in Roman law to make legal claims in court on behalf of others due to the *Senatusconsultum Velleianum*. By renouncing its protection, a mother could act as guardian. The *Corpus Iuris Civilis* required that women renounce the *Senatusconsultum Velleianum*, implying that they would not use the *exceptio* available under it as a defense against their creditors. Thus, in the legislation of Justinian, a woman's legal incapacity could be circumvented to permit her assumption of the administration of *tutela*. A mother's place in the care and education of her children had been recognized for a long time before this, and a union of the spiritual and physical aspects of *tutela* was now realized.

With one issue settled, Jacobi made an attempt to rationalize the disparity between Roman legal texts denying the appointment of mothers as guardians of children in wills, on the one hand, and, on the other, contemporary jurisprudence and actual practice allowing women as testamentary guardians through an argument for the will of the deceased: since Roman law permitted a mother to be guardian if the father had not provided testamentary guardians, his will and the law could be seen to concur if she were provided as testamentary guardian.[52] In this way, Jacobi reasoned, the law of his day might be seen to correct the *lex nova*.[53] If Jacobi's defense of the law of his own day is somewhat freely constructed, it appears to be guided by humane and just considerations, namely, the will of the deceased and the desirability of a mother's guardianship. He also confronted the frequency of such appointments in fourteenth-century Montpellier.

Where Jacobi ran into difficulty was in the discrepancies he discovered between the law of his day and the latest version of Justinianic law, the *lex nova*, specifically in the institution of a mother as guardian by reason of her husband's will.[54] Jacobi admitted that he was embarrassed by the appearance of an institution in his own day—a mother's testamentary guardianship— that had no foundation in Roman law; in fact, Roman law would seem to prohibit such an institution.[55] To clarify the role of a mother as guardian, Jacobi introduced a discussion of the order of succession to *tutela* for which he relied on and amplified the latest Justinianic stipulations. Mothers and grandmothers were to supersede all legitimate guardians, either agnates or cognates, if they renounced the *Senatusconsultum Velleianum* in the judge's presence, swore to act in the ward's interest, renounced all other aid, and made an inventory, giving sureties for the property of the ward.[56] In fact, *Novella* 118, 5, prohibited guardianship in regard to all women except the mother and grandmother but accepted them if they renounced without oath, any remarriage, or aid coming from the *Senatusconsultum Velleianum*.[57] Rebecca Winer noted the similarities across southern Europe in regard to the role of the grandmother: "The place of the grandmother in the normative Catalan view of guardianship reveals that legislators considered the widows of a man's family to be more suitable prospective guardians than any male relatives."[58]

Jacobi concluded his discussion with his belief that a mother named guardian in a will was in need of confirmation by the judge and that she must renounce the *Senatusconsultum Velleianum* and all other aid.[59] Whether Martha and her contemporaries went through such a formal procedure is unknown. They may have, as their contemporaries in Perpignan and the Crown of Aragon did. What is interesting is that Jacobi sought to confront the risks that a mother such as Martha might take in assuming guardianship by envisioning certain precautions for the woman as testamentary guardian, nevertheless sanctioning what, in a strict interpretation of Roman law, would be an extralegal situation. Such an empirical position is understandable in Jacobi who was both a teacher and a practitioner of the law. He was familiar with the Montpellier customs where renunciation of the *Senatusconsultum Velleianum* was invoked in local notarial practice, particularly in the case of surety. For him, the renunciation of the *senatusconsultum* was a means of sustaining testamentary guardianship for women. In the law of practice, which prevailed in fourteenth-century Montpellier, it was common practice for women to be named testamentary guardians in their husbands' wills.[60] The role Martha enjoyed very likely reflects this situation where practice ignored or overruled legal strictures.

The 1204 Montpellier customs, still the standard for local practice in Martha's day, make reference to this Roman law protection in article 38 where one finds reference to renunciation of the *Senatusconsultum Velleianum*, in the matter of sureties. This article reads:

> If a woman stands surety for someone else (male or female), she is
> held responsible in those cases that the laws permit. For, according
> to Roman law, intercession of a woman prevails: in the ignorance of
> the creditor; in the knowledge of her who obligates herself, in gifts
> (largesse); by reason of her own affairs, through *renunciation* [my
> emphasis]; through remission (release) of pledge [or] of mortgage;
> according to a renewal of the obligation after two years; if the surety
> is recognized by instrument in the presence of three witnesses;
> through free will; through dowry; and if she practices a trade and
> guarantees in that capacity, or with the wish of her husband, she is
> effectively obligated.[61]

As Pierre Tisset commented, the list of circumstances in which women could
be legally obligated as sureties "runs from the error of the creditor and the
fraud of the women" "to the instrument drafted in the presence of three
witnesses and to the general renunciation." The renunciation in question is
the *Senatusconsultum Velleianum*. Pertinent to the issue were texts from both
the *Code* and the *Digest*.[62] The fullest endorsement of a woman's contractual
rights in which a woman's ability to act as *fideiussor* or guarantor in a contractual agreement was, thus, affirmed.[63] This statute 38, in fact, provides direct
endorsement of the situation that the *Senatusconsultum Velleianum* was originally introduced to obviate. Certainly, the institution of guarantor was a
cornerstone of medieval business law and practice. The fact that women
could function as sureties for others implied that they were able to contract
obligations themselves, and one observes this currently in the notarial evidence of practice. Montpellier usage also acknowledged that a woman was
viewed as capable of effective obligation if she exercised a trade and acted by
reason of it.

Notarial documents are rife with renunciations, causing a debate about
the real-life application of such formulas. In a study of Roman legal renunciations, Peter Riesenberg made a compelling argument that there was substance
behind these formulas of renunciation, not simply the desire for the notary
to increase the word count of his contracts in order to augment revenues, nor
indeed the conflict between Roman and customary laws that Edmond Meynial had seen in the tensions surrounding the recovery of Roman law.[64] John
Pryor concurred with Riesenberg's reasoning: "It is a fallacy to think that in
the Middle Ages lawyers and notaries wasted words, ink, or paper."[65] Riesenberg saw the emergence of a new economy placing greater pressures on the

assurance of individual contractual freedom and increasing the complexity of business; these developments in turn necessitated the renunciation clauses.[66] Medieval jurists admonished renunciation of "every possible benefit and exception," leading Riesenberg to assert that "the renunciations were more than empty phrases."[67]

Renunciations began to appear in the documents of twelfth-century southern Europe and spread widely in the western Mediterranean, contributing to a broad continuum in legal culture and business. Riesenberg cited the date of 1171 for the first appearance of a renunciation clause in Montpellier in the cartulary of the Guilhem lords.[68] Very common in the early fourteenth-century notarial contracts of Montpellier in Martha's day, renunciations of Roman law provisions may have been as much a ritual of business as an actual legal protection by this time.[69] The medieval economy had grown tremendously, and individuals were accustomed to freedom of contract. Yet the continued inclusion of these clauses provided additional reassurance to the engagements at hand and reinforced the structure of trust on which the medieval economy depended. Renunciations in Montpellier contracts served to provide a basis for women's legal agency, both in business operations and within the court system in the first half of the fourteenth century. In all likelihood, Martha appeared before a court to make such renunciations when she became guardian of her sons. Whether she made an inventory with sureties is unknown.

One can trace actual legal practice in the south of France through notarial acts. The living law is reflected in the contracts that people established, with the record keeping of the medieval notary guiding the construction of legal obligation. In fourteenth-century Montpellier women like Martha were frequently named in their husbands' wills as guardians of their minor children and curators of their adolescent and young adult children. As noted earlier, *tutela* applied to children under age fourteen and *cura* generally from fourteen to eighteen or twenty, although this was not rigid. In 1339, Martha was still acting in the capacity of guardian to her older sons, but thereafter she appeared in acts alongside the boys without this designation.[70] Guiraudus would have been twenty-five in 1340 and Jacobus twenty-two, making it unlikely she would have continued to exercise curatorship. She continued to be their collaborator, involved in their business perhaps as a lifetime administrator of the estate of her late husband.

The inclusion of renunciations was common in acts passed by women as guardians, but rarely does one find specific enumeration of the pretexts involved.[71] Generally, the notary provided a very abbreviated list or simply the formula "*renuncio*" or the abbreviated "*ren.*" Occasionally, in an extended form of a contract, the actual renunciation of the *Senatusconsultum Velleianum* can be noted.[72] In the numerous acts that Martha recorded with the notary Guillelmus Nogareti, he almost always included the mention of renunciations, but in a very abbreviated fashion without specification of the *Velleianum.* There is often in the notarial act a general renunciation clause in Martha's contracts, "*cum omne renunciatione,*" inserted without specifics.[73] Because of the lack of specificity in most acts, it is not possible to compare the differences in renunciations in the hands of women versus men; men too renounced Roman law protections, though clearly not the *Vellianum* that addressed the situation of women. In acts recorded for men, there is the same lack of specificity in most of their renunciations of Roman law protection.[74]

Both the marital authorization and the renunciation of the *Vellianum* removed obstacles to a woman's performance of the duties of guardian or her actions in other legal and economic capacities on her own or on behalf of others.[75] Women engaged in business transactions of many different kinds in the role of guardian and also as executors of the estates of their husbands, with appointment by testament.[76] In other contexts, wives, widows, and single women could act alone.[77]

In Montpellier practice, as Petrus Jacobi discerned, women enjoyed considerable agency, functioning as sureties for their husbands and as testamentary guardians of their children. Roman law may have resisted endorsement of these roles for women, but fourteenth-century southern France used the resources of this law, through renunciations of Roman law actions, along with reinforcement of women's legal position in municipal statutes, as the means to create considerable legal capacity for women.[78] The actions of Martha that form the central threads of this study reveal considerable agency and a capacity to act in court to defend the interests of her family and to manage her own interests.[79] We do not know to what degree Martha was aware of the underlying support for her legal position. But there were lawyers in the Cabanis extended family, Stephanus de Cabanis and Jacobus de Cabanis, who could have counseled her.

Unless they entered the Church, most medieval women married if they had some economic means.[80] Marriage, dowry, guardianship, and inheritance were among the most important institutions affecting the status and life experience of women in the Middle Ages. A woman's marriage, accompanied by the constitution of her dowry, set her place in the economic and social hierarchy. Women could be testamentary heirs and could dispose of their own property through wills. Guardianship invited independent economic activities conducted by women on behalf of the family fortune. The loss of her husband opened the door for Martha to become guardian of her children.

There remains the issue of whether our understanding of agency and the degree of privilege with which we endow it in the twenty-first century would have had any resonance for Martha or among women of the Middle Ages more generally. At the very least, it is likely that medieval women obeyed different impulses from those of late twentieth- or twenty-first century women. Their lives were guided by their own values. With few exceptions— Christine de Pisan, certainly—we are ignorant of their opinions and of what was most important to them.[81] We have only their acts, and a modest sampling of those, it is true, to inform us on a superficial level of what they did within the constraints of the law and society in which they lived.

CHAPTER 7

Guardianship in Practice: Commerce and Industry

> I [Jacobus] de Cabanis, merchant of Montpellier, son and universal
> heir of Lord Guiraudus de Cabanis [merchant] of Montpellier, of age,
> who am twenty years old, with the authority and consent of the Lady
> Martha, reverend [mother] and my *curatrix* in these present matters
> that I the said Martha, present in this matter, know to be true.
>
> —Acquittal for a *societas* partnership and new
> partnership, 18 March 1338

With her legal position as guardian established, it remained for Martha to seize the reins of her husband's business and, in the years following 1326, to begin grooming her sons for an active role. As a widow with young children, she was very vulnerable, making her family ties all the more important. She had married into an important extended family that would provide much support for her and her sons. Martha may have partnered with Guiraudus during his lifetime and thus been well versed to take over the business. There exists, however, the possibility that she had to learn everything at his death.

This chapter argues for Martha's initiative and her business acumen. It is possible that she was motivated by the need to keep everything going after Guiraudus's death while her sons learned the family business. Martha was not an international merchant in the mold of male merchants. She did not travel across the Mediterranean on business. She was the entrepreneurial head of a large household and family business that had many different facets, from long-distance trade to the import of silks and mercery of Lucca to industrial processing of linen. Although the documents remaining reveal her many business talents and considerable agency, it is not my intention to argue that she escaped the legal strictures of her patriarchal era.[1] She was caught inevitably in the diminished capacity of her gender, but she maneuvered skillfully within the constraints under which she lived.

In a pattern that stretches back to the Capetian monarchy, sons often kept in place the collaborators of their fathers.[2] This was certainly the strategy Martha adopted in regard to the Cabanis business entourage. Major collaborators and lesser personnel were there to assist her as she took over from her late husband in the 1320s. Present in Martha's and in her sons' notarial acts were trusted partners (*socii*) and assistants of the Cabanis entourage. They might act as procurators, and they often acted as witnesses in the notarial contracts.[3] Procurations were delegations of legal authority frequently employed in the Middle Ages in a variety of capacities. Petrus del Euze, merchant and colleague of the late Guiruaudus, was present in the earliest act regarding the Cabanis, a procuration on 22 December 1326 that named him procurator, contained in a document of 18 March 1328, in which Petrus received an acquittal on Jacobus's behalf from a legal specialist (*jurisperitus*) of Montpellier. It is possible that this payment was made in regard to the settlement of Guiraudus's estate, coming as it did two years after his death.[4] Petrus would be an active collaborator with Martha and her sons until his death in 1339. Johannes de Suehlis, linen specialist (*canabasserius*) and partner of the Cabanis, was closely involved in Cabanis business from the late 1330s. Other partners that emerge in that era were Bernardus de Felgueriis, merchant; Petrus de Ferrariis, merchant, mercer, and linen specialist; and Jacobus Oliverii, merchant and draper. They may have been colleagues of the late Guiraudus's or brought on board by Martha after his death. The relatives, likely blood cousins, Johannes Naturalis, Guiraudus Naturalis, and Guillelmus de Cabanis, served as procurators of the Cabanis. In addition to partners, additional personnel—Berengarius Gombergua, Johannes de Grabellis, Petrus de Albinhaco, and Bernardus Fornerii—were frequently present as witnesses and procurators in the family contracts. Bernardus de Rodesio was both factor (business assistant) and procurator, along with other factors. Then, too, the family notary, Guillelmus Nogareti, and his entourage of assistants and scribes were often involved in Cabanis business. This numerous group of associates and assistants would have been essential to Martha in running the family business and in introducing her sons to the intricacies of medieval affairs.[5] Close business collaborators were represented in the partnerships that Martha and later her sons Guiraudus and Jacobus undertook.

Because of her widowhood and her duties as guardian, but also because of her personality, Martha stands out for her business engagement, though her profile was not an uncommon one among Montpellier women.[6] Agnes de Bossones, a member of the urban elite and widow of Petrus de Bossones, merchant, changer, and *burgensis*, was a real estate mogul and philanthropist. Martha's in-law, Bernarda de Cabanis, wife of Jacobus, a draper, was an entrepreneurial mercer and moneylender. There is always the factor of individual personality in the actions people take. Given the depth of Martha's involvement in business, it would be difficult to argue against her aptitude for and commitment to these activities. Moreover, her activities illustrate the close ties and collaboration that could exist between mothers and sons, particularly in widowhood and guardianship.

In the late 1320s and early 1330s, records show Martha acting on behalf of Jacobus, undoubtedly because he was his father's universal heir. In that capacity, Jacobus would have inherited the bulk of the estate of his father, not dispensed in bequests, and the debts and credits related to it. Then, in the years 1336–40, Martha was recorded as *curatrix* for both Guiraudus (ages 21–25) and Jacobus (ages 18–22). Guiraudus and Jacobus were over fourteen, the age of practical majority, and under twenty-five, the age of formal Roman law majority, during the early years of evidence for their business contracts. Martha's youngest son Johannes was just fourteen at the beginning of this period (1336) and initially under guardianship (*tutela*). That Martha continued to serve as *curatrix* until her older boys were in their early twenties reflects their positive working relationship but also the importance of her involvement and expertise for the Cabanis business enterprise.[7] It may also represent the status that Guiraudus likely created for her in his will as an administrator of his estate for her lifetime, as long as she did not remarry, a feature of some Crown of Aragon wills.[8]

Martha de Cabanis appeared repeatedly in the private notarial register of Guillelmus Nogareti from 1336 to 1344. In the late 1320s and early 1330s, she was using the notary Johannes Holanie, though not with the frequency that she would develop in her relationship with Guillelmus Nogareti. Martha had many business techniques in her toolbox that were part of standard operating procedures for Montpellier merchants. She appeared in large partnership arrangements, the basis of the Cabanis business structure, in the role of *curatrix* of her older sons, to capitalize the Cabanis textile—silks, mercery of

Lucca, and wool cloths—and linen processing businesses.[9] She hired legal representation in the form of procurations to further her own and her family's business interests.[10] She managed real property transactions and restructured her own real estate holdings. Though she was not involved in the day-to-day sales of the wholesale mercery of Lucca business of her sons, as recorded in notarial contracts, she may well have acted in a supervisory capacity for the mercery shop that was likely in the Cabanis house.

Happenings within the town and the region would have been important to Martha as she adjusted to her life as a widow and guardian. The 1320s and early 1330s were marked by continuing climatic crisis and agricultural shortages. News of local, regional, and broader geographic scope circulated by word of mouth but also by more official means such as town criers, permitting inhabitants to be informed about their world. The year 1330 brought great drought, followed by rains and a flood of the Lez River in 1331 with the drowning of two hundred people. An eclipse of the sun was noted in May 1333. All inhabitants of Montpellier must have been affected by the disaster of that year when young men, who had consumed raw herbs from extreme hunger, died in the streets of Montpellier.[11] Some provisions were available from Burgundy and Venice, but no food came in from Lombardy or Sicily or Catalonia because of a Genoese war and the problem of piracy.[12] The early 1330s would have provided multiple challenges for all urban inhabitants, including members of the urban elite such as Martha.

Even in years of good harvest in some regions, grain might be scarce elsewhere, and if there was no water transport to inland sites, there existed no means of transferring surplus to regions of scarcity. The south of France in good years could export grain.[13] By the same token in years of poor harvest, thousands of bushels of grain were imported from across the Mediterranean into Montpellier by Italian companies such as the Bardi of Florence and by individual Montpellier grain merchants who controlled the local market. Urban inhabitants and people from the countryside around Montpellier purchased grain on the urban markets. Martha's guardianship began in a turbulent era.

We have trace of Martha and her son Jacobus in 1328, two years after Guiraudus's death, as noted above. Martha was referred to as guardian (*tutrix*) of Jacobus in a 1328 act certifying her agreement to an acquittal of obligations for her late husband. Jacobus was ten in 1328. Martha was undoubtedly in the wings when Petrus del Euze became Jacobus's procurator in December 1326.[14] Jacobus was noted as the son of the late Guiraudus and his universal heir in the 1328 act. Petrus del Euze was a colleague of Jacobus's father, merchant and fellow mercer, recorded in 1327 selling black silks, worth 60 *agneaux*, to a buyer from Pomayrols.[15] As noted above, Petrus del Euze would be in business with the Cabanis until his death in 1339.[16]

In 1333, Petrus del Euze was termed a partner (*socius*) of Jacobus, already called a mercer by the notary when Jacobus would have been all of fifteen. Petrus and Jacobus sold taffeta together on 20 May 1333.[17] Jacobus was also in business at fifteen with Jacobus Oliverii, draper of Montpellier, with whom he was a partner (*socius*). Oliverii gave an acquittal on their behalf earlier in April 1333.[18] Thus Jacobus was immersed early on, with Martha's consent, in the textile business. These acts do not mention Martha, as legally Jacobus at over fourteen could appear before the notary without a guardian. However, this would not have happened without Martha's approval nor without the close collaboration of Petrus del Euze, who was undoubtedly mentoring Jacobus. The late Guiraudus's colleagues introduced Jacobus to a diverse array of economic activities at a young age. Though her sons would have specialties, they had diversified investments from the beginning and would continue to build on those as well as on their involvement in mercery and linen.

It is likely that we capture, in the remaining evidence, only a portion of the business activity in which Martha was involved. The notarial record is very spotty for Montpellier in the era before 1350.[19] The private register, an extraordinarily rich repository of information, maintained by Guillelmus Nogareti for the Cabanis, begins in 1336 and lasts through 1342, with cancellations of obligations noted into the first half of 1345.[20] Martha was last mentioned on 18 March 1344 in the notarial record in a cancellation of one of the major partnerships she had initiated as guardian.[21] Likely, there was another Cabanis register with continuing chronology that has not survived. With much less frequency, Martha and her sons used the notary Johannes Holanie in 1328, 1333, 1336, and 1342. Even with the very small surviving notarial archive in Montpellier before 1350, one finds acts of the same individuals in more than one notary's registers. This is a reflection of the small world of Montpellier business as well as the omnipresence and indispensible role of the medieval notary.[22] Holanie is the notary with the most surviving registers—five general registers extending from 1327 to 1344—in the period before 1350.[23] Extended family members like Bernarda de Cabanis used Holanie as well; a relative by marriage and business associate, Johannes Naturalis, used Holanie, and Maria Naturale, daughter of Petrus de Cabanis, used

Holanie and Nogareti. Nogareti clearly had other clients besides the Cabanis, as did Holanie. Nogareti very likely kept general registers as well as the Cabanis private register. It is thus difficult to assess what percentage of the business involvement of Martha and her sons comes through in the surviving evidence. It is necessary to acknowledge that we see through a glass darkly. But, that said, the remaining evidence is unusually rich for the time period.[24]

Martha's collaboration with her sons as *curatrix* of Jacobus and Guiraudus and *tutrix* of the youngest brother, Johannes, is illustrative of the importance of kinship ties in business.[25] The importance of kinship in business cannot be overstated for the Middle Ages, though the Montpellier evidence showed a level of kinship under 20 percent in the luxury trade, except in the woolen cloth trade.[26] In partnership, the levels rose to as high as 50 percent in maritime partnerships and to above 30 percent in some financial transactions. There was significant collaboration among siblings and same-name kin; fathers and sons and mothers and sons were also mentioned.[27] The collaboration between brothers as *socii* (partners) was the most common kinship link in business. Jacobus and Guiraudus represented the typical *socius* partnership for which there was no surviving contract.[28] Jacobus and Guiraudus were partners, but Martha was never mentioned as the *socia* of either of them or of her younger son Johannes.[29] Rather, her role of guardian was evoked. It was Jacobus, in particular, who must have shown a real knack for business early, perhaps explaining his designation as his father's universal heir. He may, of course, just have been his father's favorite. His early partnerships with Petrus del Euze and Jacobus Oliverii of 1333 suggest they recognized his talent and trusted him enough to collaborate.[30]

Martha as the guardian of her children engaged in industrially and commercially oriented partnerships. As guardian, she was also involved in property transactions related to the linen processing business. In her own behalf, she handled matters of real property. Her sons, especially Jacobus, were deeply invested in a real property investments and management.[31] Martha was further implicated in many commercial and financial matters through procurators in affairs that may have related to the administration of her late husband's estate.

There has survived no mention of lawsuits associated with the estate of the late Guiraudus. The 1328 acquittal of a *jurisperitus*, mentioned above, is the only suggestion of legal affairs relating to Guiraudus's estate.[32] Martha may have escaped major difficulties in assuming control of her late husband's estate on behalf of her sons. This was not always the case in the experience of widows, named as guardians of their children. Agnes de Bossones, guardian of her three minor daughters in 1301, faced a dispute with family members, perhaps the sons of her late husband by a first marriage that involved her litigation in the courts of both the king of Majorca and the king of France in Montpellier. She was involved in litigation for several years.[33] Maria Lamberti, widow of the late merchant Petrus Lamberti, and *tutrix* of her son, sought the approval of the court of the king of Majorca in Montpellier to sell off the real property of her late husband to repay a Lombard (an Italian creditor), who was threatening the estate with an auction of certain goods of Petrus. The court agreed, and Maria proceeded with the assistance of three sworn brokers who were able to find only one buyer.[34] Susan McDonough traced the court appearances of the widow Silona Filholine acting as tutor and curator of her children, when she defended herself against creditors who saw her as fully versed in her husband's business affairs. McDonough viewed Silona as characteristic of women in Marseille whose husbands were often away at sea or traveling on business and who were "when capable involved in their husbands' businesses and ran their homes."[35] They litigated to defend their assets. Rebecca Winer traced the ligitation of Raimunda de Camerada, widow of Pere de Camerada, a powerful royal servant in Perpignan and Roussillon; Raimunda was still dealing with debts relating to her guardianship twelve years after the death of her husband.[36] Martha was fortunate if she indeed encountered minimal difficulties as a guardian and administrator, but the slim records of these early years do not permit conclusions.

Martha's business interaction with her two older sons was frequent. As a woman in her mid-to-late thirties or early forties in the years of the Nogareti register, 1336–42, she could well have been directly engaged in the affairs of her husband and in transactions regarding her own real estate fortune before his death. Or she may just have been a keen observer of his actions and a quick study. Since Guiraudus was dead by late 1326, Martha had been operating alone for at least ten years as widow and guardian of her children when the Nogareti register evidence begins. Grooming her sons early—Jacobus was her procurator as early as 1335 at age seventeen in an acquittal for a house rental—she could relinquish greater authority to them by 1340.[37] Even as early as 1333, Martha allowed Jacobus an active role in the family business as soon as he reached the practical age of majority of fourteen.

Though Martha operated independently in the raising of her sons and in their initiation into the family business, she undoubtedly consulted kinsmen of the Cabanis family, who were probably never far afield. The business involvements of Martha's sons with members of the larger Cabanis family can be traced in detail, as noted in Chapter 3.[38] In all likelihood, Martha could have sought advice in informal ways, had she so chosen, from male and female family members such as the members of the Petrus's branch or the draper Jacobus's family, especially Jacobus's wife, the mercery specialist Bernarda. However, she acted alone or with her sons in most cases, supported by members of the trusted Cabanis business entourage that was in large measure inherited from her husband's business operations.[39] They were invariably present as witnesses to Martha and her sons' contracts. Her strategy seems to have gained momentum from 1336 on—at least it has left considerable trace—when she and her sons began to use Guillelmus Nogareti frequently as their notary.

To understand the nature of Martha's actions in her affairs and as guardian in the affairs of her sons in the family business, it is useful to consider the chronology and venue of the contracts. The following analysis is based on the Nogareti register with its approximately 327 acts spread over seven years, 1336–42, with, in addition, ninety-six cancellations of obligations upon their fulfillment extending as late as 1345.[40] The location of the passage of contracts helps define Martha's business operations. Numerous notarial acts relating to family business, her own and the acts related to her sons, were drawn up in Martha's house, as one would expect for members of the wealthy urban commercial elite. As noted in Chapter 4, Martha and her sons shared a house, the family home near Arc Saint-Nicolas. When she was the primary client, the notary noted the act was drawn up in her house. When she was acting as guardian in the family business or her sons were the principals, the notary called it the house of the brothers, that is, Martha's sons. If all were involved, the notary might speak of the house of those hiring in the case of a procuration. Rather than interpret the notary's designation of the place where an act was instituted in light of gender inferiority for Martha, is important to note that the notary often went where it was most convenient for his clients. But many of the Cabanis acts were passed at the notary's atelier in his own house.

We can trace Martha's direct involvement in twenty-three contracts of the Nogareti register, spanning the years 1336–42.[41] She was noted in one cancellation clause for a large partnership.[42] The years 1338 and 1342 saw Martha participating in seven and six acts, respectively. Nine acts explicitly state that the contractual recording by the notary took place in her house; six more state that they were being written in the house of the brothers that would have been the same structure. Once she was with her son Jacobus at the notary's atelier. It must have been easier for Martha, managing her household responsibilities, to do business in her house. She was in close proximity to her sons' mercery shop over which she may have had supervisory duties, and she was certainly involved in financing the business, as we will see. She would thus have had the responsibilities of management of a large urban mercantile dwelling and those of a thriving commercial and industrial business and of significant real estate interests.

Capitalization is an important dimension of business practice. The early years of record in the Nogareti register provide some insight into how Martha and her husband's colleagues maneuvered in financing the Cabanis business. The revenues from real estate would have provided some cash flow, the commercial properties yielding more than the long-term agricultural leases.[43] The profits from trade could be substantial, and these could be plowed back into the business. Still, to get things going, to generate the huge sums that Martha and the boys would invest in trade and industry, it is necessary to look elsewhere. Among the financial engagements of the Cabanis brothers, they were involved in managing monastic investments and farming of ecclesiastical revenues. Because the record begins early, it is likely that Guiraudus before his death or Martha under her guardianship set up these arrangements. On 4 July 1337, the abbot of Vallemagne entered into a mutual acquittal with Petrus del Euze and Martha's son Jacobus, *socii* (partners), for credits, loans, deposits, *commenda* contracts, and other obligations.[44] Jacobus was all of nineteen in 1337. With the acquittal, all instruments deriving from these engagements were thereby annulled. In a second act of the same date, Petrus del Euze, acting for himself and as procurator for Jacobus, confirmed owing Berengarius, abbot of Valmagne, 100 *l.p.t.* final accounting ("finali et legitime computo").[45] It is likely that the Cabanis, with Martha's approval, were capitalizing some of their commercial ventures with investments from local clergy. Then, too, this final accounting may have reflected the farming of ecclesiastical revenues.

Another avenue of attraction of investment capital lay, in fact, in the farming of ecclesiastical revenues. Merchants could bid to collect revenues due ecclesiastical institutions and personages. The expectation in farming revenues was that one would collect a sum greater than the bid, thereby generating a profit. On 4 November 1338, the canon and sacristan of Maguelone, Johannes de Cardona, granted Petrus del Euze and Jacobus an acquittal for 150 *l.t.* in diminution of 300 *l.t.* owing from the revenues of the last payment term of Michaelmas.[46] Del Euze engaged in a similar transaction with another merchant Bernardus de Felgueriis and was clearly the Cabanis specialist in this type of venture.[47] By 19 July 1339, Petrus del Euze was deceased, but on that date Cardona confirmed to the guardian of del Euze's children and to Jacobus and Guiraudus de Cabanis and Bernardus de Felgueriis the payment of 800 *l.p.t.* that they had owed for the purchase of the farm of ecclesiastical revenues on 9 May 1338.[48] The collection of ecclesiastical revenues could have eased the problem of cash flow in the complex commercial ventures of the Cabanis. The process meant that they would have had access to cash for a period of months before payment was due, with the turnaround time generally less than a year. There was, of course, a significant investment of time and labor in the collection of such revenues. The influx of capital from these engagements would have permitted Martha to orchestrate the large partnerships that underpinned the Cabanis operations.

Another source of funds was clearly the late Guiraudus's estate that had devolved on her son Jacobus. Martha was in control of these resources as guardian. On 18 March 1338, Jacobus, with Martha present and with her approval and consent as reverend mother and *curatrix*, drew up a *societas* partnership with Petrus del Euze, wherein Martha put in 2,000 *l.t.p.* from the goods of Jacobus ("I the said Martha place in the name of the institution of curator . . . from the goods of the said Jacobus 2000 *l.t.p.*).[49] Petrus put in 1,000 invested in diverse merchandise.[50] It is very clear that Martha as *curatrix* controlled the funds that Jacobus inherited as the universal heir of his father. The partnership was to run for four years. This was the largest *societas* partnership that left a record in the Montpellier notarial contracts before 1350.[51] This partnership came on the heels of a general acquittal of engagements with Petrus del Euze that had very likely involved a similar partnership for the previous four years. In the course of the act, Martha, Jacobus, and Petrus broke and annulled the earlier instruments of obligation in a general acquittal and absolved any further obligations that might be claimed on the basis of underage status or other reasons.

As a form of partnership, the *societas* in Montpellier saw greater investment of funds than the maritime or land *commenda*.[52] Jacobus at twenty years of age relied on maternal support. Martha as a sedentary investor, and not a traveling merchant—and in this she did not differ from many major male investors—had to manage family business interests from her home base in Montpellier. She had a rhythm of partnership investment, renewing a large *societas* every four years, with acquittal for the previous engagements preceding the new obligations.

This 1338 partnership between Jacobus and Martha with Petrus del Euze underpinned the active marketing of textiles, particularly silks and silk-related products, by the Cabanis brothers. They sold mercery of Lucca, raw silk, dyed silk, and China silk to local clients and foreigners from Toulouse, Narbonne, Cahors, Burgos, Valencia, and Castile, with a predominance of clients from Toulouse, Cahors, and parts of Spain.[53] Of these clients, Toulousans were dominant, representing over 60 percent of the clientele for sales of mercery of Lucca in Montpellier. Mercery likely referred to ribbons and threads but also may have included silk yarn, laces, gold thread, narrow ware, cloth of gold, velvet adornments, perhaps even silk head coverings.[54] Mercery of Lucca represented the elaborate damasks and brocades that were produced in Lucca and were a particular specialty of the Cabanis.

In silks, mercery of Lucca, and other textiles such as wool cloth, the young heir Jacobus plunged right in. There is no evidence that he underwent any formal apprenticeship outside the family home. Guiraudus's former colleagues would have been essential to the successful continuation of the Cabanis business, and Martha was the power behind the scenes, funding her sons' business investments. She and her late husband's colleagues partnered with the boys during their adolescence and young adulthood.

The medieval textile industry included the production and the finishing of cloths of many different fabrics. Wool cloth was the specialty of northern Europe, particularly northern France and the Low Countries.[55] Wool imported from England fueled the production of high-quality woolens that had a reputation among export products in the medieval Mediterranean world by the twelfth century. In the thirteenth century, the fairs of Champagne were the point of exchange of wool cloth for products of the Mediterranean world, particularly silks and spices.[56] Northern French provinces such as Burgundy produced linen from the flax plant, but so did Languedoc. Linen cloths were a valued product. Hemp from the cannabis plant was another valuable product, used to make canvas and rope, particularly important in maritime matters. The canvas/linen merchants (*canabasserii*) of Montpellier dealt in both linen and hemp fabrics.[57] Silks in the Mediterranean world made their way as raw fabric to Western Europe where they were finished at sites such as Lucca before cultivation of the silk worm permitted European production of silk. Cotton was also a feature of medieval textiles, coming from the eastern Mediterranean to Europe.[58] The Cabanis family specialized in mercery and silks on the one hand and in linen on the other, with some interest in wool cloth as well.

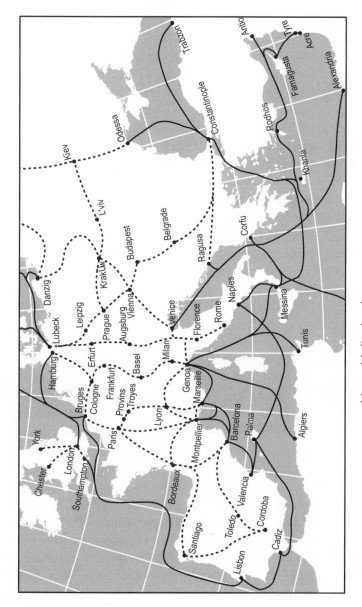

MAP 4. Medieval trade routes.

Montpellier's contacts with northern France included the Champagne Fairs and Paris. According to local transport contracts, the fairs were nineteen to twenty-four days distant from Montpellier, while Paris was usually attained in twenty-two to twenty-four days of travel.[59] Two main routes linked Montpellier and the south of France to the fairs: the Rhône Valley route and the Regordane.[60] The Rhône Valley route, involving travel partly on water, partly on land, lay for the most part outside French territory, across the Rhône in lands dependent on Provence and the empire. The Regordane ran entirely within France from Montpellier or Nîmes to Alès and then north across the Cévennes to Le Puy, Brioude, Issoire, Clermont, and on north. This latter was the traditional route used by merchants coming from Montpellier. Martha's sons Jacobus and Guiraudus shipped saffron to Paris. They were involved with the Champagne Fair towns in financial exchange as their father had been and as many Montpellier merchants were.[61]

The commercial business of the Cabanis brothers was handled in the traditional Montpellier fashion with the extension of commercial credits to their clients in this luxury trade. The credit sales of products took the form of recognitions of debt, whatever the item, silks, mercery of Lucca, wool cloth, linen, or spices. [62] Most recognitions of debt were established with an "on demand" term of repayment. In the case of mercery of Lucca, the actual repayment time extended from one month to a year, with two months the most commonly found delay. Repayment was at times scheduled for another town at a later date. In this fashion, the Cabanis and many other local merchants used the Languedocian fair town of Pézénas as a repayment site.[63] Towns on what might be considered a commercial circuit served this purpose as both debtors and creditors or their representatives would be frequenting these towns in the course of their trade.

Foreign exchange was often closely linked to commercial transactions as a means of obtaining credit for medieval merchants and underpinning trade. One borrowed money on a marketplace where one had purchases to make and arranged to reimburse the funds in another location in another coinage after the sale for profit, presumably, of the merchandise purchased.[64] Martha was not directly involved in this dimension of Cabanis business, nor were women recorded in foreign exchange contracts in Montpellier, though they were involved in lending money.[65] The Cabanis money exchange practices were closely tied to their commercial dealings. In five exchanges of the years 1339–42 that they recorded in Montpellier, they offered credit to spice merchants of Aurillac and Paris, to a Spaniard, and to the factor of an Italian merchant of Avignon.[66] The sums to be repaid were large: 500 *l.t.* and 945 *l.t.* for merchants of Aurillac, 500 *l.t.* for a spice merchant of Paris, 292 *l.t.* in money of Barcelona for a merchant of Valencia, and 810 florins for the Italian merchant of Avignon. In the latter case, Bernardus de Rodesio, procurator of Jacobus and Guiraudus, extended credit in the exchange to a factor of the Falletti of Avignon.[67] The Aurillac exchanges were to be reimbursed in Montpellier; thus they have the aspect of "dry exchanges" which in contractual terms closely resembled loans.[68] The Parisian spice merchant Guiraudus de Ganhaco operated through his procurator, a merchant of Alès, who promised repayment at the Lagny Fair, another of the Champagne Fairs that ran from 2 January to 22 February; the contract of exchange was established on 2 December 1339.[69] A Valencian merchant promised repayment in Valencia within two weeks of his engagement.[70] The basis for this extension of credit in the case of the Valencian was undoubtedly the Cabanis desire to acquire saffron and leather in that marketplace. It was to the Cabanis' advantage to have funds in Spain. Spices, saffron, and eastern spices sold to northern clients, as well as silks and mercery marketed in Spain, created the context for exchange borrowing on the part of clients of the Cabanis. In the case of repayment scheduled for one of the Champagne Fairs, the Cabanis or their agents would have needed capital in the north to acquire French cloths or Burgundian linen, which formed part of their exports to the Levant. They might also have procured the Burgundian wool that supplied some of the wool processing operations in the Montpellier hinterland.[71] The Cabanis may have traveled to both Champagne and Paris over the course of their careers and to territories of the Crown of Aragon, like their father.

The decades of the 1330s and 1340s were an ideal moment for the Cabanis' involvement in mercery and silks, and though there were challenges related to the worsening climate, bad harvests in some years with resulting famine, and the beginnings of the Hundred Years War, the Montpellier economy experienced resilience in these decades.[72] There is evidence of a silk-finishing industry in Montpellier already in the late thirteenth century. In 1294, a Montpellier merchant acknowledged his debt to a local mercer for silk that he promised to pay off in two silk cloths per week, one cloth (*senhay*) with stripes of gold and the other in the "little work of Montpellier," suggesting the town had a known specialty in silk-finishing production.[73] The merchant may have been otherwise commissioning the weaving of gold thread into silks. Dyeing, embroidering, and trimming featured among the local finishing activities. The silk involved likely reached Montpellier as raw fabric that was then treated and decorated.

Women were represented in textile finishing industries. They were trained in apprenticeship to spin gold that was used in embroidery, in brocade, and in decoration of cloth, to make silk corduroy (*cordurarie de serico*), to produce mercery, to do linen embroidery, and to tailor cloths.[74] Women were involved in sales of silk and mercery. The mercer Bernarda de Cabanis made loans to rural women and couples, accepting repayment in mercery; she trained rural women in the production of mercery and sold mercery in Montpellier.[75] Towns in the south of France, such as Alès in the Cévennes north of Montpellier, enjoyed individualized designations of workmanship, as did Montpellier, noted above.[76]

The Cabanis brothers as mercers and merchants fit into a tradition of trade and production of mercery and finished silks that stretched back into the thirteenth century and perhaps beyond.[77] From the perspective of Montpellier, Lucca emerged in the thirteenth century as the prime mover in silks in the western Mediterranean basin, furnishing lots of product to Montpellier and other western European towns. The artistry of the Lucchese industry was present in products traded in Montpellier: *argento de Lucha cerico*, a cloth of silk of Lucca, possibly silver brocade, and *cerico et auro de Lucha*, which may have been gold brocade.[78] Montpellier early on imported silks as well from the Levant, the southern Caspian Sea region of Ghilan, and even China.[79]

Montpellier's specialty in scarlet dyeing, first emerging in the twelfth century, laid the groundwork for a silk-dyeing industry that is also visible by the end of the thirteenth century.[80] Jewish participation at this date in the local industry is likely. The dyeing trade was a common occupation of medieval Jews in Provence and Italy.[81]

Montpellier was well equipped for a silk-finishing industry. The presence in Montpellier of a well-developed metalwork industry, products of which may well have graced Martha's home, as noted in Chapter 4, dovetailed with the finishing work on silk cloths, in particular. The metalwork industry of Montpellier furnished a significant complement to the silk-finishing industry in Montpellier in this era. Wives of goldsmiths were involved in the precious metal industry, hiring workers and contracting apprenticeship to teach the spinning of gold thread. Gold work done on cloth in Montpellier was predominantly a feminine undertaking. Three apprenticeship contracts in 1327 to learn the spinning of gold involved girls apprenticed to a goldsmith, to the wife of a grain merchant whose specialty was spun gold, and to the wife of a goldsmith. These materials were, in turn, undoubtedly used in embroidery of silk.[82] Gold thread production—the spinning of gold thread—was present in Montpellier, as it was in many Mediterranean towns.[83]

Martha's husband Guiraudus was a mercer, as were several other members of the extended Cabanis family. Her older sons were designated as mercers from an early age, and their brother Johannes was apprenticed later in the mercery trade in 1342 at the age of twenty.[84] Jacobus was active in the textile trade by 1333. Martha was facilitating her sons' partnerships with former colleagues of their father and financing these enterprises to further their business. By the 1330s, there had emerged an emphasis on Lucchese merchandise that was reflected in the new formula that appears in silk sales in Montpellier: *merces de Luca*, mercery of Lucca.[85]

The demand for silks cloths and embroidered silk garments, produced by the Montpellier finishing industry, was high during the presence of the Avignon popes in the south of France. Given Montpellier's involvement in marketing silks and elaborate damasks and brocades, often of Lucchese origin, it is no surprise that the town represented a market for the luxury fabric consumption in Avignon.[86] Martha's sons' connections with Avignon would have facilitated their involvement in the finished silk market.[87]

Beyond the silk and mercery business, another significant sector in which Martha and her sons engaged was linen processing and marketing. The second major area of investment of the Cabanis business during Martha's guardianship was in the processing and exporting of linen. In a bilaterial *commenda* of 10 February 1339 (n. s.), Martha, acting as *curatrix* of Jacobus and Guiraudus, crafted a partnership with Johannes de Suelhis, linen merchant, in which the Cabanis investment was 1,100 *l.t.p.* that was transferred as 880 gold deniers, with the gold *denier ad leonem* valued at 25 *s.t.*[88] The arrangement was to run for four years. This was a bilateral *commenda* because the working partner also contributed to the capital of the venture. Suelhis invested 341 *l.* and 15 *s.t.p.* He was to receive a salary of 200 *l.t.* from the profits of the enterprise and the Cabanis brothers the residual profits from their *commenda* investment. Suelhis was to profit solely from the money that he put into the business. Martha, Jacobus, and Guiraudus agreed to these terms. As in the partnership with Petrus del Euze, the sums that Martha was wielding were significant.[89] Suelhis promised to repay their principal investment with a proper accounting at the end of the term, vowing to trade and negotiate with these funds under the ordinances of the pope and the king of France and other princes. Suehlis committed to his engagement with renunciations of Roman law protections, swearing on the Evangelists (the Gospels) to uphold the terms of the contract. Then it was the turn of Jacobus and Guiraudus, who acknowledged they acted with the authority, advice, and consent of their mother and *curatrix*; Martha confirmed that was true.[90] The contract was duly cancelled at the Cabanis house at its completion on 13 May 1344, with all parties, including Martha, expressing satisfaction, over five years after its inception.[91] The cancellation, like the original obligation, was drawn up in the brothers' house with Guillelmus de Conchis as witness, along with Petrus de Albinhaco and the notary Nogareti. Martha was supervising the inception of this business arrangement and still involved at the formal cancellation of the engagement.

Johannes de Suelhis was to use the funds of the 1339 partnership to negotiate in his trade, that of *canabasserius* or linen/hemp merchant, for a period of four years. In 1340 and again in 1341, Suelhis drafted *commenda* partnership contracts for the export of linen clothes of Autun and of Aurillac to the Byzantine Empire and to Cyprus on behalf of the Cabanis.[92] His assistants were involved in these travels. Suelhis hired several apprentices in this period to assist him in his trade.[93] He was thus actively fulfilling his side of the partnership agreement. Wool cloth and linen were common exports from Montpellier to the eastern Mediterranean basin.[94]

For production and processing of fabrics, the Cabanis family had mills called *molendinum, bladeria, paratoria*, and boilers (*candoraria*) near the Lez source at Saint-Clément la Rivière.[95] Jean Combes identified the *paratoria* as mills for the preparation of linen and canvas, along with boilers that were part of Montpellier industry.[96] To further the processing business, the Cabanis brothers rented a stream to Johannes de Suelhis at Saint-Clément la Rivière with their processing mill (*molendino nostro paratorio*) and the *paratoria et bladeria* that they had on the Lez River with all the water and the usual meadows for four years for the fee of 140 *l.t.* each year, due at Lent.[97] Suelhis accepted the rental terms. Witnesses to the engagement were Petrus Ricardi, cleric, Jacobus Oliverii, merchant and relative by marriage of the Cabanis, as well as sometime partner, and the notary Nogareti.

The boilers and mills of the Montpellier hinterland were used in processing linen and wool, though the surviving documents do not provide details of the process.[98] If the process began with the flax fibers, they would have been retted, loosening the fibers from the flax stalk. Then came the removal of woody parts of the stalk, called scutching. The fibers were combed before being spun into yarn and then woven into fabric.[99] The raw fabric would then have been treated.

Johannes de Suehlis, the Cabanis agent and himself a linen/hemp merchant (*canabasserius*), was occupied with pastures for sheep and with the purchase and sale of raw wool, suggesting that there might have been wool processing (fulling) in the Cabanis mills, as well as linen production.[100] Suelhis bought and sold wool fleeces for his own account, sometimes in exchange for grazing grasses from the Bois de Valène, a forest owned by the municipal administration of Montpellier.[101] Suehlis obtained some wool from his brother Bernardus.[102] On several occasions, he sold grasses of Valène that he farmed from the consuls of Montpellier for the feed of grazing animals, in all likelihood sheep.[103] On his own account, he purchased wood that was probably destined for industrial fuel.[104] He sold wood from the forest of Valène on behalf of his partners, Jacobus de Cabanis and Petrus de Ferreriis.[105] On other occasions, he bought wood with Jacobus.[106] The fabric processing activities of the Cabanis near the source of the Lez would have demanded a source of energy for the boiler. Suelhis bought the wood from men of the immediate region, Montferrier, Prades, and Assas, to run the bleaching and finishing operations in which the Cabanis were investing.[107]

This industrial work was undoubtedly labor-intensive. The Cabanis had Johannes de Grabellis rent them a *garrigue* area not far from the Lez to permit the coming and going of men and animals from the processing plant.[108] On 9 January 1342, the mills were rented out to Hugo Fabri, who took charge of them for his own account and agreed to restore them with the equipment repaired and intact at the end of his rental. This rental contract provided details of the equipment at the mills such as boiler and caldrons, involved with the textile processing industry.[109]

As noted earlier, the region of Montpellier did not possess rivers with strong currents, with the exception of the Hérault River at about thirty kilometers distance from the town to the west.[110] The Lez River flowed a little to the east of the center of town, and two tributaries of the Lez traversed the medieval city, permitting the treatment of raw wool and the bleaching of linen and canvas, probably done in boilers in either thread or fabric form, and in the treatment of leather. The topography of Montpellier contained two quarters, the Flocaria and the Blancaria, since the twelfth century, where artisans in these industries would have lived.[111]

In regard to the funding of ventures in mercery and in linen, Martha used the contractual instruments of her day. As a form of partnership, the *societas* in general saw greater investment of funds than the maritime or land *commenda*.[112] Martha was sanctioning the use of funds from the paternal inheritance that had come to Jacobus as universal heir of his father. Jacobus, at twenty or twenty-one years of age in the early ventures, relied on maternal support. Martha, acting on behalf of Jacobus as a sedentary investor and not a traveling merchant, did not differ from major male investors in managing the business interests of her son. Martha most often represented the interests of her sons in the role of guardian. Her successful management of these enterprises speaks volumes about her competence.

Martha's husband Guiraudus was very likely already established in the mercery business that would become the specialty of his sons. An important segment of the medieval urban economy was in the hands of retailers/wholesalers, including both men and women, who at times made small sales and at other times participated in large transactions. The retail market was developing apace in the fourteenth century.[113] The Montpellier transactions do not distinguish between "retail" and "wholesale" operations, and it is very difficult to separate out these two markets, unless through the inadequate measure of the size of the transaction.[114] Moreover, Montpellier inhabitants, male and female, dealt in both dimensions of the market. Women like Martha were familiar with international, regional, and local trade and fully cognizant of the standard credit and investment mechanisms of their day. They were also involved in finance, in trade, in artisanal industry and apprenticeship, and in agriculture. With Martha's guidance, her sons Jacobus and Guiraudus were able to perfect a significant specialty in mercery of Lucca and a presence in the processing and exporting of linen. Early in their careers, they relied on partnership with members of their father's business entourage and on extended family members, setting a pattern of guidance and collaboration that would persist even as they came of age.

The Cabanis fortune diversified beyond the commercial and industrial enterprises just discussed. The family also developed and managed a large landed fortune, some of it inherited as well from the late Guiraudus. Chapter 8 will explore the family's landholdings, with Martha operating first as guardian and then independently and ultimately tracing a real estate strategy with her sons for the family fortune.

CHAPTER 8

Real Property

I Petrus Borzes, wine merchant, inhabitant of Montpellier, for me
and mine, confirm to you Lady Martha, wife of Guiraudus de
Cabanis, late merchant of Montpellier, present, stipulating, and
receiving for you and yours that I hold from you and wish and ought
to hold in *emphyteusis* and under your direct domain, counsel,
approval, and right of first refusal . . . that whole piece of vineyard
land.

—*Emphyteusis* recognition to Martha, 26 January 1338

Land was the major source of wealth in the Middle Ages, and merchants,
though they focused on trade and finance, sought to acquire real estate, both
urban and rural. Martha and her sons were heavily invested in land and
housing. Martha had real property in her own right, probably from her own
family. She likely had a dowry that consisted of real property she would have
administered even if it remained globally, as it probably did, within the family holdings. Martha had substantial real estate interests in her own right, the
origins of which, with one exception treated below—the gift from her mother
Jacoba—cannot be determined. Martha's holdings could have come to her
in a variety of ways: family inheritance from paternal or maternal relatives,
earlier gifts from Jacoba or bequests from her father Raymundus Franchi, her
dowry, the resources that Guiraudus presumably furnished in the form of an
augment at the time of their marriage, additional bequests from Guiraudus
in his will, or simple acquisitions.[1] As noted earlier, statutory regulations
prohibited dowried daughters from receiving a further share of the paternal
inheritance in intestate situations, but in practice the testator, in his will,
could make additional bequests.[2] These are some of the possible origins of

Martha's real property holdings. Martha used rentals, *emphyteusis* leases, and real estate exchanges as a means of management and exploitation of real property investments. Martha's interest in real property investment and her transactions appear to have traced the way for her sons' real estate investments. But in some ways Guiraudus and Jacobus diverged from Martha in real estate strategy, Guiraudus in salines, Jacobus in foreclosures, as we will see. In the years 1336–42, Martha was in the process of converting some of her rural real estate to commercial real estate—especially tables—in town.

Jacobus's extensive property holdings were likely part of Guiraudus's estate as universal heir. There were also joint holdings among Martha and Guiraudus's sons that may have been an offshoot of Guiraudus's estate. This chapter will explore the property holdings of Martha and the Cabanis family and the general landholding context of medieval Montpellier. Land-related contracts were considerably different from commercial and financial documents, and the administration of a real property fortune required different techniques from that of trade. The Cabanis landed fortune is thus best treated separately from investments in trade and finance.

Family ties to land were very strong in the medieval era. With the growth of towns from the eleventh century on, new bases for landownership emerged. Freehold had always existed in the countryside, but in towns it was increasingly common. Frequently, however, there were dues attached to urban holdings in the form of the *census* or *usaticum*, and on top of this hierarchy was the concept of eminent domain (*dominium directum*), that is, abstract property rights, referred to in the *emphyteusis* recognition at the beginning of this chapter.[3] It was thus possible for there to be multiple layers of urban property rights. Nonetheless, disposing of urban tenures was much easier than in an earlier rural feudal context.[4]

Historians have frequently inquired into the relationship between merchants and landholding in the Middle Ages.[5] Land was often enmeshed in the feudal and seigneurial structures of earlier centuries, though less so in the south of France than in the north.[6] The acquisition of land on the part of merchants has sometimes been seen as the first step in the process of withdrawal from active commercial engagement that could lead, with the proper alliances and royal patronage, to ennoblement or at least to rentier status.[7] Such a pattern has been suggested for northern France.[8] But this was not always the case in southern Europe, as studies of Italian towns such as Genoa have demonstrated.[9] The merchant and the noble might remain active in trade while owning large amounts of land.[10] Between such extremes, Montpellier presents an intermediate case along the spectrum of possibilities. The Cabanis fortune included significant investment in real property, along with commercial and financial dealings.

Martha exercised her role as guardian in real estate as well as in commercial matters. Using the notary Johannes Holanie, in 1336 the three Cabanis brothers, with Martha acting as *curatrix* of Jacobus and Guiraudus and *tutrix* of Johannes, gave out a garden, house, and well at the Villeneuve gate in lease (*accapitum* and perpetual *emphytheusis*) for the price of 40 *l.p.t.* for the lease and 15 *l.t.* annually in payments, a very lucrative *usaticum* (real estate revenue), to a gardener.[11] Another gardener had the right to use the well that was next to this orchard. This complex was in a suburban neighborhood on the south side of town, just outside the city walls, suggesting the dispersal of real property holdings of the family, only some of which we can track through the remaining evidence.

In the same year, 1336, Jacobus served as the procurator of his mother Martha on the basis of a procuration established when he was seventeen on 24 February 1335 by Guillelmus Nogareti.[12] The act was an acquittal, written by the notary Johannes Holanie, to an inhabitant of Castelnau, Guillelmus de Valhanquesio, for a rent payment, 40 *s.t.*, that he had made for a shoemaker in regard to the latter's rental of a house. The payment had been made to another of Martha's procurators, Petrus de Albinhaco, but Jacobus was acknowledging it on behalf of his mother. This payment seems to have come on the heels of a lawsuit (*dica*) over the rent. With Jacobus seventeen years old in 1335, Martha had begun to rely on him in some business dealings.

Martha and her sons had significant real estate holdings that we can glimpse in instances when they are collecting dues or buying, selling, or exchanging property. Thus, the record of holdings that can be reconstructed is only partial. As a comparative example, in the case of the fortune of the late Petrus de Cabanis, likely uncle or great uncle of the Cabanis brothers, Jean Hilaire has calculated from the 1336 intestate proceedings to resolve controversies among the children that there was about 2,700 *l.*, of which 400 *l.* was in liquid, the rest in real estate, including multiple houses in Montpellier.[13] There were also debts and the need to return the dowry of a widowed daughter-in-law. Martha's husband Guiraudus's estate has left no direct trace, outside the bequest to poor girls to marry for which Jacobus was still receiving acquittals in 1342, but the capital available to Martha, in the two large partnerships in 1338 and 1339, discussed in Chapter 7, suggests a fortune greater than that of Petrus de Cabanis. Real property revenues may have been the source of some of the capital for the partnerships. Martha had a complex real estate fortune to manage, including some holdings of her own and some of her sons'.

The Nogareti register contained seventy acts relating to real estate, sixty-seven of which concerned members of the Cabanis family. Of the sixty-seven Cabanis real estate contracts in the Nogareti register, Martha appeared in ten real estate transactions of her own.[14] Jacobus was involved in forty-six transactions alone, in person or through representation. Jacobus as the universal heir of his father would have inherited landed property. He was a powerhouse of real estate entrepreneurship. Jacobus and his brother Guiraudus together participated in five acts. In two more, they were noted with their younger brother Johannes. Guiraudus appeared alone in one act. Finally, Jacobus appeared with Johannes de Suelhis, a business associate, in one transaction. In the same sense that the inherited property holdings of the children reveal something of the success of Guiraudus their father, by the same token, Martha's economic success as a widow and guardian of her husband's estate in the preservation and expansion of Cabanis family's property holdings reflects favorably on her ability to manage the late Guiraudus' estate and pass on to her sons her real estate talents, as well as on her business sense. She would have managed the real property holdings of the family for a period of eight to ten years prior to Jacobus's practical majority at fourteen.

The Nogareti documents permit an in-depth investigation into the relationship of merchants and land in Languedoc. A whole range of real estate operations is represented by these acts. Rentals were a form of short-term investment at fixed rates.[15] Rentals transferred the right to the use of real property, with subletting to third parties a possibility. Moreover, no payment was made upon completion of the transaction, but significant periodic payments were made by the lessee to the lessor in exchange for the right of the lessee to make use of the property. For the landlord, rentals did not represent a form of loan or financing, but rather a type of investment with a fixed rate of return.

Emphyteusis contracts differed from real estate rentals. *Emphyteusis* was a form of long-term land lease for a fixed payment in cash or kind. *Emphyteusis* holdings functioned as a form of long-term investment for the Cabanis, carrying the important right of first refusal (*ius prelationis*).[16] In *emphyteusis* concessions, they retained abstract property rights (*dominium directum*), not involving use, and could step in as buyers in the case of the sale of the use. *Emphyteusis* contracts were in some ways similar to a contract for sale of real estate, except that it was only the use of the property that was leased for a lengthy period (thirty years) in exchange for a large initial payment and a nominal periodic payment by the buyer to the seller. The seller retained the right of first refusal, that is, the opportunity to repurchase the *emphyteusis* rights of use sold to the buyer if that buyer attempted to sell the buyer's *emphyteusis* rights to a third party. The residual right of first refusal and the right to the periodic nominal payments themselves might be sold to a third party by the seller. The layers of medieval land ownership, associated with real property, are illustrated in this kind of lease. Since a large payment was made upon completion of this type of transaction by the buyer to the seller and since there was a possibility that the seller, in the future, might make a large payment to the original buyer upon exercising the original right of first refusal, *emphyteusis* contracts had the credit effect in some circumstances of a long-term loan, with the nominal periodic payments to the seller acting as an outward sign of the continuing interest of the seller in the buyer's purchased rights to the property. Thus, *emphyteusis* might be seen as a form of long-term financing of an interest in real property.[17]

In a radius around Montpellier of about twenty kilometers, the Cabanis had coastal *salines* to the south toward the sea and to the north landholdings in Boutonnet, near Montferrier, and around the source of the Lez River to the north of Montpellier. Martha had vineyards to the southeast of the town at Montaubérou, in particular (see Map 2, Chapter 1). Though urban in orientation, Martha and the Cabanis were well integrated in the local geography. Inhabitants of Montpellier held urban and rural land, vineyards being the primary agricultural investment in the region. The connections between town and country were strong.[18] Martha and her sons had significant investments in the region surrounding Montpellier.

As guardian, Martha was present in real property transactions, as she was in enterprises relating to trade and industry in the years up to 1340. Martha was involved in the rental of a stream and a mill as part of her partnership enterprise in linen processing with Johannes de Suelhis. Suelhis was a key link in the Cabanis linen enterprise as one of the Cabanis partners managing their linen industrial enterprise in the rural areas surrounding Montpellier. With Suelhis, Martha as *curatrix* had made large partnership investments in the linen processing industry as discussed in the previous chapter. There was need for rural land to accommodate the linen processing procedure.

In another act as *curatrix*, on 9 April 1339 Martha, with Jacobus and Guiraudus, hired Firminus Salamonis, merchant, and Petrus de Albinhaco, *clericus*, as their procurators to make recognitions to the king of Majorca as holder of abstract rights over some of their urban and rural holdings that were not specified and to promise to pay the accustomed dues (*usatica*). Martha and her sons were sometimes the holders of abstract rights and sometimes that of use.

In the years 1336–40, when we trace Martha in her role of guardian most intensely, we find that she also found time to manage her own real estate investments. She began a campaign of exchanging rural lands (all but her vineyards at Montaubérou) in return for commercial holdings in town. In an exchange of lands (undated but likely in 1336) with Petrus del Euze, the familiar Cabanis business associate and sometime partner in commercial investments, Martha traded two vineyards that she held in *allod* (freehold) at Clapiers, a small town about five kilometers directly north of Montpellier, along with abstract real estate rights over lands at Clapiers, in return for Petrus's rights of dues (*census*) over a table in the fish market and over holdings in the quarter of the pepperers.[19] These dues produced 65 *s.* in one case and the third part of a gold *obole* (half a gold denier) in the other. The act was passed in Martha's house with Nogareti writing and with Berengarius Gombergua, priest, and Bernardus de Rodesio, merchant, as witnesses. She was still pursuing the strategy of exchange with her mother's gift of lands at Boutonnet in 1342 for tables in town (see below).

Martha's own fortune in real property included urban and rural holdings: commercial tables and houses on the one hand and vineyards and other agricultural lands on the other, a different profile altogether from that of Jacobus, as he pursued aggressive rural property acquisition for a variety of purposes, including industrial processing plants.[20] We do not know whether Martha had reclaimed her dowry, but her personal real estate management demonstrates that she controlled real property in her own name. She engaged Jacobus as her procurator to manage some of her holdings. If the lands and houses she did control were from her dowry, there was no indication of a withdrawal from her guardianship responsibilities for the real property of her sons, as the 1336 suburban land transaction near the Villeneuve gate, discussed above, shows.

Martha was recalibrating her own investment strategy toward an urban concentration. She pursued for herself a program of divestment of rural holdings, with the exception of vineyards, for the acquisition of commercial assets in town. Such a strategy permitted adjustments for inflation in urban investments and allowed for conversion by sale into cash if necessary. Commercial property in town was rented short-term, a more flexible form of investment than the long-term rural lease. Was Martha preparing for the future, with assets she could manage more easily? Perhaps. Women of the urban elite did not traipse around the countryside managing real property. Then, too, different real property strategies were advisable at different life stages. The 1336 act above illustrates that Martha, as guardian, followed a more traditional pattern of long-term leases for the holdings of her sons. This was a stable strategy that she underpinned with diversification of real property investments for the estate.

Martha would retain her interests in the prized Montaubérou vineyard location where grapes brought high prices and vineyards there were in much demand by Montpellier inhabitants. Four contracts relating to Martha's rural holdings were drawn up in her house by the notary on the same day, 26 January 1338. These were concessions and recognitions of long-term leases termed *accapitum* or *emphyteusis*.[21] A lease usually ran for thirty years, though it was possible for the lessee to exit the contractual arrangements earlier through the sale of use. Martha as lessor was the holder of abstract rights in these transactions that she handled on her own. The lands in question were vineyards in the Montaubérou area in a location called Als Trencatz where high-quality grapes were concentrated. The wine merchant, Raymundus de Lunascio, took a vineyard at Als Trencatz in lease for 19 *l.* 10 *s.* current *p.t.* with payment spread over three years at the feast of St. Gilles (1 September).[22] The dues (*usaticum*) of 20 *s.t.* were to be paid yearly at the feast of St. Peter. If the vineyard was worth more, Martha agreed to grant the surplus to Lunascio as a gift (*donatio inter vivos*). Then Lunascio drew up an official recognition of *emphyteusis* for Martha.[23] On 29 July 1342, she certified the sale of this vineyard by a merchant, Raymundus Clayranni, to a cordmaker at Als Trencatz.[24] She received an approval fee (*laudiminum*) for the sale of 4 *l.* 6 *s.*, current money, and 19 *l.* 10 *s.* for the establishment of the *emphyteusis*. Payment from the earlier Lunascio transaction had apparently dragged on, as we see Martha collecting the 19 *l.* 10*s.* in 1342 at the time of the sale of the vineyard that had presumably changed hands in the interim, passing from Lunascio to the merchant Clayranni. Martha retained her abstract rights over the Montaubérou vineyards.

On the same day, 26 January 1338, Martha gave out another lease at Als Trencatz to another wine merchant, Petrus Borzes, for the same dues, with a recognition following.[25] In the Borzes lease, the vineyard was noted as located next to another property of Martha's that she gave out in lease on the same day to the cultivator Jacobus Mazellarii. On 5 April 1340, the butcher Jacobus Symonis acknowledged to Martha that 40 *s. t.* was still owing of 11 *l.* 5 *s.t.* for a lease of a vineyard at Als Trencatz, contracted on 26 January 1338.[26] The payment was owed at the feast of St. Gilles of 1340. Martha was following up on the payment owed by Symonis in a recognition of debt of 5 April 1340, when the butcher acknowledged still owing her 104 *s.t.*[27] Clearly, in these lease arrangements, Martha had to be vigilant in collecting her just due.

From the contracts in the Nogareti register and from internal evidence referring to additional obligations, it is clear that Martha was regularizing her vineyard leases at the beginning of 1338. The wine merchants were present in 1338 when the acts were initially drawn up, as were witnesses to the acts. Close Cabanis associates, Berengarius Gombergua and Petrus de Albinhaco, served in this capacity. Petrus Riberie, mercer, who may have been in the Cabanis mercery shop for his own business, also witnessed these transactions. We do not know whether Martha derived wine from the grapes of her vineyards, but many Montpellier inhabitants did so.

In the area around Montpellier, grape vines were the most important component of local agriculture in the Middle Ages, as today, although olive trees and cereals were also cultivated.[28] It is quite probable that medieval vineyards, in contrast to the vineyards of today, were located on the high points of land, while the plain was reserved for cereals. The vine is a plant indigenous to Languedoc, but its exploitation had to await the first century BCE when Roman colonizers imported grapevines. The episcopal, seigneurial, and monastic cartularies of the region reveal that, by the twelfth century, vineyards were present in considerable numbers.[29] According to the *Cartulaire de Maguelone*, they were located within a radius of a few kilometers around Montpellier at Montpelliéret, Boutonnet, Montaubérou, where Martha had holdings; on the banks of the Merdanson and the Lez; at Saint-Jean de Védas, Lavérune, Juvignac, and La Valette; and in pockets to the east of Montpellier about fifteen kilometers distance in the territory of Mauguio and to the southwest at twenty to twenty-five kilometers distance at Gigean, Montbazin, Poussan, and Balaruc. There were also vineyards between Montpellier and the sea in the marshy lands separating the town from the lagoons.

Grapes were an important item in the local rural economy. Wine was a preferred local beverage, and self-respecting urban inhabitants had vineyards for their own use.[30] Martha's holdings were substantial enough to suggest that her lands may have provided grapes for commercial as well as personal purposes. Jacobus dealt directly in the grape trade, as he recorded a series of grape purchases himself and through agents.[31] Holdings at prized sites such as Montaubérou and at Soriech would have maximized the chances for profit in the wine and grape trades. It is possible that Martha and Jacobus combined efforts to produce the wine needed for their household, selling off surplus grapes or wine. Though leases and rentals of vineyards, Martha controlled a valuable real property investment. In those real estate acts where she acted alone as the principal—and she frequently did—she was often surrounded by members of the Cabanis entourage serving in the capacity of witnesses to her acts—Berengerius Gombergua, Bernardus de Rodesio, and Petrus de Albinhaco.[32] These entourage members were present in the acts of her sons as well. There is little doubt in these transactions that Martha had full responsibility for her acts and engaged independently in real estate activities, setting an example for her sons.

Active widows in Montpellier, such as Martha and Agnes de Bossones, acted alone before the notary. In the first quarter of the fourteenth century, Agnes acquired houses on the Herbaria Square that she later gave in dowry to her oldest daughter.[33] While she held them herself, she managed the property through assistants and *factores*. The widow Maria Naturale, an in-law of Martha's, managed her commercial tables through procurators in a more passive approach to real property. Wives were also present in real property transactions. Shennan Hutton suggested for Ghent, "Whether a Ghent woman publicly performed property management depended on three factors: her choice, external pressures, and negotiation with others. A woman's choice was likely influenced by her talents, skills, age, experience, and her internal reaction to hegemonic discourses. Women's choice spread along a continuum between the two extremes of total passivity and completely independent activity."[34] A similar situation seems to have prevailed in Montpellier.

Women were present as buyers and sellers of urban houses: nineteen of ninety-two sales and thirteen purchases were made by women.[35] Women were also noted in land sales and purchases, with fifty-six sellers and twenty-eight buyers of 262 sales being women. In vineyard transactions specifically, women accounted for twenty-nine sellers and sixteen buyers in 151 sales. A whole range of Montpellier society was represented among the family background of women real estate participants, from merchants and changers to artisans and agricultural workers. Women were heavily invested in the real estate market in Montpellier.

Urban real estate was an important dimension of the family landed fortune. The Cabanis family house, located near Arc Saint-Nicolas in the mercers' quarter, may have been part of her late husband's estate and was clearly the family dwelling (see Map 3, Chapter 2). On the Herbaria Square, located up the street from Notre-Dame des Tables in a continuation of the central commercial quarter of Montpellier, the Cabanis had a house called that of the children of Guiraudus de Cabanis, making them neighbors, or at least investment property holders, with the grandson of Agnes de Bossones, who held numerous houses on the square and considered it his own.[36] And one of the witnesses on the Bon Amic side in the Herbaria lawsuit, brought by the town consuls in 1336 to demonstrate the public, not private, nature of the square, was a Jacobus de Cabanis (Cabanas), draper, who said that, when he lived with Petrus Bon Amic, he had seen him collect rent for the houses on the square.[37] Jacobus the draper was likely the Jacobus of the third Cabanis branch. Asked for further details on how long Johannes Bon Amic had possessed the Herbaria houses, Jacobus, who was well informed, stated in his testimony that Johannes had had them since the death of his father Petrus and that Petrus had had them from the time of his marriage with the mother of Johannes. Before that, they had been his maternal grandmother's (Agnes de Bossones).[38] The intersection of Bossones, Bon Amic, Cabanis, and other elite lives was inevitable in a town the size of Montpellier. In the Montaubérou vineyard region, Martha had vineyards that bordered Bon Amic holdings.[39] In rural surroundings as well, the close connections of these elite families can be observed.

As noted earlier, in one case Martha enjoyed her mother's generosity. On 12 February 1342, her mother Jacoba made a living gift (*donatio inter vivos*) to Martha of a field at Boutonnet, a suburb to the northeast of Montpellier, which Martha then traded for commercial tables in a land exchange.[40] Jacoba dictated this act in her own house in the presence of Berengarius Gombergua, the priest who was a frequent presence as witness in Martha's acts, and two tawers (*blanquerii*), who were perhaps colleagues of Jacoba's husband or at least representatives of the same trade that Petrus de Tornamira had practiced. They may have been well known to Jacoba and Martha.

Martha put the gift of land to good use. The subsequent land exchange (27 February 1342), following the gift by two weeks, with son Jacobus as Martha's procurator, involved trading the land at Boutonnet in return for tables in the Butchery and in the fish market and a shop, all belonging to a local merchant Raymundus Fabri who received the Boutonnet property.

Martha was absent from this act that was drawn up at the workshop of Fabri, with Jacobus representing her. The priest Berengarius Gombergua, her close assistant, was one of the witnesses. These tables were next to other tables of Jacobus and an honor of his and were located on the public road leading from the consular house to Notre-Dame des Tables. They carried annual dues of 10 *s.t.* and 40 *s.t.* with the king of Majorca, called the lord of Mont-pellier, as the holder of abstract rights.[41] Martha paid an additional 75 *l.t.* in current money for the greater value of the tables that were recognized as hers in full possession. Clearly, this was a costly investment, but one that Martha could count on to produce annual rental revenues. That these newly acquired tables were near tables of Jacobus and near holdings of her son Johannes suggests that Martha had a strategy of consolidation of family property as well as a desire to divest herself of rural holdings in favor of urban commercial property, more lucrative or at least more productive of steady income and potentially easier to administer.

Martha may have felt strongly about having her own real estate portfolio, distinct from that of her sons, Jacobus and Guiraudus, who were married by 1341, with their own families. At some point, the family home may not have been able to accommodate them all and the family business. Then, too, the political troubles brought on by the weakness and decline of the kingdom of Majorca and the beginnings of the Hundred Years War created uncertainties that could have affected Cabanis real estate strategies.[42]

The rate of return on commercial property in economically desirable areas of the town of Montpellier was greater than that of rural real estate. Martha's commercial holdings were rented out for short periods of time com-pared to the long-term *accapitum* or *emphyteusis* leases, allowing for adjust-ments to cope with inflation, currency devaluation, and other vicissitudes for which fine-tuning in economic terms was more feasible than in long-term "fixed-rate" arrangements characteristic of leases that she used for rural lands and that Jacobus used frequently.[43] As she grew older, Martha may have come to prefer urban property investments with more flexible management strategies. She may have chosen to leave to her sons, particularly Jacobus, the investment in and management of rural agricultural and industrial exploita-tions as time went by.

Further evidence of Martha's resources invested in urban real estate is found in her rentals as landlord on 2 March 1340 of an atelier and one-half of a soler (*solarium*) of a house in the den Camburac area (*Trivium* and *Quadrivium den Camburac*) of Montpellier, located not far from the family home at the entrance to the Coirataria quarter and of one-half of an atelier with a soler in the same area.[44] This property was a likely component of Martha's dowry, given her father's profession of tawer. The first of these rentals involved a woman, Garcendis Folhaquerie, as lessee; the second a reseller, Petrus Rosseli. Both were for four years, and the second brought in 10 *l.t.* of money current at the time of payment. The rent for the first is illegible. In both of these transactions Martha was present and acting on her own. In other instances, Martha used her son Jacobus as procurator in managing her real estate holdings.[45] These rental holdings were not far from the Cabanis family home at Arc Saint-Nicolas. It is likely that Martha preferred to remain in town. She was present if business could be done in her home and exceptionally at the notary's atelier. She may have traveled rarely, if at all, to her rural properties.

Other family holdings were nearby. Martha's daughter-in-law, wife of her son Jacobus, was the holder in common with her sister of houses in the rue de l'Aiguillerie and in the Old Aiguillerie that were rented out by Petrus de Albinhaco as procurator of Jacobus. These properties may have been the result of an inheritance bequest that the sisters decided to hold in common, rather than sell and divide the proceeds. It is possible that Jacobus's wife brought her share in these holdings to him in dowry. Petrus de Albinhaco represented Jacobus and Johannes de Affriano, legal specialist and husband of Jacobus's wife's sister, on 9 May 1341 in a rental of a house of these two sisters to a dyer that was situated next to other holdings of the wives (see Map 3, Chapter 2). The Cabanis and Affriano wives were not present in this act for any kind of approval, but it is possible that such an approval was recorded elsewhere.[46]

Since the will of Guiraudus has not survived, it is impossible to know the origins of the joint real property holdings of the Cabanis brothers. The joint real estate transactions of Jacobus and Guiraudus included holdings (a group—*tenentia*—of modest houses—*domus*) in proximity to the above rental housing of Martha, in the quarter of the Coirataria and the Little Coirataria, fronting on the Carreria Correiarie. This was not far from Martha's rental at Trivium den Camburac. The brothers rented these to a silk merchant of Montpellier for eight years at 60 *l.t.* a year.[47] The combined Cabanis real estate in this part of town, not far from the family home, was substantial. Jacobus was most heavily invested in real estate as the universal heir of his father. Those collaborations with Guiraudus probably reflect the brothers' partnership or properties that they had inherited in common from their father. The joint real estate transactions involving Jacobus and Guiraudus included urban and rural property. Jacobus had other house rentals in this area as noted below, and Guiraudus also had other properties of his own.

Geographically, Jacobus's rental holdings were spread throughout the town with concentrations in the area of Pila Saint-Gély (the Saint-Gilles gate) at the specific location of Trivium den Camburac. The Via Francigena, the important commercial and pilgrimage road coming form Italy and crossing southern France to Spain, entered Montpellier at the Saint-Gilles gate and traversed the urban center along streets such as the rue de l'Aiguillerie. Jacobus's holdings were thus prime real estate.

Jacobus acquired lands, houses, real estate revenues, and other holdings. He obtained the usufruct of a house and a soler in the pepperers' quarter for four years at 35 *l.t.* per year.[48] The rationale behind such an acquisition could have been that the pepperers' trade in Montpellier was sufficiently important to promise prime revenues in the subletting of this property.[49] Jacobus shared Martha's interest in commercial urban property.

The advantage of rents over long-term leases is evident in the flexibility of response that a landlord had to changing economic conditions, inflation or deflation of the coinage, and the decay and need for upkeep of the property itself. Rentals allowed more consistent supervision of the property, greater possibilities of intervention, and more freedom of adjustment of revenues to assure profits. Within Montpellier, Martha and Jacobus had the opportunity to oversee their holdings in sufficiently consistent fashion to make the rentals attractive as a means of real estate exploitation. The uncertainties of the Hundred Years War may have contributed to their choices. (see Chapter 9 below).

As in the case of commerce, Martha's real estate interests may have provided the model for some, though not all, of her sons' later activities. There were some dimensions of Martha's sons' enterprises that they may have developed on their own: investment in salt marshes (*salines*) is one. At Villeneuve-lès-Maguelone they had *salines*, from which they sold salt to the *gabelle* or salt monopoly of the king of France.[50] Guiraudus possessed some *salines* on his own as well.[51] The seacoast southeast of Montpellier was a noted salt-producing region in the Middle Ages.[52]

Early on, Jacobus represented his mother in property transactions and acted alone in his own holdings. His program included commercial assets in town but also traditional holdings in the countryside. He was also aggressively acquiring real property. Jacobus can be documented loaning money to rural inhabitants and then foreclosing on the rural holdings that had been pledged as a guarantee of the loan transaction. Jacobus's investments in real estate ran the gamut from urban to rural and were expanding aggressively as he developed his foreclosure strategy.

Jacobus can also be traced in rural property exploitation through long-term leases of *emphyteusis* and *accapitum*. Holdings leased in this fashion had annual returns of dues payments (*censum* or *usaticum*) ranging from modest to middling in size (12 *d.* to 45 *s.t.* in the remaining Montpellier evidence). Fifteen such transactions remain for Jacobus in the Nogareti register. The holdings were scattered, with vineyards at Soriech, Montels, Fenouillède, Castelnau, and the *decimaria* (tithing district) of Notre-Dame des Tables, as well as in the diocese of Béziers and in the commune of Lunel.[53] The vineyard leased at Castelnau was directly identified as having come to Jacobus from his father.[54]

In the rural context, in collaboration, brothers Jacobus and Guiraudus, with their partner Jacobus Oliverii acting for himself and on their behalf, sold a vineyard at Castelnau on 11 February 1339 for 15 *l.p.t.* to a Montpellier inhabitant.[55] The *usaticum* (dues) payment of 12 d. t. for the abstract rights of this property went to the heirs of Raymundus de Capite Vilare, jurist, of an old and important Montpellier family.[56] The Cabanis brothers themselves possessed abstract rights over some rural holdings; a recognition of debt was recorded on their behalf for dues owed them for a vineyard at Terinieyras for which 30 *s.t.* was outstanding.[57] Their rental of mills to Hugo Fabri with the expectation of repair of the mechanisms was already mentioned in Chapter 7. They took on as renters a portion of the *garrigue* near the Lez River for the purpose of movement of men and animals in and out of their textile processing facilities. This rental, recorded by Johannes de Grabellis for two years on 24 April 1339, cost the Cabanis 60 *s.t.*[58]

For partners who had significant involvement in international trade and finance, management of a real estate fortune was a demanding responsibility. To cope with such a challenge, on 2 September 1342, Jacobus and Guiraudus participated in a management arrangement of sweeping proportions (*meiar-iam*) in which the Montpellier merchant Johannes Pauli, assumed responsi-bility for all fields, vineyards, and gardens that one or both of the brothers possessed in the territories of Saint-Clément la Rivière, Saint-Barthélémy d'Aubagne, and Saint-Jacques de Prades.[59] In the case of Jacobus, this arrangement may have been extremely useful, given his acquisitions in this area in the years of the Nogareti register (1336–42). Jacobus had many purchases and recognitions of debt owed him for *emphyteusis* tenures like his mother. This agreement alleviated the need for the brothers to oversee directly the agricultural holdings that they had amassed separately or together.

The involvement of the Cabanis in the region just north of Montpellier, first orchestrated by the partnership that Martha facilitated with Johannes de Suelhis, led to additional involvement of her son Jacobus in this area. Jacobus extended loans to borrowers who were likely agriculturists in this region; one was specifically identified as such.[60] Guiraudus occasionally joined him in these endeavors. The credit operations of the Cabanis relative by marriage, Bernarda de Cabanis, come to mind here, as she too extended credit via loans to agriculturalists.[61] The Cabanis furnished funds to rural inhabitants, perhaps as a means of purchasing or facilitating the purchase or acquisition of land through foreclosure. The loans were to men in areas such as Prades where Jacobus was particularly active in accumulating real estate.[62] The later Middle Ages witnessed the extension of urban credit to rural inhabitants, resulting in rural lands in urban hands. David Nicholas observed the beginnings of an active rural real estate market in urban hands in Flanders at the end of the thirteenth century.[63] Montpellier followed a similar pattern without the emphasis on fief-holding by urban elite inhabitants that was a feature of the feudal landholding structures of the north.[64]

Jacobus loaned money to Petrus Symonis of Prades with "on demand" terms on 28 June 1340.[65] The loan was cancelled on 17 August 1340, on Jacobus's behalf by Petrus de Albinhaco, and, on the same day, Petrus Symonis confirmed to Jacobus having received from him 20 *l. t.* for the purchase of meadowland at a site termed "al Lanun Vetus," at the Old Lez in an auction sale.[66] These two transactions suggest that Symonis may have satisfied his debt by accepting the purchase offer of Jacobus, minus the loan sum. It is unlikely that the initial loan involved such a large sum, but the fact that Symonis was having land auctioned implies that he was in difficult financial straits.

In another context, Jacobus and Guiraudus made an "on demand" loan on 13 March 1341 to Berengarius Baudilii and Guillelmus Arimanni of Prades of 40 *s.t.*[67] The previous year, on 30 March 1340, Jacobus had bought lands at Prades from Anthonius Ariman[ii].[68] Then, on 19 December 1341, the brothers made another loan of 12 *l.t.* to Berengarius Baudilii.[69] A Jacobus Baudilii was one of those making recognitions of *emphyteusis* to Jacobus.[70] Here Jacobus may have been using his real estate contacts to further the brothers' loan business. An additional loan by Jacobus went to a cultivator of the diocese of Notre-Dame de Ro where Jacobus had *emphyteusis* holdings, and the brothers together lent money to a man of Les Matelles in the hinterland north of Montpellier.[71]

While none of these loans are directly connected to land transactions as in the Symonis contracts, still the last name similarities and the coincidence of Cabanis land holdings in the vicinity of the borrowers' origins render it plausible that loans advanced to family members were the first step in pressuring land sales. If foreclosure was the ultimate aim, then perhaps the more innocent tactic of purchasing lands at low prices or favorable rates was employed. Then, too, one may be observing a simple system of patronage of rural inhabitants by the mercantile elite. As just noted, such an extension of urban credit to a rural world was a common feature of fourteenth-century town and country relations in Western Europe.[72]

In the case of holdings in common, it is interesting to note that all three brothers, Jacobus, Guiraudus, and Johannes, were associated with holdings in abstract property rights that may have come to them as part of a family holding. If they were not entailed, in a manner similar to the *fideicomissum* of Florence, they may have been assigned as some sort of joint inheritance or fortune held in common.[73] In a land exchange, the three brothers surrendered their abstract rights over a garden, houses, and wells outside the fortifications of Montpellier near the Villeneuve gate, worth 15 *l.t.* 6 *d.* in annual payment, in return for all abstract rights worth 115 *s.t.* annually over lands at Via Croza alias Tor de Sirvent that were part of the estate of a woman, along with 300 *l.t.* current money to cover the greater value of the rights exchanged by the brothers. The motive for this exchange was the establishment of a chantry on the late *testatrix*'s behalf.[74] The Cabanis had been willing to accommodate this intention, and it provided them with significant cash. Earlier, in 1336, the three brothers and Martha, as guardian, had given out this property in *accapitum* lease—a garden, house, and well at the Villeneuve gate—for the price of 40 *l.p.t.* in lease and 15 *l.t.* in annual payments.[75]

The real estate interests of the family suggest the degree of diversification of assets characteristic of urban mercantile families. Martha's son Jacobus's case is particularly revealing through the depth of involvement in real property that one observes in his transactions. He had what would seem to be clearly articulated strategies for the profitable management of his holdings. There is no indication, however, that Jacobus or indeed that the Cabanis in general were in any way contemplating a withdrawal from active commercial and industrial participation. Some members of the extended Cabanis family were not involved in business: the sons of Petrus de Cabanis—Stephanus, *legum professor*, and Jacobus, *jurisperitus*—were the obvious cases in point, but they had real property fortunes. Jean Hilaire argued that the bulk of the fortune of Petrus de Cabanis was in real property.[76] With Martha's sons, real estate investment from the profits of commercial and industrial undertakings seems probable. Martha and her sons had a diversified fortune, with investments flowing both ways between business and real estate. Some of the revenues derived from real property—the 300 *l.* of the exchange, for example—may in turn have been plowed back into trade. Jacobus and Guiraudus's generation was not the first to have substantial lands, and some of the holdings that they enjoyed must have had their origins in paternal and maternal fortunes.

Other Cabanis women have also left a trace in real estate transactions. Of three Cabanis women whose activities can be traced, Maria Naturale, daughter of the late Petrus de Cabanis, had the least independent and least active economic profile. Maria also had considerable investments in commercial tables, an efficient way to derive returns. In 1336, she was the recipient of funds from the inheritance of the late Johannes Naturalis, her husband.[77] Maria was the mother of at least four children, two boys and two girls, all over the age of fourteen by 1336. Moreover, her brother Jacobus de Cabanis, the universal heir of their father Petrus, owed her 300 *l.p.t.* in regard to their paternal inheritance and in payment gave her two contiguous houses of his inside Montpellier in the quarter of the Sainte-Croix drapery.[78] Though this was an intestate situation, Maria was clearly not disadvantaged by the exclusion of dowried daughters from paternal inheritance.

A whole series of real estate transactions involving the children of Maria and the late Johannis Naturalis were drafted in the 1336 notarial register of Johannes Holanie.[79] Son Johannes sold son Guiraudus a house near Notre-Dame des Tables. Daughter Sibienda received her legacy from her father's estate through the sale by her brother Johannes of another house in the Soqueria quarter, a sale which Maria, Guiraudus, and Flos ratified; Sibienda gave an acquittal to her brother Johannes that all of her 200 *l.* legacy had been satisfied except for 40 *s.t.* in annual real estate revenues in the town of Lattes.[80] A further act detailed a deposit of 100 *l.p.t.* to Stephanus de Cabanis, *legum doctor* of Montpellier, their uncle, and 20 *l.p.t.* to Guiraudus Naturalis, their brother, by Johannes and Sibienda to hold for the occasion of Sibienda's entry into religious life.[81]

Earlier in 1336, Jacobus Oliverii, merchant of Montpellier and son-in-law of Maria, had acted on Maria's behalf as her *socius* to rent two tables of hers in the Old Butchery of Montpellier to a local butcher for a year beginning at Easter for 22 *l.p.t.*, in payments of 10 *s. t.* each Saturday.[82] In 1333, Maria had made another Montpellier butcher her procurator to seek repayment of debts.[83] In the Nogareti register, Maria's activities were confined to real estate transactions—sales of tables in the Butchery to a butcher and rental of a house in the Butchery to a butcher—handled by Oliverii as her procurator.[84] She relied on family connections, especially on her son-in-law, to handle her affairs. This was not an uncommon stance for Montpellier widows whose involvement in real estate was frequent but sometimes indirect.[85] While the evidence remaining regarding Maria is certainly limited, it would seem that she was involved only through representatives in the management of her own affairs and participated in an indirect fashion in the administration of her late husband Johannes's estate and in her children's affairs. She appeared on all counts to operate much as a rentier might, living off real estate investment with specialized holdings in tables and houses in the Butchery of Montpellier.

The topographic compactness of Montpellier would have favored encounters among women of the urban elite. No evidence links Martha directly with other elite Montpellier women, though she did do business—rentals—with women of lesser status. She must have interacted with other Cabanis women, including Bernarda de Cabanis, the mercery businesswoman. In contrast to rentier widows such as Maria Naturale, who lived from real estate and were free of business management concerns, Martha was busy with the family business as well as with the management of her landed fortune, and, of course, the large Cabanis mercantile household.

It is useful to set the details of the Cabanis real estate holdings in a broader historical context. Most heavily represented in possession of abstract rights of direct domain in Montpellier were members of the old urban elite (*milites, burgenses*, and *domicelli*), as well as ecclesiastical figures such as the bishop and provost of Maguelone and ecclesiastical institutions.[86] Commercially oriented groups were acquiring such holdings in considerable numbers by the fourteenth century, in search, perhaps, of a diversification of their assets and profits from trade. The Cabanis undoubtedly fit here. Abstract property rights represented on a yearly basis a small return on real estate investment that might be capitalized at a high level when they were sold or if the lands that the rights encumbered were sold or exchanged, necessitating the payment of rights of approval (*laudimium*) to the holder of abstract rights. In these instances, the profits were generally substantial, resulting in a 4 to 5 percent return on the sale price of the rights, whereas the yearly payments due might, in fact, be quite modest.[87] The Cabanis received 15 *l.* 6 *d.* in annual payment from the transaction involving holdings near the Villeneuve gate, a higher than normal return suggesting either that these were recent acquisitions with rates set higher than the traditional rates of several deniers (*denarii*) or at most several sous (*solidi*) or portions of an impressively large family landed fortune. The 300 *l.* payment to the Cabanis accompanying the Villeneuve gate exchange suggests the latter. Turnover rates for rights over lands and houses might account for an increase in value, but, in general, the rates stayed fixed over time and represented in the late thirteenth and fourteenth centuries a low rate of return on a large capital investment.

Many methods of deriving income from real estate were employed in this era; house and land rents, sharecropping, long-term leases (*accapitum* and *emphyteusis* tenures).[88] Women were present in smaller numbers as lessees in these engagements. They were particularly dominant in the renting out of tables and shops in the markets of Montpellier, accounting for about one-third of the total surviving transactions; occasionally, they were recorded as tenants of shops. Martha endorsed this investment strategy with her land exchanges in return for urban tables. Maria Naturale was also invested in urban tables.[89] Women in Montpellier were familiar with the means of generating real estate revenues from methods such as sales of rights in lands, houses, and shops for specific periods of time.[90] They were also active in land exchanges. Women as a group showed a preference for short- rather than long-term contracts in exploiting real estate holdings. In sum, women had important interests in urban and rural property, exploiting the full gamut of real estate techniques.[91]

Women often acted with their children in land transactions, and Martha's interactions with her sons in real estate would have been the norm. Couples were frequent participants as sellers of land. Real estate sales were at times accompanied by formal approvals of family members, for, in southern France as elsewhere in medieval Europe, there was a strong predilection for families to guard jealously the kin's right of oversight in matters of real property.[92] Property was a conservative form of investment in contrast to trade, where the risks multiplied with distance and difficulty of travel. Returns on land investments were more limited but generally less speculative, except for the peasant classes whose livelihood depended upon a successful harvest.

Widows with the responsibility for the welfare and support of children and with the need for accountability in estate management might choose to avoid aggressive speculation. Real estate seems to have been the sector in which women were most active in Montpellier, and in this they shared some of the characteristics of a rentier class. Agnes de Bossones is representative of this trend.[93] She had two clusters of property, one near the Montpelliéret gate and the other near the church of Saint Denis, in the quarter of Montpelliéret, outside the walls of the Commune Clôture fortifications. She also had houses, including some on the Herbaria Square, and her family mansion within the walls, not far from Notre-Dame des Tables.

Martha represented a departure from this trend because she combined an interest in real estate with an active involvement in business. In Martha's case, the steady flow of real estate revenues would have assisted in the capitalization of the commercial and industrial sectors of Cabanis business. Martha keep close track of revenues due her, following up in the case of long-term leases when she had not been fully paid. Both she and her sons were engaged in exchanging land holdings for better deals or better placement of investment. Martha set an example that her sons certainly followed in diversification of investments. Hers is an impressive legacy.

CHAPTER 9

Collaboration: Mother and Sons, Inc.

Before the third hour (9:00 a.m.) we Martha, wife of the late Guiraudus de Cabanis, merchant of Montpellier, and Guiraudus de Cabanis, son of the said couple [crossout] with the wish of my said lady mother which I Martha confirm to be true . . . in like manner we make, order, and constitute certain, true, and undoubted procurators of ours Jacobus de Cabanis, my son of the said Martha and my brother of the said Guiraudus, present and receiving, and Master Bertholomeus Lespinhani, royal notary, and each of them together. Thus, etc. specially and expressly to ask for, make faith, and seek for us and for each of us in us and in each of us to become and to be bourgeois (*burgenses*) of the New Bastide of Saint-Pierre de Beauvais.

—Procuration, 16 September 1342

From guardianship, Martha's relationship with her sons evolved to where her interests and those of her sons were conjoined in many ways. They collaborated in what I call Mother and Sons, Inc. Such collaboration did not preclude independent operations as individuals, but, in significant matters, such as the establishment of initiatives through procuration, they worked together. Martha's guardianship evolved over the period 1326–40 into collaboration with her two older sons that underpinned the workings of the Cabanis business enterprise. Her strategies changed as well in regard to her own property. This is most evident in her real estate restructuring, with the conversion of some rural lands into commercial urban holdings. She had begun early on to use her sons as procurators to manage some of her real estate assets. By 1340, she had surrendered her role as *curatrix* and assumed a position of collaborator. The two older boys were emerging as men by 1340, with their own specialties and strengths. When we lose track of the Cabanis in the mid-1340s, Martha was launching new initiatives and planning for the future.

The business tactics of men and women were similar. Female participants in the luxury trade used credit recognizances (recognitions of debt) in the capacity of buyer and seller, as did their male counterparts.[1] Martha as the guardian of her children was engaged in industrially and commercially oriented partnerships. On her own, she handled matters of real property. She was further implicated in many commercial and financial matters through procurators in affairs that may have related to the management of her late husband's estate. Martha's interaction with her two older sons was frequent and continued after she relinquished her role as guardian.

Colleagues of Guiraudus were particularly instrumental in assisting Martha in the years when her sons were very young. Petrus del Euze was a key collaborator of Martha and the Cabanis in the early years of her curatorship. He was dead by 19 July 1339, but we catch him in sixteen transactions in the Nogareti register in the years 1337 and 1338.[2] He was engaged in partnership with Martha and Jacobus. He acted as the partner (*socius*) of Jacobus in managing ecclesiastical obligations and cessions of actions. He was Jacobus's procurator in accounting measures. As noted in Chapter 8, he exchanged land with Martha, likely in 1336, taking two of her vineyards at Clapiers and providing her with rights of eminent domain with *census* rents over tables in the fish market and the pepperers' market, as part of Martha's strategy to consolidate her real estate holdings in commercial urban properties.[3] Along with Petrus de Albinhaco, the priest Berengarius Gombergua, the Cabanis apprentice and factor Bernardus de Rodesio, and the merchant Firminus Salamonis, Petrus del Euze was essential to Martha's operations. Partners and the business entourage sustained the operations of every significant merchant.[4]

The mercers' trade, which included all three of Martha's sons, was one of the most important retail/wholesale occupations in Montpellier. Martha was never identified in mercery sales, but she negotiated the financing of her sons' enterprise. In this respect, she acted more like an older established male merchant might have, supervising younger family members in business. The mercery trade offers an interesting nexus for the activities of women. Women were active in the luxury market of Montpellier, particularly associated with mercery, encompassing a broad range of activities from silk cloth sales to production of ribbons, thread, and decorative accessories.[5] Although the mercery trade was a focus of female apprenticeship, no woman in the notarial documents was termed a mercer before 1350.

Although Martha herself did not engage in any direct sales of silks and mercery, women's activities can be traced in silk sales and purchases, an active branch of Montpellier commerce. In the silk trade, the sale transactions of women were often related to their positions as wives and widows of silk-industry personnel. In 1293, Maria Orlhaco, wife and then widow of the mercer Bernardus, sold silk on four occasions; her clientele consisted of Jews of Montpellier and Uzès.[6] Maria was already involved in business with her husband before his death and continued in the business that her husband had run as a mercer and in which she had participated. In this, her experience was similar, though not identical, to Mergriete Scettorf of Ghent.[7] Mergriete was active as a wife and then as a widow. In another case, the wife of a wood merchant bought a large quantity of silk from Ghilan for 40 *l. melg*, from a local mercer; she may have been acquiring goods for her own enterprise, silks and mercery, common to merchants' and artisans' wives.[8]

Apprenticeship contracts to teach women techniques of silk embroidery, mercery, spinning of gold thread, and other textile-related arts were common in Montpellier.[9] Spun gold thread would have been used to decorate fabrics.[10] As noted earlier, mercery was a broadly used term for silk textiles and their adornments, but also for also ribbons, fabric decorations, tassels, and gold threads.[11] A range of artisans and their wives trained young women in textile arts. A mercer taught the daughter of a Montpellier immigrant mercery for eight years.[12] The wife of a shoemaker and her husband apprenticed a young girl to learn the wife's trade of mercery.[13] The wife of a wood merchant accepted the daughter of a cultivator in apprenticeship.[14] The daughter of a cultivator apprenticed with the widow of a changer to learn corduroy making.[15] As noted earlier, there was an important metalwork industry in Montpellier that was linked to bye industries such as gold thread production. The wives of goldsmiths were often engaged in the spinning of gold thread and trained young women in apprenticeship in this art.[16] Women throughout Mediterranean Europe were involved in the spinning of gold thread, in cloth trimming, and in the making of brocade.[17]

Though women were associated with the silk industry, they were not mentioned as sellers of mercery of Lucca, the renowned brocades and damasks of the Lucchese silk-finishing industry that represented the Cabanis brothers' specialty in Montpellier.[18] The Cabanis had women clients,

however: widows of Toulouse, who purchased this product in person, traveling from Toulouse to Montpellier to do so, or who dealt through procurators
to purchase mercery of Lucca in Montpellier.[19]

Bernarda de Cabanis, wife of Jacobus, draper, and a Cabanis relative by
marriage, participated in the mercery trade. She taught young women of the
cultivator milieu the mercery trade, though she was not a member of the
mercers' guild.[20] She took Florencia, daughter of a cultivator, Arnaudus Val-
erie, as her apprentice, to live and work for her and to learn her trade via
apprenticeship, paying Arnaudus 40 *s.* per year for each of three years for
Florencia's work.[21] The mercers' statutes of 1328 made no mention of the
participation of women.[22] There were clearly some levels of economic engagement in Montpellier that were denied to women, even a skilled artisan like
Bernarda. However, a lack of formal membership in a guild did not mean a
lack of training and expertise or a failure to participate in artisanal activities
on the part of women. With her association with the mercery trade, Bernarda
shared a general textile orientation with her husband the draper but no more.
She was active in lending money, for which she accepted repayment in kind
in mercery. These activities supported her mercery trade, as she was also
recorded selling mercery to mercers of Montpellier.[23] On 28 May 1333, she
sold mercery worth 30 *l.t.p.* to the mercer Berengarius Gasqui and his wife.
On 4 December of the same year, she made another sale to Bernardus
Rebolh, mercer, of diverse types of mercery.[24] In these transactions, she
accepted recognitions of debt currently used in the luxury trade in Montpellier. Bernarda understood the production and marketing of mercery in Montpellier. She would have been able to provide invaluable assistance to Martha
in gauging how her sons could participate in the mercery trade after the death
of Guiraudus, even if Martha herself was not a direct participant. Martha was
likely never trained formally as a mercer and appeared somewhat removed
from the mercery trade, financing the operations of her sons through partnerships, described in Chapter 7.

The textile business, with its extensions into apprenticeship training, the
metalwork industry, and the industrial processing of wool cloth and linen,
was easily the industry par excellence in the Middle Ages. The Cabanis participated at many levels in this sector, financed through large partnerships that
Martha organized with Petrus del Euze and Johannes de Suelhis. Neither
Jacobus nor Guiraudus was recorded in apprenticeship, but their younger
brother Johannes, born in 1322, apprenticed as a mercer in 1342 for two
years.[25] He had likely had some earlier training, as he was termed mercer in

the apprenticeship contract, and he received a salary of 25 *l.* current money for his work. He was furnished with food and drink, perhaps during the workday, and could have continued to live in the Cabanis home during his formal apprenticeship.

Of Martha's sons, Guiraudus, the eldest brother, born in 1315, had married as early as 1338, by age twenty-three. Son Jacobus, born in 1318, was married by 1341, also by age twenty-three. Johannes's marriage, if he married, has left no trace. The two older boys married early, therefore not following the Mediterranean marriage model that would have elite sons marrying later in life, as noted in Chapter 3. One wonders whether the death of their father played a role in their marriages at a young age.

The division of business responsibilities of Martha's older two sons, Guiraudus and Jacobus, her main business partners, is also of interest. Jacobus may well have had the more gregarious personality. A natural salesman, he was probably voluble and ambitious. He was his father's choice as universal heir, a nomination that would have occurred in the late Guiraudus's will and that required Jacobus to accept the estate with all its obligations, positive and negative. In Jacobus's case, such an appointment meant a significant real estate fortune as well as involvement in the family's commercial and financial investments. Jacobus would collaborate more closely than his brother Guiraudus with their mother Martha, perhaps because of his designation as universal heir, though both brothers would interact with her. The youngest son, Johannes, was much less evident in the remaining notarial evidence.

Guiraudus, Jacobus's brother, close collaborator and partner (*socius*), was the detail man of their business, the accountant who was present in more cancellations, though Jacobus was also present in many. Over the period 2 October 1338 to 6 May 1342, there were seventy credit sales of mercery of Lucca in the Nogareti register, construed as recognitions of debt that were paid off at the terms stated in the contract.[26] Guiraudus was present at the majority of sales of mercery of Lucca, the brothers' specialty, acting for himself and for his brother. Jacobus was often absent. The notary frequently represented both brothers when they were not present, with a member of the Cabanis entourage present among the witnesses to these sales contracts.[27] Both brothers were present together in only one act.[28] Their factor Bernardus de Rodesio, who ran their mercery shop from his appointment on 22 September 1338, was also present in only one sale.[29] Rodesio in the role of procurator received a general acquittal from a Lucchese merchant in June 1342, perhaps the result of payment for Lucchese merchandise for the Cabanis mercery shop.[30] Most of Rodesio's sales may have been from traffic through the shop itself, bypassing the notary, except for large transactions that he would have passed on to the brothers.

The Cabanis factor, Bernardus de Rodesio, was hired in late September 1338 to run the mercery shop as a factor and business negotiator (*factor and negociorum gestor*).[31] The factor contract provided him with food, drink, clothes, and shoes, as well as a salary, the profits of 250 l. each year for four years.[32] He very likely lived in the Cabanis home as a result. Bernardus would have been involved in both retail and wholesale transactions, but he was clearly not the dealmaker for large sales that were recorded by the notary Nogareti. In the one mercery transaction he was recorded in, in July 1339, the location of the act was unspecified, and it may well have been at the shop.[33] With the Cabanis mercery shop likely located in the family house, as I have suggested, Martha's oversight would have been central to its operations. Bernardus de Rodesio, along with Firminus Salamonis, acted frequently in the capacity as procurator to tidy up business deals with formal cancellations of obligations regarding mercery of Lucca transactions.[34]

Overall, Guiraudus held down the mercery of Lucca business with his overwhelming presence. Also noteworthy is the efficient management of resources and division of responsibilities reflected in the fact that the brothers were together before the notary only once in the mercery of Lucca transactions recorded over these years. They had discrete areas of responsibility, a structure that Martha may have decided on early in their careers. For his universal heir, their father Guiraudus may have already assessed the potential of his sons and chosen Jacobus as his successor.

In the years 1338–40 most of the Cabanis contracts in their specialty of mercery of Lucca were drawn up in the French quarter of Montpellier, *parte regia*. Nogareti was a public notary authorized by the king of France. He may well have had his atelier in the French quarter of Montpelliéret, in that part of the quarter that lay within the *Commune Clôture* walls. In the years 1341 and 1342, the place of the transaction was explicitly noted as the notary's atelier. In only one instance was the contract at the brothers' house, with both brothers present. This was a transaction involving a colleague Petrus Cotelli, merchant of Toulouse, and a major player with the Cabanis in the sale of armor as well as mercery of Lucca in their affairs in Avignon.[35] The sum involved—11 gold marks, translating to 1515 *l.t.* or 769 florins and 2 gros—was enormous. The payment would be facilitated through letters patent of a Portuguese cardinal, written in Avignon, and Cotelli agreed to pay if the cardinal did not. Another Cabanis factor, Bernardus de Ruthena, was also mentioned. Cotelli, who had other business with the Cabanis as well, may have been entertained at the Cabanis house and shown the merchandise in stock in the mercery shop. Martha would not have been far afield.

Martha and her sons had additional extensive business personnel that I have discussed at length in *The Art of the Deal* and detailed in Chapter 7.[36] Some of these individuals may have lived in the Cabanis home. The Cabanis also hired apprentices for several years at a time, one in 1339 and another in 1342, whom they committed to support in food, drink, and shoes, in both sickness and health. In the case of an apprenticeship of 26 May 1339, when they took Americus Roque as an apprentice, the boys were only twenty-one and twenty-four.[37] Martha must have supervised this arrangement, even if partners and members of the Cabanis entourage dealt specifically with the mercery training. Americus's father apprenticed him to learn the trade of the Guiraudus and Jacobus (*artem vestram*). Guiraudus was present at the drawing up of the contract, acting on his own behalf and for his absent brother Jacobus. The length the apprenticeship was to run is illegible, but it was multiple years (*annos proximos*). Americus promised to be faithful and honest and not to leave his apprenticeship before the time of commitment was up. He undoubtedly lived in the Cabanis home, given the level of support offered. He may have begun by providing menial labor until he learned to be of some assistance in the mercery business as time went on, and he had acquired some training.

Another apprenticeship was scheduled in the first half of 1342; it would seem to follow on the completion of the first apprenticeship.[38] This time the hiree, Johannes Benachi, was to receive a salary of 8 *l.t.* for the period of two years of his apprenticeship, with material support. Johannes may have been an immigrant as he had a surety (*fideiussor*) certify for him.[39] This act was drawn up at the notary's atelier. The apprentice Benachi, with a salary, must have had some skills to bring to the Cabanis, though he said that he wanted to learn their trade. He too may have lived with the Cabanis.

A further dimension of Cabanis business practice lies in the movements of Martha's sons, particularly their absences over the seven-year period of greatest evidence, 1336–42. When transactions took place before the notary with the brothers physically absent, it is possible that they were not in town, perhaps traveling on business. If they were absent, members of their entourage, partners, or lesser personnel, perhaps empowered by procurations, would have substituted for them. Martha would have remained at home to manage the mercery shop, the real estate, and other commercial undertakings as well as the family household during the departure of one or more sons.

After the establishment of the partnership on 18 March 1338, a *societas* and procuration for commerce in mercery and other products with Petrus del Euze that followed on an earlier *societas* the obligations of which were mutually acquitted, both Jacobus and Guiraudus were absent from the Nogareti register until 22 September 1338. This was a period of six months, long enough for a trip to the Levant to enhance their international commercial expertise. They would have been twenty and twenty-three years old respectively. Trips to the Levant usually saw the drawing up of partnerships in the spring and the return of the traveling merchants in the fall. Frequently, the time frame was April to October.[40] In this case, a trip would have been late March to late September. Immediately upon their return, the brothers established the factor contract with Bernardus de Rodesio to run the mercery shop.

The Cabanis interest in textiles and their exports in the Mediterranean world can be documented in the years 1338–41 with partnerships in international trade targeting both Cyprus and Romania (the Byzantine Empire).[41] They used a ship of the joint Narbonne-Montpellier fleet, the *Sainte-Marie-de-Vauvert* as well as the *Saint-Jean*, a cog of Perpignan, and the *Santa-Clara*, a ship of Majorca. The joint fleet of Narbonne and Montpellier sailed to Cyprus and the Byzantine Empire regularly in the period 1336–46 while other ships of Perpignan, Barcelona, Majorca, Venice, Pisa, Genoa, Lucca, and Aigues-Mortes also moored at Aigues-Mortes, the international port of Montpellier, to take on cargo for the Levant.[42] Martha orchestrated the 1338 *societas* with Petrus del Euse that invested 2000 *l.t.* in a partnership for trade on land and sea.[43] Shortly after the formation of this partnership, the brothers may have departed for the Levant. Whether they made subsequent trips to the eastern Mediterranean is unknown.

Following on the *commenda* in 1339 with Johannes de Suelhis, surviving evidence provides a glimpse of international investments that were likely much more numerous than what we can capture in the surviving documents. With Johannes de Suelhis acting on their behalf, in October 1340 Jacobus and Guiraudus sent seven bales of linen from Autun to the Byzantine Empire in the charge of the assistant (*juvenis*) of a Montpellier linen/canvas merchant on a ship of Perpignan anchored at Aigues-Mortes.[44] In May 1341, the brothers exported French wool cloths, dyed in scarlet in Montpellier with a Montpellier merchant to the Byzantine Empire on a Majorcan ship, moored at

Aigues-Mortes.[45] In September 1341, they again sent scarlet cloths with a merchant of Béziers, inhabitant of Montpellier, to Cyprus on the *Sainte-Marie-de-Vauvert* of Montpellier and Narbonne.[46] Again in September 1341, Johannes de Suelhis, acting for the brothers, sent white linen of Autun to Cyprus on the same ship.[47] A likely rhythm of spring and fall investments in partnerships that exported wool cloths and linen was in place.

Some fruits of this trade surfaced as sales in Montpellier. In October 1341, the Cabanis sold 1,376 *l.t.* worth of sugar and pepper to a merchant of Aurillac representing Parisian and Aurillac clients, as noted earlier.[48] These eastern Mediterranean and south Asian products would have been acquired in Levant ports to which the Cabanis had directed their exports of scarlet cloths and white linen in spring 1341. Whether the brothers shipped eastern spices to Paris or Champagne (common destinations of re-export from Montpellier) cannot be determined. Their main product of re-export to northern France was saffron from Catalonia.[49]

On only one other occasion in the remaining evidence was Jacobus again absent for multiple months, from 16 or 26 September 1340, when he made Bernardus de Rodesio his procurator, to 10–20 March 1341, the occasion of a mercery of Lucca sale where he was representing himself and Guiraudus.[50] It is possible that he took another long trip to the Levant in this period, though winter was a less desirable sailing time than summer. Such an absence on Jacobus's part could explain why Guiraudus had such a dominant role in the mercery of Lucca sales. Guiraudus was never again absent from the surviving sources for a period of sufficient length to promote a Levant trip.

There were other possible destinations for the brothers' travel. The boys' father Guiraudus left a trace in Perpignan and in Marseille, and he had debts at the Champagne Fairs, suggesting that he may also have traveled there.[51] As noted in Chapter 7, financial engagements in the form of money exchange contracts often targeted repayment in Champagne.[52]

Champagne and Paris were twenty to twenty-four days travel from the south of France. There were seven transport contracts in the Cabanis records, five with the explicit intent of shipments of saffron to Paris.[53] The contracts state that the goods would be restored to the brothers or their representatives. In some cases, Jacobus or Guiraudus may have journeyed to Paris, but they would have had to make a more rapid trip—twelve days on horseback—as none of their shorter absences were more than about six weeks at the most. More likely, they had a colleague who represented them in saffron sales in Paris. They had Parisian clients for spices, as noted above, and could well have had a network of contacts in northern France. The model for such representatives could be their Valencian contact, Petrus Calvo of Montpellier, resident in Spain, who acted as their agent, importing silks and mercery from Montpellier and sending saffron and leather to Montpellier on the Cabanis behalf.[54] Cities of southern France would have been within easy traveling distance for the brothers. Narbonne, Carcassonne, Perpignan, Avignon, and Marseille all could have been visited with an absence of ten days at most.

Martha would have been directly exposed to her sons' broad geographic clientele that included merchants from Toulouse, Burgos, Cahors, Valencia, and Castile who visited Montpellier. Under her guidance, her sons were investors in the Levant trade and exported wool cloths to Cyprus and the Byzantine Empire.[55] The Cabanis connections with Spain led them to import saffron and leather that they could ship to the Champagne Fairs and to Paris.[56] Martha's mental map, established in the company of her father and grandfather and then her husband, would have included much of medieval France and the Mediterranean world, giving her the basis for her deep involvement in her sons' business.

The installation of the papal court in Avignon deeply affected Montpellier. There existed a flow of inhabitants in both directions between Montpellier and Avignon, as noted earlier. Some Montpelliérains were associated with the papal court in Avignon.[57] Others served in foreign lands as collectors of papal taxes or as messengers or members of the papal administration. They were particularly involved in transfers of funds from as far afield as Scandinavia and Castile and Portugal back to the papal chamber.[58]

Merchants of Avignon came to Montpellier to purchase a variety of spices for the papal court. The dense contacts between Montpellier and Avignon, in the realm of painting, enamels, and gold work, were discussed in Chapter 4. There is no minimizing the impact that Avignon as a market and artistic center had on Montpellier during Martha's lifetime, and her sons participated directly in complex commercial and financial arrangements involving the papal capital. The Cabanis' business in Avignon in silver armor and mercery of Lucca left considerable trace in regard to their close Toulousan client for mercery of Lucca, Petrus Cotelli.[59]

Just as the papal presence in the south of France influenced market strategies, so too royal politics also bore heavily on the lives of Martha and her sons. Inhabitants of Montpellier in the first half of the fourteenth century had a concept of "Francia" (France) by which Martha and her co-citizens may have understood the region of Paris, the Île de France, or perhaps a broader geographic region dominated by the king of France. With the purchase of the episcopal quarter of Montpelliéret in 1293, the king of France solidified his influence in the area of Montpellier through the rector and his court, representing French justice seconded by a commercial court. The creation of the court of the Petit Scel belongs to a pattern of French royal expansion in the south of France from the late thirteenth century where, in many places in the second half of the thirteenth century, courts carrying the title "*sceaux aux contrats*" and endowed with considerable independence of action were instituted by the king of France.[60] Martha and her sons would refer to the jurisdiction of this court in their documents of procuration.[61] These southern courts of voluntary jurisdiction were an imitation of an earlier movement in northern lands where, since the second half of the twelfth century, ecclesiastical courts had gained the competence to ratify contracts by the apposition of a seal and specialized courts of the wardens of the Champagne Fairs and of the Châtelet in Paris were functioning.[62] In the Midi, the notarial act continued to stand alone, without the need for further authentification. But submission to a voluntary jurisdiction such as the Petit Scel provided additional assurance to the acts carrying its seal and the promise of the rapid execution of judgment and justice in the case of nonfulfillment of the terms of the contract. French jurisdiction in Montpellier and its region opened up new possibilities for business.

Martha's home near Arc Saint-Nicolas was in the more commercially dynamic quarter of Montpellier, the section of town under the king of Mallorca's jurisdiction. In an act of procuration of 9 April 1339, as noted earlier, Martha, Jacobus, and Guiraudus, with Martha acting as *curatrix* and giving her consent, hired procurators Firminus Salamonis and Petrus de Albinhaco, members of their mercantile entourage, to make recognition of their urban and rural landholdings under the abstract rights of the king of Majorca, with a promise to pay the accustomed dues.[63] Inhabitants of Montpellier used both court systems and successfully played one king off another, resulting in considerable independence for the town's inhabitants in Martha's era.[64] When Martha and son Guiraudus hired procurators—son Jacobus and a notary Bertholomeus Lespinhani—to obtain for them the status of *burgenses* of the new bastide of Saint-Pierre de Beauvais in the region of Toulouse, to be discussed below, they were seeking to benefit from the protection offered by the new court of voluntary jurisdiction founded there under the auspices of the king of France.[65] Such a connection would have facilitated Cabanis business in Toulouse. To live in Montpellier during Martha's time was a balancing act between the two kings, France and Majorca. Progressively, as the first half of the fourteenth century wore on, the king of Majorca became a weaker figure, until the king of France purchased the quarter of Montpellier from him in 1349.

The last stage of the possession of Montpellier by the king of Majorca began in 1344 with new aggression on the part of the king of Aragon, the redoubtable Peter IV, who, in 1344, annexed Majorca, Roussillon, and the Cerdagne, territories of the kingdom of Majorca.[66] The French defeat at Crécy in 1346 ruled out any interference on behalf of James III, king of Majorca, by Philip VI to assist him in the recovery of his lands. James was left to plot continuously for the recovery of Majorca until his death in 1349. It was to finance this enterprise that he sold Montpellier on 18 April 1349 to Philip VI for the sum of 120,000 gold *écus*. Included in the cession were the town of Montpellier, the palace and château of the king, the jurisdiction of the bailiff, the castellany of Lattes, and all dependencies. Philip VI confirmed the privileges and liberties of the town on 8 May 1349; the inhabitants and the consuls had already taken a new oath of loyalty to the French king. Consular election mechanisms remained unchanged. A court of the governor replaced that of the bailiff, representing French justice in the former Majorcan quarter of Montpellier. The court of the rector and the court of the Petit Scel remained in Montpelliéret, with the jurisdiction of Montpellier and Montpelliéret remaining separate until 1551.[67]

The decade leading up to the purchase of Montpellier saw inhabitants of the town leaning more in the direction of France. The Bastide of Beauvais initiative of Martha and her sons reflects this trend. Inhabitants of Montpellier and other southern French towns typically identified themselves with a political overlord when pressed. In inquest testimonies where they were questioned about their political loyalty, they were asked to state whose subject they were. Martha and her sons Jacobus and Guiraudus were not witnesses in any surviving lawsuit, so we do not know for certain how they would have identified themselves, but it is likely their first loyalty was to the king of Majorca. Their real estate recognitions of the abstract rights of the king of Majorca would suggest that, and this was likely the orientation of most of the mercantile elite of Montpellier. However, increasingly, this identity was not exclusive (see Map 1, Chapter 1).

There are inquests of litigation surviving where political identification was given. In witness testimony from a French inquest of 1299 regarding the lagoons and the jurisdiction of the French king over trade entering

Aigues Mortes, we see a range of self-identification.[68] Some witnesses added a political orientation to their geographic identity. Two men of Frontignan called themselves "men of the king of Majorca." One was a merchant and fisherman, one a mariner. A mariner from Collioure, a port of Perpignan in Roussillon, also held allegiance to the king of Majorca. It should be noted that the majority of the inhabitants of Montpellier, those of the seigneurial quarter at least, were subjects of the king of Majorca in 1299. The hinterland of Montpellier was small, but, clearly, within a thirty-kilometer radius, Majorca held sway. Five men, three from Mèzes, two from Agde, called themselves "men of the lord Bishop of Agde." There was no mention of the king of France to whom residents of Aigues-Mortes were theoretically subject.

Of nineteen witnesses in an inquest of 1332 regarding religious asylum in Montpellier, ten stated their allegiance to the king of Majorca; five more responded more obliquely that they lived in the Majorcan quarter of the town, that is, Montpellier.[69] A French royal notary did not state his specific lord, but he lived in the French quarter, Montpelliéret, and was probably a French subject. Finally, one bourgeois (*burgensis*) who had served as bailiff for the court of the king of Majorca actually identified himself as a French subject, though he lived in the Majorcan quarter. Further, one witness had dual allegiance, to the Majorcan king in civil matters and, oddly, to the bishop's court (the *officialité*) in criminal affairs. Another cleric who lived in the Majorcan quarter was under ecclesiastical jurisdiction. The question of allegiance was quite complicated for any inhabitant of Montpellier, Martha and her sons included. Martha and her sons lived in the Majorcan quarter of Montpellier, thus under the king of Majorca, but they did business with French royal jurisdiction in mind.

For the period when we can trace their activities closely, Martha and the Cabanis brothers could take advantage of their two masters, as did all the inhabitants of Montpellier, though one, the king of Majorca, was increasingly weak. The political conditions of the town would have been key to the business operations of the Cabanis in northern France, at Paris and Champagne, in western France at Toulouse, and in central France at Cahors and at Aurillac. Here the French held sway. But in Roussillon at Perpignan, in Majorca, and in Spain at Valencia, and probably more generally throughout the Mediterranean, the role of the king of Majorca was key. In the end, the dual political overlordship of Montpellier undoubtedly worked to the advantage of merchants in their business deals and litigation.

From the perspective of Montpellier, the political conflict between Majorca and France was further complicated in the late 1330s and early 1340s by events of the Hundred Years War. The town itself and its trading networks would be affected.[70] The burden of French taxation and the harassment to enlist troops punctuated the decades of the 1330s and 1340s for Montpellier. The town contributed heavily to restore the port of Aigues-Mortes in 1336.[71] By 1337, the date of the opening of hostilities between the French and the English in the north on land and on sea, Edward III had honed his army and his tactics with five years of war in Scotland.[72] In 1337, Philip VI of France began a benighted campaign of taxation to raise funds for the war. The towns of Languedoc were targeted. Montpellier protested that it did not have to pay a subsidy because of its ties to the kingdom of Majorca, and the king adjusted the level of the levy. A royal letter of August 1337 exempted subjects of the king of Majorca from payment.[73] In spring 1338, Montpellier proposed a loan to the French king of 2,000 *l.t.*, but this did not immediately spare the town from a military summons.[74] In 1338, French royal officials tried to impose a tax on Majorcan subjects, but the French king reined them in.[75] By 1339, the king of Majorca, James III, protested to Philip VI about the harassment of his subjects.[76] In the summer of 1339, French officials arrested three hundred Montpelliérains, and French sergeants occupied the houses of the consuls. Again Philip VI intervened, as there were subjects of the king of Majorca involved.[77] An effort to impose a war subsidy recurred in early 1340 in Montpellier; the French seneschal of Beaucaire put out an order to muster heads of household in Montpellier. This order was rescinded, and Montpellier made an offer of a subsidy of 2,000 *l.t.* This sum was followed by 2,500 *l.t.*, offered in return for a safeguard and pardon for offenses that French royal investigators had turned up.[78] As John Henneman commented, "The [French] crown thus obtained 4,500 *l.t.* from Montpellier, none of it in the form of a war subsidy."[79]

In 1341, the French king changed tactics, since taxation to support the war effort was minimally successful. He began instead to extend the salt tax (*gabelle*) from the north of France, where it was already established, to the south. Montpellier and other southern towns resisted this, arguing that the economy was poor and that the holders of saltpans should have been consulted.[80] The Cabanis as holders of *salines* would have been concerned. In spring 1341, the French seneschal of Beaucaire required support for one sergeant from every household in Montpellier, whether of French or Majorcan allegiance, for forty days.[81] Montpellier protested again, but its wealthy citizens may well have contributed. Further contributions came in 1342 and 1343.[82] In 1344, Montpellier paid 4,000 *l.t.* to replace a sales tax and to atone for monetary infractions.[83] This relentless assault of French taxation was accompanied in 1343 by a revaluation of coinage that resulted in a 76 percent reduction in the price of silver paid by royal mints.[84] Prices dropped, causing merchants difficulty but pleasing those with fixed revenues, that is, creditors and landlords.[85]

French royal officials were not well viewed in Montpellier. As Henneman noted, "The consuls of Montpellier said that they 'always sought a thousand pretexts for troubling them,' and obtained the promise that they would conduct their investigations only in the presence of the seneschal or his lientenant."[86] But that did not put an end to the French demands. In 1345, Montpellier was again required to contribute, converting support for men-at-arms into a lump sum of 2,000 *l.t.*[87] Later in 1345, French royal sergeants occupied Montpellier houses when the consuls refused to furnish crossbowmen.[88] This was not the last of royal demands, but the war would take a different turn after the defeats of the French at Crécy in 1346 and at Poitiers in 1356. The consuls of Montpellier faced rapidly recurring demands for funds from the king of France in the late 1330s and 1340s, and their citizens, whether claiming allegiance to Majorca or to France, were harassed by royal officials who intruded into their homes. Martha and her sons would have been in the midst of this turmoil as wealthy inhabitants of the town. Their trade was impacted by war maneuvers, and their networks had to be flexible to cope with hostilities across Western Europe.

The war reached Montpellier directly in 1340–41, but by then trade had already been disrupted in the north and west by the English activities in Aquitaine. In June 1341 a dispute between James III, king of Majorca and lord of Montpellier, and Philip VI, king of France and lord of Montpelliéret, turned ugly. James III was in desperate straits in his struggle with the king of Aragon. He had approached Edward III in the fall of 1340 in Ghent. At a tournament in March 1341, he openly repudiated French suzerainty, prompting the French to move against Montpellier from Toulouse in June 1341.[89] One can understand the gradual shift in allegiance on the part of the Montpellier elite toward France, given the declining fortunes of the king of Majorca. The town would be menaced more directly by the companies of *routiers* and the Black Prince in the 1350s, prompting the construction of a suburban fortification called the Palissade as of 1352.[90] War only added to the crises of subsistence, plague, and social unrest.

In these challenging times, Martha's tactics varied according to the context in which she was operating. Her technique was to establish partnerships extending for four years and, if they were satisfactory, to renew them. In 1338, Martha seems to be cleaning up previous engagements and forging ahead with this rhythm. In the *societas* partnership with Petrus del Euze, the parties first agreed to an acquittal for previous engagements and then established the partnership. The 1338 partnership would be interrupted by Petrus del Euze's death, sometime in 1339. What followed upon his disappearance is not known. In 1342, the second year of greatest recorded activity for Martha, she shifted her focus to the establishment of procurations to acquire privileges and to defend business interests in court.

A significant dimension of Martha's involvement in her children's affairs lies in the appointment of procurators, on her own behalf and in collaboration with sons. The practice of procuration that involved a delegation of legal authority had begun for Martha at the death of her husband. In all likelihood, Guiraudus had used this technique regularly to manage his business affairs before his death. Martha may have also been using the technique before we find a remaining trace. Women employed procurators currently, as did men, to draft their contracts for them before the notary, to defend them in litigation, and, in general, to carry out their business. Procuration was a common business technique permitting legal or business-oriented representation at a distance or in the absence of a principal.[91] Robert Lopez argued that procuration was the cornerstone of medieval business in combination with partnerships and loans.[92] There is no evidence in the documents of Montpellier or Marseille that women were appointed as procurators, but they employed procurations, as did their male colleagues, with great frequency in the conduct of their affairs.[93] Martha alone and with her sons used procuration regularly.

Procuration would be central to the management of the family affairs for Martha and for her sons. In December 1326 Petrus del Euze was named procurator of Jacobus, age eight and the universal heir of his deceased father Guiraudus.[94] As noted earlier, by 1335, Martha was using Jacobus as her procurator. He showed up in an act of 30 April 1336 acting as her procurator (by appointment of 4 February 1335 in an act of Johannes Holanie). In the 1336 act, Jacobus gave an acquittal to a man from Castelnau for 40 *s.t.* owed to his mother from an obligation of 15 May 1335 that a shoemaker owed for a rental of a house.[95] Jacobus was drawing up the formal acquittal on his mother's behalf.

There were thirty-four procurations recorded in the Nogareti register, registering the appointment of legal representatives by the Cabanis family.[96] In seven of these, Martha hired procurators alone or with her sons for real estate management, to represent their business interests in law suits, and to establish *burgensis* status in a town of western France. When she was hiring a son to represent her, she appeared alone. In all other cases, she was collaborating with Jacobus and Guiraudus, or with one of them, to hire legal representation. Most often those hired were members of the Cabanis mercantile entourage, Firminus Salamonis or Petrus de Albinhaco. The pretext might be the management of real property or the pursuit of or defense in matters of litigation outside Montpellier in ecclesiastical and civil courts.[97] By 1336, Martha was using both Jacobus and Guiraudus as procurators in family affairs, and she continued to do so in a land exchange as late as 1342 when the evidence ceases.[98]

In the Nogareti evidence, five of the seven procurations Martha drew up were written in her house, one took place the notary's atelier, and, in the remaining procuration, the venue was not given. For reasons of convenience, on 9 April 1339, as noted earlier, members of the Cabanis entourage were given a delegation of authority to make real estate recognitions to the king of Majorca and to promise to pay the accustomed dues.[99] The properties themselves were not itemized, but it is likely they were numerous.

On 12 February 1342, Martha received holdings at Boutonnet from her mother in a *donatio inter vivos*.[100] In procuration of 19 February, Martha alone hired one of her sons (name illegible) to sell or exchange land in the suburb of Boutonnet.[101] On 27 February, she exchanged the Boutonnet lands for tables in town. The boundaries of the properties described were similar, and this is the same piece of land that was exchanged two weeks later for tables and a shop in the butchery/fish market through the services of Jacobus as procurator.[102] The process of adjusting her real estate holdings was laid out in these three acts as she disposed of rural or suburban property and invested in lucrative commercial properties.[103] By 1342, Martha would use Jacobus, in particular, to carry out such operations.

In four cases, two in October 1341, with Martha and Jacobus hiring, and two in 1342 (August and September) with Martha, Jacobus, and Guiraudus hiring, the family sought the assistance of legal specialists, *jurisperiti* and notaries, to pursue litigation in both civil and ecclesiastical courts.[104] In two of the procurations, Petrus de Albinhaco, described as *clericus* and *familiaris*, was joined by Guillelmus de Albinhaco, who was a legal specialist and perhaps his relative. The basis for the lawsuits was not specified, but the number of procurations suggests that litigation was an accompaniment of business. Merchants had to be ready to defend their interests. Jacobus and Guiraudus used procurators regularly in their affairs, as did many medieval merchants. Everything from representation in sales and purchases to the pursuit of debts and the defense in court might be necessary.[105]

Martha's most sophisticated and innovative use of procuration came in September of 1342 when she, in the Cabanis house, along with son Guiraudus, hired her son Jacobus and the French royal notary Bertholomeus Lespinhani to seek for the Cabanis that they become *burgenses* of the new Bastide of Beauvais in Upper Languedoc.[106] The two of them, Martha and Guiraudus, were acting in like manner, as equals, *pariter*.[107] This was a particularly precise act, with the hour of the day included along with the normal dating protocol. Martha and Guiraudus authorized these two to pay whatever was due for the said status, with full power, and special mandate. With business interests in Toulouse, Martha was positioning the family to take advantage of the expansion of French royal rights in southern France, particularly in this region.[108] The Bastide of Beauvais near Toulouse was the site of the establishment of a new commercial court of law.[109] The Cabanis as *burgenses* of Beauvais would enjoy special merchant status and access to this court. They had significant business interests with Toulouse in mercery of Lucca, and such privileged status in the immediate region would be important. In trusted Cabanis strategy, Petrus de Albinhaco, mainstay of the Cabanis business entourage, was one of the witnesses to this act of procuration.

With Martha's careful tutelage, her sons were poised to flourish when we lose track of their affairs in the mid-1340s. Jacobus and Guiraudus were already referring to the Beauvais court for legal protection in October 1342 in a sale for them by Johannes de Suelhis of dyed linen of Autun to a merchant of Toulouse.[110] The procuration to obtain *burgensis* status represents the expansion of the Cabanis business and the careful monitoring of legal protection orchestrated by Martha. Access to a court of French royal voluntary jurisdiction in western France would prove useful to business.[111] This was perhaps the crowning achievement of Martha's business strategy, first as the guardian of her children and then, increasingly, as their collaborator. The fact that she was still intimately involved with them in business suggests that she had a commitment to their affairs. The date of this venture, 1342, speaks to her continued collaboration in the family business with her sons, several years after she would have been expected, legally or morally, to have stepped aside. Guiraudus was twenty-seven in 1342, and Jacobus was twenty-four. Both sons had been active in business for ten years. Even if Guiraudus's will had given Martha lifetime control of his estate, she could have delegated that responsibility if she had wished. Instead, she pursued new initiatives until we finally lose track of her in the cancellation of one of her partnerships in 1344.[112] Through her procurations, Martha showed brilliant business acumen, consistent with her significant involvement in some of the largest partnerships surviving in the notarial evidence of Montpellier before 1350.

Conclusion

The environment in which Martha de Cabanis operated was vastly different from the rural seigniorial world and most of the north of Europe. Hers was the urban, commercial, and cosmopolitan milieu of Mediterranean Europe. But women all over Europe lived in a world of gender rules and differences of experience shaped by gender. They lived in the patriarchal society of the Middle Ages. To complicate the place and actions of women within such a society, Marie Kelleher traced gender ideas in the statutes of the Crown of Aragon and followed women in court proceedings, revealing multiple layers of legal discourse and identity.[1] Judith Bennett has argued for a patriarchal equilibrium for women across time, based on wage disparities and a less developed occupational identity.[2] However, the effects of patriarchy and gender were complex.[3]

This case study of Martha de Cabanis was written to explore what women could do in fourteenth-century medieval southern Europe. I have sought to demonstrate the real commercial and legal agency of Martha, all the while providing the reader with an entrée into a medieval city and into the life of the urban commercial elite of the first half of the fourteenth century. Although southern France was a patriarchal society, like the rest of medieval Europe, women of Montpellier like Martha operated with considerable independence and success across a wide range of activities. They relied heavily on occupational connections and family ties, creating communities of support. Martha was a member of the urban elite, a privileged status that gave her both resources and position. My interpretation of Martha's experiences, based on documents of practice, is a bit more optimistic than the picture painted by Marie Kelleher and definitely more hopeful than the patriarchal equilibrium described by Judith Bennett.

It has been possible to trace Martha's actions and interactions with her sons over a period of almost twenty years, from 1326 to 1344.[4] Surviving notarial contracts preserve Martha's and her sons' investments in commerce, industry, and in real property. Martha's domestic surroundings—her house, its furnishings, and its decoration, and her possible mobile wealth in personal effects from jewelry, art objects, fabrics, and clothing of the period—have been recreated from remaining evidence. Martha's activities, as the head of a large urban household, as guardian of her sons, and in her own right, furnish convincing proof of her agency.

Marriage and inheritance funneled property, both mobile and real, into women's hands. They could expect a dowry from their fathers and an augment from their husband that, while not on a par with London dower, brought some security to the couple and later to the surviving widow. They could make wills and dispose of their property as they wished. There is no evidence that Martha herself made a will; it was, however, very common for women of her status to do so.[5] Married women of Montpellier without children could not dispose of their goods through a will without their family's permission. Women with children were freer to frame their wills as they chose but were restricted in the amount they could leave to their spouses.[6] For mothers, their most common beneficiaries were their children. Beyond the statutory constraints, a woman's social and legal status—whether she was of noble background, of the urban elite, of the artisan class, or of urban agricultural background—affected her legal rights and the range of her activities.[7] Martha was a woman of the urban elite, a woman of privilege, who enjoyed many options in her decisions.

Women were capable of defending their interests and the interests of their children, whether in claims for the early return of dowry and the preservation thereby of the family patrimony or in disputes regarding the estates of their late husbands.[8] Widows enjoyed the greatest range of agency, but wives could also act decisively. The courts admitted women's litigation and treated women as witnesses in lawsuits without gender distinctions. Martha's establishment of procurations to defend the family business and her acquisition for herself and her sons of *burgensis* status in order to benefit from the French voluntary jurisdiction of the Bastide of Beauvais illustrate her extensive use of and familiarity with the court systems of her day.

Martha de Cabanis shared the challenges of other widows but confronted necessities specific to the raising of three sons. For Martha, it was essential to assure a career formation for her sons so that they could carry on in their father's footsteps. In the process, she revealed herself a very involved and effective businesswoman.

The relationship of Martha with her children reflects the connections between mothers and sons.[9] In Martha's case, familial closeness seems to characterize the parent–child and extended family relationships. Her extensive interaction with her sons in business leaves open the possibility of significant affective ties, although there is a limited survival of documents addressing familial emotions.[10]

While Martha was recorded in many fewer notarial acts than her sons, she was present in highly significant acts financing the family business and expanding initiatives to western France. She was deeply involved in matters of litigation and debt recovery through procurations. The rhythm of her contracts and the pattern of her involvement suggest that she was vested with considerable initiative, not simply the pawn of her husband's partners who needed her to sign off on investments. Her partner, Petrus del Euze, died in 1339, and Martha was on her own after that, with activities that can be traced to 1344. The partnership and linen processing arrangements with Johannes de Suelhis reflect her and her sons' involvement with someone who was more of an employee. There is no way to be certain where original initiative lay in these partnerships, but Martha's role seems quite explicit. And it continues to be in late ventures (1342) like the acquisition of *burgensis* status in the Bastide of Beauvais. Stephen Bensch and Rebecca Winer found similar examples of widows involved for long periods in the management of their husbands' estates.[11]

Notarial evidence portrays Montpellier women in active economic roles in the late thirteenth and in the first half of the fourteenth century. Though we have evidence of strong families in the urban setting, the Cabanis family branches being illustrative of these, it is also the case that the traditional configuration of the medieval family was not always the norm. Urban families were more fragile than rural families because of the difficult living conditions in towns, due to crowding and the ease of spread of disease. Immigration could cause a disruption of traditional family ties. If women's influence in the early Middle Ages was through family channels, in later medieval towns, for some individuals, as David Herlihy noted, family structure, rather than evolving along patriarchal lines, tended to fragment with "proliferation within the city of small, truncated, and incomplete households."[12] Women assumed more independence, though their exact involvement in business undoubtedly reflected individual personalities, as it does today. There were many times when women acted without a base in family enterprise in their own trades. They also acted with other family members on behalf of family business enterprises.[13] Martha's experience illustrates this dual role. Women's economic involvement was not a direct parallel of men's roles, but Montpel-liéraines like Martha and Bernarda de Cabanis were well integrated into the Montpellier economy.

The history of women in the upper echelons of urban society is inevita-bly favored with more specific detail than survives for women in artisanal or agricultural work. The economic operations of women of the extended Cabanis family furnish three models of mercantile women's activities, run-ning the gamut from Martha, the active widow, managing the family business and collaborating with her sons as they matured, to Bernarda de Cabanis, the elite tradeswoman, wife, and moneylender, to the widow Maria Naturale, the most passive of the three, who nonetheless had real estate investments that she supervised through agents and sons and sons-in-law.[14] The methods by which these women in Montpellier overcame the legal constraints on women are revealing of a community of family and business associates who assisted and probably advised their activities. The Cabanis women appeared in a wide range of economic activities.

Elite women engaged in a great variety of activities and utilized multiple approaches in their economic involvement. The skills developed in the man-aging of a patrician household would have assisted elite widows after the demise of their spouses. Business and household management were closely intertwined for elite women like Martha, who belies any suggestion of domestic confinement such as that suggested by Régine Pernoud and Shu-lamith Shahar.[15] Rather, they navigated the patriarchal society to minister to the needs of their families and the family fortune. Martha had three major occupations: business, household management, and motherhood. She excelled at all three.

Women can be documented in most but not all of the specialties of medieval Montpellier. They were active in international and local trade, though as sedentary investors in most cases, as were many of the merchants of Montpellier. Martha's involvement in commercial transactions stemmed from her role as guardian of her sons. She demonstrated considerable business acumen in trade and industry. Though not formally admitted to guild mem-bership, women worked in specialties such as the silk and mercery trade and in the precious metal auxiliary activities. They were apprenticed in crafts that might be classified as women's work: textiles, decorative arts, and the food trades. There were thus clear gender distinctions in the apprenticeship and work contract evidence from this corner of Languedoc in the region's largest city.

The prestigious occupations of the mercantile elite were exclusively masculine in Montpellier. Women were not noted in the pepperers', spice merchants', or apothecaries' trades, among the most illustrious in Montpellier. They were not part of the legal or paralegal professions. Women were participants in the lending and deposit banking dimensions of Montpellier finance, but not in money exchange transactions. Martha focused her efforts on the earlier specialty of her late husband Guiraudus in textiles, developing and expanding her sons' activities in that sector. Women were notably not involved in the spice trade, the sector par excellence of international trade, and were not noted in the extant transport contracts by which luxury goods were shipped to markets at the Champagne Fairs, in Paris, or in Spain and Italy.[16] Martha's sons dealt in spices and shipped merchandise to Paris and the Champagne Fairs, but Martha did not. She was not mentioned selling mercery of Lucca, the specialized luxury products that the Cabanis brothers, in particular, handled, but Bernarda was noted in mercery sales and in mercery apprenticeship. Martha may have earlier been involved in the mercery business during her married life; however, when our evidence begins, she was otherwise occupied as guardian, setting the Cabanis business on a secure footing and assisting her young sons in their entry into business. She was instrumental in arranging the financing and the partnerships that underpinned the major business operations of her sons. At the same time, she carefully adjusted her real property holdings to concentrate on urban commercial investments.

Given the depth of her involvement in business and real property, Martha's aptitude for these engagements stands out. She had definite management skills. Here again, her profile was not an uncommon one among Montpellier women, but we have much more detail about her actions than survives for other women.[17] Agnes de Bossones was equally impressive but with somewhat different emphases in real property and philanthropy, a true *maîtresse femme*.[18] The demands of home and family could be reconciled with economic ventures. The notarial contracts of Montpellier portray Martha and her compatriots in active economic roles in the first half of the fourteenth century, with the impressive participation of women of the mercantile elite and of lesser strata. Kelleher and Winer find examples of women comparable to Martha in the Crown of Aragon, such as Romia, widow of Pere de Gernolosa, and Raimunda de Camerada, as does Hutton with Mergriete Scettorf of Ghent.

There is something rather tragic in this Cabanis family history. A young mother would never remarry but would dedicate herself to her sons and the family business. Her two older sons missed out on a carefree youth. Jacobus was active in business at fifteen, only seven years after the death of his father. His older brother may have been as well. These two married early. These facts are the signs of stress on a merchant family when the father died during the youth of his children. With the youngest son Johannes, things were different. By his apprenticeship at age twenty, his older brothers and Martha had the family business flourishing. Martha could afford to have him trained in more traditional fashion. He went outside the family sphere and apprenticed himself to a mercer of Montpellier, Raymundus Arulhe, for two years at a level of expertise that suggests he already had some skills (*discipulum et juvenem*). One can only wonder whether he would be invited into the family business at the end of his training. Perhaps his upbringing, very different from that of his older brothers, could have created a rift of sorts. But Martha was probably skillful enough to overcome that. Johannes may have been her baby even then.

The disappearance of evidence after 1345 prevents us from knowing the end of the story. The arrival of the plague in 1348 meant that life in Montpellier would have changed dramatically for the Cabanis, their family, and colleagues within a few years of our acquaintance with them. When notarial evidence resumes in the early 1360s, we no longer find these individuals. The Cabanis surname would persist, but with a different set of first names.

Martha had positioned her sons well by the mid-1340s. That they lived in an era of relative prosperity in Montpellier, the end of a long process of growth that began in the eleventh century and accelerated in the twelfth and thirteenth, certainly made things easier for success. The story of Martha, placed in the context of the collective experience of women, provides insight into the world of women in Montpellier and furnishes depth and detail regarding women's lives in the Middle Ages. Martha's story presents to the modern reader the limits of what was possible for medieval women in the context of a patriarchal society. Martha represents what an elite woman could do in a mature medieval urban economy before the Black Death.

The survival of notarial evidence for Martha and her sons leaves uneven data available. There remain an act of 1326/1328 and a few acts in the early 1330s and in 1336.[1] Then from 1336 there is a run of information (several hundred contracts) over seven years until 1342, recorded in one private notarial register by the notary Guillelmus Nogareti and largely dedicated to Cabanis business transactions.[2] Additional interventions—acquittals of business obligations and cancellation clauses—have left their trace in the Nogareti register as late as 1345. Then the evidence ceases.

I have worked with a photocopy of the Nogareti register, made in the 1970s. Subsequently, the register was "restored" with the pages plasticized, rendering some of the handwriting illegible. The Nogareti register containing most of the Cabanis acts presents some problems in consultation because of the way it was bound. In the late 1970s, I benefited from the careful renumbering and dating of the contracts of this register by then assistant archivist (*archiviste adjointe*) Madame Annette Sahraoui, of the Archives Départmentales de Montpellier. The register has 94 folios, including blank folios and fragments, with approximately 330 contracts (not counting acts within acts). There are two series of acts, one that runs forward and the other in reverse. Hence, folio citations will, for example, be f. 10v and f. 10Rv to distinguish between the series. The bound version of the register with a simple numbering of acts (1–327) contains the following chronology:

1336—Acts 157–159
1337—Acts 160–177
1338—Acts 1–8
1338—Acts 178–207
1339—Acts 9–54
1339—Acts 208–250

1340—Acts 55–72
1340—Acts 251–271
1341—Acts 73–122
1341—Acts 272–300
1342—Acts 123–156
1342—Acts 301–327

For the Nogareti register and the other notarial registers of the Montpellier archives, I have been guided in my citation of notarial folios by the archivists' renumbering in pencil of otherwise older, inconsistently numbered folios of the surviving registers. Any ambiguity should be resolved by verifying the date of the document in question.

The medieval notary was more important than the modern notary public who stamps his name and signs next to our signatures to certify that we are who we say we are for contractual purposes.[3] With some legal training, he functioned more like a paralegal and in some ways shaped the law through the documents he wrote. In the south of Europe, where written Roman law traditions were strong, individuals of varying rank and social status went before the notary to have important documents drawn up. The notary often produced copies for his clients and kept a record in a register, frequently in the somewhat abbreviated form of minutes. Notarial contracts had the force of proof before the law.[4] At the time Martha lived, in the first half of the fourteenth century, notarial documents in Montpellier were written in Latin. The notary might interpret the language for his clients if they were not familiar (and most were not) with that learned tongue.

Women like Martha are identified in the Montpellier documents in a variety of ways. It was notarial practice to include the names of husbands, often noting the latters' occupation or honorific title, and whether they were alive or deceased. Generally, the notary did not list women's occupational status. If women were not married, their fathers' names and occupations were generally given with the indication of "deceased" if that was apt. At times, a notary provided both sets of identification and a geographic place of origin. When women were identified only with their fathers, it is a reasonable assumption that they were single.[1] For immigrants, both men and women, the notary noted their geographic origins, at times incorporating these labels in their last names as place-name surnames or simply calling them "inhabitants "of Montpellier, meaning nonnative inhabitants. Men and women native to Montpellier were often described as "of Montpellier," not "inhabitant of Montpellier." Occasionally, the notary provided a vernacular surname in one act and a Latin version of the same name in another.[2] The same practice can be found in some legal documents such as witness testimony. A woman might also be identified with a feminine form of her husband's surname. In Martha's case, I have called her Martha de Cabanis for the sake of simplicity, though this form does not appear in the documents. She was termed, Martha, wife of the late Guiraudus de Cabanis, in most instances. In contrast, her in-law Maria Naturale, widow of Guiraudus Naturalis, was given a feminine form of her husband's last name by the notary.

For the names of kings and the ruling ladies of Montpellier, I have used the English version of a name, thus for kings of France, Philip, not Philippe;

for the kings of Aragon and Majorca, James, not Jacme; and for ruling ladies, Marie of Montpellier and Eudoxia Comnena. I have used the traditional name Guilhem for the lords of Montpellier, given that they are most commonly known by that vernacular name. In the case of inhabitants of Montpellier, I have used the Latin form given in the notarial documents.

APPENDIX 3. A NOTE ON MONEY

The most commonly quoted coinage in the Montpellier notarial registers was the silver coinage of Tours, *livres tournois*, or *libras turonensium*, a French royal coinage. The local money of the region of Montpellier was Melgorian coinage of Melgueil.[1] Though stable, it was generally of low value. The monetary situation in France about 1300 was very complicated, with some forty coinages in circulation.[2] Majorcan coinage was essentially ousted from Montpellier by French royal coinage in the later thirteenth century.[3] There was almost no mention of Majorcan coinage in the surviving notarial registers.

Denominations included pounds (*livres*), shillings (*sous*), and pennies (*deniers*), abbreviated *l.*, *s.*, and *d.* There were 12 *deniers* in a *sous* and 20 *sous* in a *livre*, with 240 *deniers* in a *livre*. An *obole* was half a denier. There was a system of money of account as well as real coins in circulation. Sums were given most frequently in *turonensium parvorum*, which were real coins, *petits tournois*. The coins in circulation were *deniers* or *gros deniers*, worth 12 *deniers*. One does not find *sous* or *livres* in circulation as real coins. Also mentioned occasionally were gold coins, florins of Florence or *agneaux* and *réaux* of France, silver and gold *marcs*, and other foreign coinages.

In the first half of the fourteenth century, the king of France manipulated the precious metal content of coins for his profit, causing the value of individual *tournois* coins to fluctuate. In some years, such as 1342–43, money quotations were in "current money," as a result of the unstable monetary situation before a reform on 26 October 1343.[4] Monetary debasements and revaluations were the plague of medieval merchants who risked seeing their investments lose value if they were quoted in other than current money whose value was sometimes specified in real coins, not money of account.

NOTES

INTRODUCTION

1. Andrée Courtemanche, *La Richesse des femmes: Patrimoines et gestion à Manosque au XIVe siècle* (Paris: Vrin, 1993), 246n1, called attention to this intervention.

2. On Provence, see Francine Michaud, *Un signe des temps: Accroissement des crises familiales autour du patrimoine à Marseille à la fin du XIIIe siècle* (Toronto: Pontifical Institute of Mediaeval Studies, 1994); Andrée Courtemanche, *La Richesse des femmes*; idem, "Women, Family, and Immigration in Fifteenth-Century Manosque: The Case of the Dodi Family of Barcelonnette," in Kathryn Reyerson and John Drendel, eds., *Urban and Rural Communities in Medieval France: Provence and Languedoc, 1000–1500* (Leiden: Brill, 1998), 101–27; and Susan McDonough, *Witnesses, Neighbors, and Community in Late Medieval Marseille* (New York: Palgrave Macmillan, 2013). On Barcelona, see Carme Batlle i Gallart, "La Casa burguesa en la Barcelona del siglo XIII," in *La Societat barcelonina a la baixa edat mitjana: Annexos d'història medieval* (Barcelona: Universitat de Barcelona, 1983), 1:9–52; idem, "La Casa i els béns de Bernat Durfort, cuitadà de Barcelona, a la fi del segle XIII," *Acta Historica et Archaeologica Mediaevalia* 9 (1988): 9–51; idem, "La Vida y las actividades de los mercaderes de Barcelona dedicados al comercio marítimo (siglo XIII)," in Luigi de Rosa, ed., *Le Genti del mare mediterraneo* (Naples: Lucio Pironti Editore, 1981), 1:291–339; Teresa-Maria Vinyoles i Vidal, *Les Barcelonines e les darrieres de l'Edat Mitjana (1370–1410)* (Barcelona: Fundació Salvador Vives Casajuana, 1976); idem, "L'Esdevenir quotidià: Treball i lleure de les dones medievals" in Mary Nash, ed., *Més enllà del silenci: Les Dones a la història de Catalunya* (Barcelona: Generalitat de Catalunya, 1988), 73–89; and Stephen Bensch, *Barcelona and Its Rulers, 1096–1291* (Cambridge: Cambridge University Press, 1995). See, on the Crown of Aragon, Marie Kelleher, *The Measure of Woman: Law and Female Identity in the Medieval Crown of Aragon* (Philadelphia: University of Pennsylvania Press, 2010), Rebecca Winer, *Women, Wealth, and Community in Perpignan, c. 1250–1300* (Aldershot: Ashgate, 2006); Dana Wessell Lightfoot, "The Projects of Marriage: Spousal Choice, Dowries and Domestic Service in Early Fifteenth-Century Valencia," *Viator: Medieval and Renaissance Studies* 40, 1 (2009): 333–53. On Languedoc, see Cécile Béghin-LeGourriérec, "La Tentation du veuvage: Patrimoine, gestion et travail des veuves dans les villes du Bas-Languedoc aux XIVe et XVe siècles," in *La Famille, les femmes*

et le quotidien (XIVe–XVIII siècles), textes offerts à Christiane Klapisch-Zuber et rassemblés par Isabelle Chabot, Jérôme Hayez, et Didier Lett (Paris: Publications de la Sorbonne, 2006), 163–80. On Florence, Christiane Klapisch-Zuber, " 'The Cruel Mother': Maternity, Widowhood, and Dowry in Florence in the Fourteenth and Fifteenth Centuries," in *Women, Family, and Ritual in Renaissance Italy*, trans. Lydia G. Cochrane (Chicago: University of Chicago Press, 1985), 117–31; and Isabelle Chabot, "Widowhood and Poverty in Late Medieval Florence," *Continuity and Change* 3(1988): 291–311. On Venice, Stanley Chojnacki, *Women and Men in Renaissance Venice. Twelve Essays on Patrician Society* (Baltimore: Johns Hopkins University Press, 2000). And, most recently, see Lucie Laumonier, "Exemptions et dégrèvements: Les Montpelliérains face à la fiscalité (fin XIVe et XVe siècles)," *Bulletin historique de la ville de Montpellier* 35 (2013): 34–47; idem, *Solitudes et solidarités en ville: Montpellier, mi XIIIe–fin XVe siècles* (Turnhout: Brepols, 2015); idem, "Vivre seul à Montpellier à la fin du Moyen Âge," Doctoral thesis, Université de Sherbrooke (QC) and Université de Montpellier 3, 2013. See also Kathryn Reyerson, "La Participation des femmes de l'élite marchande à l'économie: Trois exemples montpelliérains de la première moitié du XIVᵉ s," in *Les Femmes dans l'espace nord-méditerranéen*, under the direction of Christiane Klapisch-Zuber, *Études Roussillonnaises* 25 (2013): 129–35; idem, "Urban Economies," in Judith M. Bennett and Ruth Mazo Karras, eds., *Oxford Handbook on Medieval Women and Gender* (Oxford: Oxford University Press, 2013), 297–310; and Kathryn Reyerson and Kevin Mummey, "Whose City Is This? Hucksters, Domestic Servants, Wet Nurses, Prostitutes, and Slaves in Late Medieval Western Mediterranean Urban Society," *History Compass* 9, 12 (2011): 910–22.

Women of the Low Countries and Germany have enjoyed similar focus by Martha Howell, *The Marriage Exchange: Property, Social Place, and Gender in Cities of the Low Countries, 1300–1550* (Chicago: University of Chicago Press, 1998); by James Murray, *Bruges, Cradle of Capitalism, 1280–1390* (Cambridge: Cambridge University Press, 2005); and, most recently, by Shennan Hutton, *Women and Economic Activities in Late Medieval Ghent* (New York: Palgrave-Macmillan, 2011).

3. Barbara Hanawalt, Caroline Barron, Marjorie McIntosh, Judith Bennett, Maryanne Kowaleski, and more recently Sandy Bardsley and Kate Staples, among others, have dealt with women in Great Britain. Barbara Hanawalt, *"Of Good and Ill Repute": Gender and Social Control in Medieval England* (New York: Oxford University Press, 1998); idem, *The Wealth of Wives: Women, Law, and Economy in Late Medieval London* (Oxford: Oxford University Press, 2007). Caroline Barron, *London in the Later Middle Ages: Government and People, 1200–1500* (Oxford: Oxford University Press, 2004). Marjorie McIntosh, "The Benefits and Drawbacks of *Femme Sole* Status in England, 1300–1630," *Journal of British Studies* 44 (2005): 410–38. Judith Bennett, *A Medieval Life: Cecilia Penifader of Brigstock, c. 1295–1344* (Boston: McGraw-Hill, 1999). Maryanne Kowaleski, "The History of Urban Families in England," *Journal of Medieval History* 14 (1988): 47–63. Sandy Bardsley, *Women's Roles in the Middle Ages* (Westport Conn.: Greenwood Press, 2007). Kate Kelsey Staples, *Daughters of London: Inheriting Opportunity in the Late Middle Ages* (Leiden: Brill, 2011).

4. Kathryn L. Reyerson, *Women's Networks in Medieval France: Gender and Community in Montpellier, 1300–1350* (New York: Palgrave Macmillan, 2016), and "L'Expérience des plaideuses devant les cours de Montpellier (fin XIIIe–mi-XIVe siècle," in Julie Claustre, Olivier Mattéoni, and Nicolas Offenstadt, eds., *Un Moyen Âge pour aujourd'hui: Mélanges offerts à Claude Gauvard* (Paris: Presses Universitaires de France, 2010), 522–28.

5. Winer, *Women, Wealth, and Community in Perpignan.*

6. Kelleher, *The Measure of Woman.*

7. McDonough, *Witnesses, Neighbors, and Community in Late Medieval Marseille.*

8. Hutton, *Women and Economic Activities in Late Medieval Ghent.*

9. Appendix 1 below discusses notarial sources in greater detail.

10. Bennett, *A Medieval Life*, 3, stated in her study of Cecilia Penifader and the peasants of Brigstock, "the most abundant and most useful sources are legal and economic documents."

11. For the use of this type of evidence, see Anthony Molho, R. Barducci, G. Battista, and F. Donnini, "Genealogy and Marriage Alliance: Memories of Power in Late Medieval Florence," in S. K. Cohn, Jr., and S. A. Epstein, eds., *Portraits of Medieval and Renaissance Living: Essays in Honor of David Herlihy* (Ann Arbor: University of Michigan Press, 1990), 39–70.

12. Margherita Datini's letters have been edited in two volumes: *Le Lettere di Margherita Datini a Francesco di Marco, 1384-1410*, ed. Valeria Rosati (Prato: Società pratese di Storia Patria, 1977), and *Le lettere di Francesco Datini alla moglie Margherita (1386–1410)*, ed. Elena Cecchi (Prato: Società pratese di Storia Patria, 1990). For the Paston letters, see Diane Watt, *The Paston Women: Selected Letters*, trans. from Middle English with Introduction, Notes and Interpretative Essay (Cambridge: D.S. Brewer, 2004).

13. Archives départementales de l'Hérault (hereafter A. D. Hérault), II E 95/374, was written as a private register for the Cabanis by Montpellier notary Guillelmus Nogareti. Martha also has acts in A. D. Hérault, II E 95/368, 370 and 371, Johannes Holanie, another Montpellier notary. See the discussion of the Cabanis notary, Guillelmus Nogareti, in Kathryn Reyerson, *The Art of the Deal: Intermediaries of Trade in Medieval Montpellier* (Leiden: Brill, 2002), passim. See also Appendix 1 below. On Holanie, see Kathryn Reyerson and Debra Salata, *Medieval Notaries and Their Acts: The 1327–1328 Register of Jean Holanie* (Kalamazoo, Mich.: Medieval Institute, 2004).

14. Nevertheless, Bennett, in *A Medieval Life*, her study of Cecilia Penifader, demonstrated that a privileged peasant woman with an extensive kinship could accumulate land and manage it effectively.

15. Judith M. Bennett, *History Matters: Patriarchy and the Challenge of Feminism* (Philadelphia: University of Pennsylvania Press, 2006), 55.

16. Ibid., 55.

17. A. D. Hérault, II E 95/370, Johannes Holanie, f. 108v, an act of 1336 in which Martha is called the *curatrix* of Jacobus and Guiraudus, who were eighteen and twenty-one, respectively, and the *tutrix* of Johannes, who was fourteen. See also Reyerson, "Women in Business in Medieval Montpellier," in Barbara A. Hanawalt, ed., *Women and Work in Preindustrial Europe* (Bloomington: Indiana University Press, 1986), 117–44.

18. Kelleher, *The Measure of Woman*, 69.

19. I do not treat Martha's spiritual life, as there remains no evidence. For a general discussion of religious orientation in Montpellier in Martha's time, see Reyerson, "Changes in Testamentary Practice at Montpellier on the Eve of the Black Death," *Church History* 47 (1978): 253–69. See also the discussion of Agnes de Bossones's spiritual orientation in Reyerson, *Women's Networks in Medieval France*, Chapter 9.

20. On widows, see Louise Mirrer, ed., *Upon My Husband's Death: Widows in the Literature and Histories of Medieval Europe* (Ann Arbor: University of Michigan Press, 1992). See also Sue Sheridan Walker, ed., *Wife and Widow in Medieval England* (Ann Arbor: University of Michigan Press, 1993).

21. Mirrer, *Upon My Husband's Death*. See also Walker, *Wife and Widow in Medieval England*. Reyerson, "Women in Business in Medieval Montpellier," makes the argument that widows enjoyed a privileged status. Further questions remain about whether the lines between married women and widows should be as sharply drawn in terms of agency.

22. Most of my scholarship on Montpellier has addressed the experience of men in business, banking, and trade, though I have treated women directly in articles and recently in *Women's Networks in Medieval France*.

23. See Reyerson, *The Art of the Deal*, for background on the Cabanis.

24. See ibid., Chapter 4, for detailed development of the business entourage. See also Chapter 7 below for a discussion of Martha and her sons' entourage.

25. For a window into this society, see Linda M. Paterson, *The World of the Troubadours: Medieval Occitan Society, c. 1100–c. 1300* (Cambridge: Cambridge University Press, 1993). The most famous southern French woman of that past age was undoubtedly Eleanor of Aquitaine, and now, thanks to the evocation of historians Fredric Cheyette and Jacqueline Caille, Ermengard, viscountess of Narbonne for much of the twelfth century, has emerged from the shadows. See Fredric L. Cheyette, *Ermengard of Narbonne and the World of the Troubadours* (Ithaca, N.Y.: Cornell University Press, 2001); and Jacqueline Caille, "Ermengarde, Viscountess of Narbonne (1127/29–1196/97): A Great Female Figure of the Aristocracy of the Midi," in Kathryn Reyerson, ed., *Medieval Narbonne: A City at the Heart of the Troubadour World* (Aldershot: Ashgate Variorum, 2005), X: 1–46, also published as "Ermengarde, vicomtesse de Narbonne (1127/29–1196/97): Une grande figure féminine du Midi aristocratique," *Narbonne: Fédération historique du Languedoc méditerranéen et du Roussillon* (1994): 1–46.

26. Claudie Duhamel-Amado, *Genèse des lignages méridionaux* (Toulouse: CNRS-Université de Toulouse-Le Mirail, 2001), on the Guilhem family. See Elizabeth Ann Haluska-Rausch, "Family, Property, and Power: Women in Medieval Montpellier, 985–1213," Ph.D. dissertation, Harvard University, 1998, 76–78, for a list of women connected to the Guilhem family. Trends observed in late twelfth- and early thirteenth-century Montpellier by Haluska-Rausch reveal different tendencies (in land, guardianship, and so forth) than those I find in a later period. These changes were perhaps due to differences in social stratum and focus, noble versus bourgeois, mercantile, artisanal, and marginal.

27. Henri Vidal, "Les Mariages dans la famille des Guillems," *Revue historique du droit français et étranger* 62 (1984): 231–45.

28. See, for example, *The Goodman of Paris*, trans. and ed. Eileen E. Power (London: Routledge, 1928). A telling example of the elite merchant wife is Margherita Datini. For a discussion of Margherita Datini, see Frances Gies and Joseph Gies, *Women in the Middle Ages* (Barnes and Noble, 1980), 184–209.

29. Régine Pernoud, *La Femme au temps des cathedrals* (Paris: Stock, 1980).

30. Susan Mosher Stuard, *A State of Deference: Ragusa/Dubrovnik in the Medieval Centuries* (Philadelphia: University of Pennsylvania Press, 1992).

31. Though the exploration of women's experiences in medieval cities is very much a work in progress, our vision of medieval women's lives now appears significantly different from that created by nineteenth- and early twentieth-century scholarship, as well as that of second-wave feminism of the 1960s and 1970s. *Femme sole* status in England, though not used frequently, it would seem, offered one means around the constraints of patriarchy. For the debates of early feminist scholarship, see, for example, Joan Kelly-Gadol, "Did Women Have a Renaissance?" in Renate Bridenthal, Claudia Koonz, and Susan Stuard, eds., *Becoming Visible: Women in European History*, 2nd ed. (Boston: Houghton Mifflin, 1987), 174–201; Kathleen Casey, "The Cheshire Cat: Reconstructing the Experience of Medieval Women," in Berenice A. Carroll, ed., *Liberating Women's History: Theoretical and Critical Essays* (Urbana: University of Illinois Press, 1976), 224–49; and Judith C. Brown and Jordan Goodman, "Women and Industry in Florence," *Journal of Economic History* 40 (1980): 73–80.

32. The best recent study of *femme sole* status is McIntosh, "The Benefits and Drawbacks of *Femme Sole* Status in England, 1300–1630."

33. Kowaleski, "The History of Urban Families in England," and Kowaleski and Judith M. Bennett, "Crafts, Gilds, and Women in the Middle Ages: Fifty Years After Marian K. Dale," *Signs: Journal of Women in Culture and Society* 14 (1989): 474–88, reprinted in Judith M. Bennett, Elizabeth A. Clark, Jean F. O'Barr, B. Anne Vilen, and Sarah Westphal-Wihl, eds., *Sisters and Workers in the Middle Ages* (Chicago: University of Chicago Press, 1989), 11–25. Most historians of women have now abandoned the idea of a medieval golden age.

34. See the *American Historical Review Forum*: Revisiting "Gender: A Useful Category of Historical Analysis," *American Historical Review* 113 (2008), especially the article by Dyan Elliott, "The Three Ages of Joan Scott," 1390–1403.

35. Bennett, *History Matters*, passim.

36. See, for example, Kathryn Reyerson, "L'Expérience des plaideuses devant les cours de Montpellier (fin XIIIe–mi-XIVe siècle);" "La Participation des femmes de l'élite marchande à l'économie," and "Women in Business in Medieval Montpellier."

37. Scholarship on the south of France has produced quantitative studies of women's activities in monographs by Courtemanche, *La Richesse des femmes*, on Manosque; Michaud, *Un Signe des temps*, on Marseille; and, more recently, in the 2000 study of

Cécile Béghin-LeGourriérec, "Le Rôle écononique des femmes dans les villes de la Séné-chaussée de Beaucaire à la fin du moyen âge (XIVe–XVe siècles)," 3 vols., Doctoral thesis, École des Hautes Études en Sciences Sociales-Paris, 2000; and Lucie Laumonier's study, "Vivre seul à Montpellier," and her *Solitudes et solidarités en ville*. Béghin-LeGourriérec compares the experience of women from three cities in medieval Languedoc, in isolation from that of men, through quantitative exploitation of the surviving notarial registers of Montpellier, Mende, and Alès, in the thirteenth through fifteenth centuries. In contrast, Laumonier's study tracing the fate of those who lived alone is very attentive to the issue of gender. Attention to the broader historical context involving men and women can assist in the analysis and interpretation of women's and men's experiences. See also the interest-ing new collection *Les Femmes dans l'espace nord-méditerranéen*, under Christiane Klapisch-Zuber.

38. I credit my second reader for this phrase.

39. Bennett, *A Medieval Life*, 10. Brigstock was not representative of all England, but Cecilia Penifader was not "wildly atypical." The same could be said of Martha.

40. On crises in the early fourteenth century, see William Chester Jordan, *The Great Famine: Northern Europe in the Early Fourteenth Century* (Princeton, N.J.: Princeton University Press, 1996). On the economy of Montpellier generally, see Reyerson, *Business, Banking and Finance in Medieval Montpellier* (Toronto: Pontifical Institute of Mediaeval Studies, 1985), and *The Art of the Deal*.

41. Pernoud, *La Femme au temps des cathédrales*, advanced the hypothesis that the position of women in France declined with the rise of the bourgeoisie at the end of the Middle Ages.

42. See Reyerson, "Changes in Testamentary Practice at Montpellier."

CHAPTER I

Note to epigraph: Alexandre Germain, *Histoire du commerce de Montpellier antérieure-ment à l'ouverture du port de Cette*, 2 vols. (Montpellier: Imprimerie de Jean Martel ainé, 1861), I: ii: "Dicta villa mercibus et mercatoribus est fundata. Notorium et manifestum est quia locus Montispessulani est clavis maris istius terre."

1. On the origins of Montpellier, see Jean-Claude Richard, "Le Problème des ori-gines de Montpellier," *Revue archéologique de Narbonne* 2 (1969): 49–62.

2. See Brian Tierney, ed., *The Crisis of Church and State, 1050–1300* (Englewood Cliffs, N.J.: Prentice-Hall, 1964), 136–38, for a translation of the decretal *Per venerabilem* (1202) and 129 for a discussion of the matter.

3. Elizabeth Haluska-Rausch, "Unwilling Partners: Conflict and Ambition in the Marriage of Peter II of Aragon and Marie de Montpellier," in Theresa Earenfight, ed., *Queenship and Political Power in Medieval and Early Modern Spain* (Aldershot: Ashgate, 2005), 3–20.

4. The best printed version of the 1204 charter is in Alexandre Teulet, ed., *Layettes du Trésor des Chartes* (Paris: Librairie Plon, 1863), 1: 255–66. The town chronicle is included in the *Petit Thalamus*, along with many municipal regulations. The printed edition of the the *Petit Thalamus* is that of F. Pégat, E. Thomas, and C. Desmazes, eds., *Thalamus parvus: Le petit thalamus de Montpellier* (Montpellier: La Société archéologique de Montpellier, 1840). Vincent Challet of the Université de Montpellier III: Paul Valéry, and his team are creating an online edition of the nine versions of the *Thalamus* that survive; see http://thalamus.huma-num.fr/. Online entries began appearing in late 2014. I have not had the opportunity to consult these to any extent. The online version, edited by Challet et al. will ultimately supersede all earlier versions.

5. On town governance, see A. Gouron, *La Réglementation des métiers en Languedoc au moyen âge* (Geneva: Droz, 1958); Jan Rogozinski, *Power, Caste, and Law: Social Conflict in Fourteenth-Century Montpellier* (Cambridge, Mass: Medieval Academy of America, 1982); and three essays by Archibald. R. Lewis, "The Development of Town Government in Twelfth Century Montpellier," *Speculum* 22 (1947): 51–67; "Seigneurial Administration in Twelfth Century Montpellier," *Speculum* 22 (1947): 562–77; and "Popular Assemblies and the Charter of Liberties of Montpellier in 1202," in *Album Elemér Malyusz* (Brussels: Librairie Encyclopédique, 1976), 49–59.

6. On the Albigensian crusades, see Joseph R. Strayer, *The Albigensian Crusades* (Ann Arbor: University of Michigan Press, 1971); Mark Pegg, *A Most Holy War: The Albigensian Crusade and the Battle for Christendom* (Oxford: Oxford University Press, 2008); and Jonathan Sumption, *The Albigensian Crusade* (London: Faber, 1978).

7. Monique Zerner, ed. *Inventer l'hérésie: Discours polemiques et pouvoirs avant l'Inquisition* (Nice: Centre d'Études Médiévales, 1998).

8. André Gouron, "Grands bourgeois et nouveaux notables: L'Aspect social de la révolution montpelliéraine de 1204," *Recueil de mémoires et travaux de la société d'histoire du droit et des institutions des anciens pays de droit écrit*, fasc. 15 (Montpellier, 1991), 27–48. Louisa Burnham has demonstrated convincingly that Montpellier had its heretical elements. See Louisa A. Burnham, *So Great a Light, So Great a Smoke: The Beguin Heretics of Languedoc* (Ithaca, N.Y.: Cornell University Press, 2008).

9. Charles Wood, *The French Apanages and the Capetian Monarchy 1224–1328* (Cambridge, Mass.: Harvard University Press, 1966).

10. For the political history of Montpellier, see Jean Baumel, *Histoire d'une seigneurie du Midi de la France, Naissance de Montpellier (985–1213)*, vol. 1 (Montpellier: Éditions Causse, 1969), and *Histoire d'une seigneurie du Midi de la France: Montpellier sous la seigneurie de Jacques le Conquérant et les rois de Majorque; Rattachement de Montpelliéret et de Montpellier à la France (1213–1349)*, vol. 2 (Montpellier: Éditions Causse, 1971).

11. Albert Lecoy de la Marche, *Les Relations politiques de la France avec le royaume de Majorque*, 2 vols. (Paris: E. Leroux, 1892).

12. The background for this purchase was presented in detail by Lecoy de la Marche, ibid., 1: 311ff. See also Jean Baumel, *Histoire d'une seigneurie du Midi* 2:166–76.

13. On the judicial landscape in the region of Montpellier, see Jan Rogozinski, "Ordinary and Major Judges," *Studia Gratiana* 15 (1972): 589–611; and "The Counsellors of the Seneschal of Beaucaire and Nîmes, 1250–1350," *Speculum* 44 (1969): 421–39.

14. A. D. Hérault, II E 95/374, G. Nogareti, f. 36Rv, as an example. On the court of the Petit Scel, see André Gouron, "L'Origine du Tribunal du Petit-Scel de Montpellier," *Fédération historique du Languedoc méditerranéen et du Roussillon*, Congrès de Mende (Montpellier, 1955), 55–70; and Gouron and Jean Hilaire. "Les 'Sceaux' rigoureux du Midi de la France," *Recueil de mémoires et travaux publié par la société d'histoire du droit et des institutions des anciens pays de droit écrit*, fasc. 4 (Montpellier, 1958), 41–77.

15. Alexandre Germain, *Histoire de la commune de Montpellier* (Montpellier: Imprimerie J. Martel ainé, 1861), 2:354, published the document of sale of 28 December 1292, signed by seventy-two canons. The actual date of sale was 6 March 1293.

16. See articles in Ghislaine Fabre, Daniel Le Blévec, and Denis Menjot, eds. *Les Ports et la navigation en Mediterranée au Moyen Âge* (Montpellier: DRAC, 2009).

17. See *Juifs et judaïsme de Languedoc*, Cahiers de Fanjeaux 12 (Toulouse: Privat, 1977) for treatment of Jewish life in this period.

18. See Jonathan Sumption, *The Hundred Years War: Trial by Battle* (Philadelphia: University of Pennsylvania Press, 1991); and John Bell Henneman, *Royal Taxation in Fourteenth Century France: The Development of War Financing, 1322–1356* (Princeton, N.J.: Princeton University Press, 1971). See also the detailed development in Chapter 9 below.

19. David Abulafia, *A Mediterranean Emporium: The Catalan Kingdom of Majorca* (Cambridge: Cambridge University Press, 1994).

20. See Joëlle Rollo-Koster, *Avignon and Its Papacy, 1309–1417: Popes, Institutions, and Society* (Lanham, Md.: Rowman & Littlefield, 2015). See also Bernard Guillemain, *La Cour pontificale d'Avignon (1309–1376): Étude d'une société* (Paris: Boccard, 1966).

21. See Chapter 8 below on real property. The Cabanis brothers, particularly Guiraudus, had investments in *salines* (salt-producing territories) in the early 1340s, probably dating from their father's activities and originally under the supervision of Martha.

22. Jeanne Vieillard, *Le Guide du pèlerin de Saint-Jacques de Compostelle* (Mâcon: Imprimerie Protat, 1978), 2.

23. See Fabre, Le Blévec, and Menjot, eds., *Les ports et la navigation en Mediterranée au Moyen Âge*, for articles on Mediterranean port cities.

24. See Germain, *Histoire du commerce*, 1: 55 ff, for a detailed discussion of the seacoast south of Montpellier.

25. See Reyerson, "Identity in the Medieval Mediterranean World of Merchants and Pirates," *Mediterranean Studies* 20 (2012, appeared 2013): 129–46.

26. On fishing, see Richard C. Hoffman, "Medieval Fishing," in Paolo Squatriti, ed., *Working with Water in Medieval Europe: Technology and Resource Use* (Leiden: Brill, 2000), 331–93.

27. Roger Dugrand, "La Garrigue montpelliéraine," *Bulletin de la société languedocienne de géographie* 2nd ser. 34 (1963): 3–266.

28. Pasturage paths still exist today. Although their origin lies in the distant past, they were given a special judicial status under the Intendants in the seventeenth century.

See J.-B. Géze, "Les Drailles du Départment de l'Hérault" (Montpellier: Office Agricole Départemental de l'Hérault, 1926). See also A. D. Hérault, 2S 39, for a report by the Service Vicinal on the *drailles*.

29. Jean Combes, "Les Foires en Languedoc au moyen âge," *Annales: Economies, Societies, Civilisations* 13 (1958): 231–59.

30. On the Guilhem and other southern noble families, see Duhamel-Amado, *Genèse des lignages méridionaux*.

31. On coinage in the region of Montpellier, see Mireille Castaing-Sicard, *Monnaies féodales et circulation monétaire en Languedoc (Xe–XIIIe siècles)* (Toulouse: Marc Bloch, 1961). See Appendix 3 below on money.

32. Georges Jehel, *Aigues-Mortes: Un port pour un roi: Les Capétiens et la Méditerranée* (Roanne/Le Coteau: Horvath, 1985).

33. See Chapter 8 below on Cabanis real property.

34. Emmanuel LeRoy Ladurie, *Les Paysans de Languedoc* (Paris: SEVPEN, 1966), 17–19.

35. Jordan, *The Great Famine*. See also Monique Bourin, John Drendal, and François Menant, *Les Disettes dans la conjuncture de 1300 en Méditerranée occidentale* (Rome: École Française de Rome, 2011).

36. Louis J. Thomas, "Note sur l'origine de Montpellier," *Cahiers d'Histoire et d'Archéologie* 1 ser. 2 (1931): 126–35.

37. See Marcel Boriès, "Les Origines de l'université de Montpellier," Cahiers de Fanjeaux 5, *Les Universités du Languedoc au XIIIe siècle* (Toulouse: Privat, 1970), 92–107.

38. Rollo-Koster, *Avignon and Its Papacy*, passim.

39. See Chapters 4, 7, and 9 below.

40. See the discussion in Reyerson, "Patterns of Population Attraction and Mobility: The Case of Montpellier, 1293–1348," *Viator* 10 (1979): 257–81.

41. See Reyerson, *Business, Banking and Finance*.

42. See Rogozinski, *Power, Caste, and Law*, 40–42.

43. Bernard Sournia and Jean-Louis Vayssettes, *L'Ostal des Carcassonne: La Maison d'un drapier montpelliérain du XIIIe siècle* (Montpellier: DRAC, 2014), 14–20.

44. Ghislaine Fabre and Thierry Lochard, *Montpellier: La Ville médiévale* (Paris: Imprimerie Nationale, 1992), Chapter 2. See also Chapter 2 of Reyerson, *The Art of the Deal*.

45. See Reyerson, "The Tensions of Walled Space: Urban Development Versus Defense," in James D. Tracy, ed., *City Walls: The Urban Enceinte* (Cambridge: Cambridge University Press, 2000), 88–116.

46. The Tour des Pins was for a long period the site of the municipal archives, which have now moved to the municipal library, constructed in the late twentieth century.

47. Bernard Sournia and Jean-Louis Vayssettes, *Montpellier: La Demeure médiévale* (Paris: Imprimérie Nationale, 1991), 146.

48. See Louise Guiraud, "Recherches topographiques sur Montpellier au moyen âge," *Mémoires de la société archéologique de Montpellier* 2nd ser. 2 (1895): 156. See also

Archives municipales de Montpellier (hereafter A. M. Montpellier), *Grand Chartrier,* Louvet nos. 237 and 238 for the 1259 acts of the king of Aragon.

49. See *The Art of the Deal,* Chapter 2.

50. See Reyerson, "Public and Private Space in Medieval Montpellier: The Bon Amic Square," *Journal of Urban History* 24 (1997): 3–27. See also *Women's Networks in Medieval France,* Chapter 7.

51. See Fabre and Lochard, *Montpellier,* for a discussion of Montpellier topography.

52. The parish church of Saint-Firmin lay within the first fortification of Montpellier in the eleventh century; the area around Saint-Firmin had once been walled in the early circular fashion characteristic of eleventh- and twelfth-century fortifications in Lower Languedoc. On the early walling of towns in the region, see Krzysztof Pawlowski, *Circulades languedociennes de l'an mille: Naissance de l'urbanisme européen* (Montpellier: Presses du Languedoc, 1994).

53. *The Art of the Deal,* Chapter 2. For discussion of the urban environment in general, see Ronald E. Zupko and Robert A. Laures, *Straws in the Wind: Medieval Urban Environmenal Law—The Case of Northern Italy* (Boulder, Colo.: Westview, 1996).

54. See further discussion of Martha's father in Chapter 2 below.

55. On issues of water supply in European towns in general, see André E. Guillerme, *The Age of Water. The Urban Environment in the North of France, A.D. 300–1800* (College Station: Texas A&M University Press, 1988); and Paolo Squatriti, *Water and Society in Early Medieval Italy, AD 400–1000* (Cambridge: Cambridge University Press, 1998).

56. Jacques Rossiaud, *Medieval Prostitution,* trans. Lydia G. Cochrane (Oxford: Blackwell, 1988). There were public baths at Montpellier.

57. Teulet, ed., *Layettes du Trésor des Chartes,* , Art. 10, 1: 290.

58. See Sournia and Vaysettes, *L'Ostal des Carcassonne,* 25, for the importance of light in domestic housing.

59. See A. M. Montpellier, Sér. EE, Fonds de la Commune Clôture, and the inventory by Maurice de Dainville and Marcel Gouron, eds. *Archives de la ville de Montpelllier, inventaire publié par les soins de l'administration municipale,* vol. 12, Sér. EE. *Fonds de la Commune Clôture et affaires militaires* (Montpellier: Tour des Pins, 1974).

60. See Reyerson, "The Tensions of Walled Space."

61. See Reyerson, "Prostitution in Medieval Montpellier: The Ladies of Campus Polverel," *Medieval Prosopography* 18 (1997): 219. See also Reyerson, "The Tensions of Walled Space."

62. See Reyerson, "Flight from Prosecution: The Search for Religious Asylum in Medieval Montpellier," *French Historical Studies* 17 (1992): 603–26. See Chapter 9 below for a detailed discussion of the demands of taxation.

63. See Reyerson, "Urban Sensations: The Medieval City Imagined," in Richard Newhauser, ed., *A Cultural History of the Senses,* vol. 2 (Oxford: Berg, 2014), 45–65.

64. See Reyerson, "Public and Private Space in Medieval Montpellier See also my forthcoming article on hucksters selling on the Herbaria, "Les Réseaux économiques entre femmes à Montpellier (fin XIIIe–mi-XIVe)," in Lucie Laumonier and Lucie Galano, eds., *Montpellier au Moyen Âge: Bilan et approches nouvelles* (Turnhout: Brepols, forthcoming).

CHAPTER 2

Note to epigraph: A. D. Hérault, II E 95/374, G. Nogareti, f. 51Rr, 12 February 1342 (n. s.): "ego facere poteram autem hanc presentem [crossout] inter vivos donationem quam vobis dicte filie mee ut supra stipultanti et recipienti facio mota maternali amori et propter ultima servicia et beneficia que mihi fecistis et facistis."

1. For an early critique of the ways in which medievalists have dealt with family, see Anita Guerreau-Jalabert, "Sur les structures de parenté dans l'Europe médiévale," *Annales: histoire. sciences sociales* 36 (1981): 1028–49.

2. On the medieval family, see David Herlihy, *Medieval Households* (Cambridge, Mass: Harvard University Press, 1985).

3. See Tamara Hareven, "L'Histoire de la famille et complexité du changement social," *Cahiers d'histoire* 45 (2000): 9–34, 205–32. See also Glen Elder, "Family History and the Life Course," in T. Hareven, ed., *Transitions: The Family and the Life Course in Historical Perspective* (New York: Academic Press, 1978), 17–64.

4. Guerreau-Jalabert, "Sur les structures de parenté dans l'Europe médiévale," 1030. See also Joseph H. Lynch, *Godparents and Kinship in Early Medieval Europe* (Princeton, N.J.: Princeton University Press, 1986).

5. See the discussion in Jean Hilaire, "*Patria potestas* et pratique montpelliéraine au moyen âge: Symbolisme du droit écrit," *Société pour l'histoire du droit et des institutions des anciens pays bourguignons, comtois et romands* 30: *Mémoires Georges Chevrier* (Dijon: Faculté de droit et des sciences politiques, 1972), 433.

6. See the papers in *Famille et parenté dans l'Occident medieval: Actes du colloque de Paris* (June 1974), organisé par L'École Pratique des Hautes Études (VIe section) en collaboration avec le Collège de France et l'École Française de Rome, Communications et débats présentés par Georges Duby et Jacques Le Goff (Rome: École Française de Rome, 1977); Diane Owen Hughes, "Urban Growth and Family Structure in Medieval Genoa," *Past and Present* 66 (1975): 3–28, and Hughes, "Domestic Ideals and Social Behavior: Evidence from Medieval Genoa," in Carol Neel, ed., *Medieval Families. Perspectives on Marriage, Household, and Children* (Toronto: University of Toronto Press and Medieval Academy of America, 2004), 125–56; Jacques Heers, *Le Clan familial au moyen âge* (Paris: Presses Universitaires de France, 1974). See also the recent studies of Lucie Laumonier, including *Solitudes et solidarities en ville*.

7. Heers, *Le Clan familial au moyen âge*, for example, 85, 186–87, 202.

8. See Bensch, *Barcelona and Its Rulers, 1096–1291*, 237–40. Bensch, 392–93, spoke of the absence of agnatic clans and weak lineage identity. Rather, the patriciate's emphasis on the urban economy and maritime trade caused greater openness and collaboration. This is not to say the Barcelona patriciate was without conflict, as *nouveaux riches* challenged the older families (ibid., 282). See also Batlle i Gallart, "La Vida y las actividades de los mercaderes de Barcelona dedicados al comercio maritime (siglo XIII)."

9. See Reyerson, *Women's Networks in Medieval France*.

10. For Tornamira references in Montpellier evidence, see Reyerson, "Commerce and Society in Montpellier: 1250–1350," 2 vols., Ph.D. dissertation, Yale University, 1974,

1:19–20. For Tornamira references, see A. M. Montpellier, BB 2, J. Grimaudi, f. 25r, 37r, 107r, and 138r. See also A. D. Hérault, II E 95/371, J. Holanie, f. 30v and 125v; II E 95/372, J. Holanie et al., f. 143r.

11. See the consular lists in Germain, *Histoire de la commune de Montpellier*, 1: 376ff.

12. Further on Tornamira homonyms, see Reyerson, *Women's Networks in Medieval France*, 171–72.

13. The father of Jacques Coeur, a prominent fifteenth-century merchant, financier, and royal official, was a furrier. This background did not deter his rise to prominence in wealth and station. See Reyerson, *Jacques Coeur: Entrepreneur and King's Bursar* (New York: Pearson Longman, 2005).

14. On the university book trade, see Sven Stelling-Michaud, "Le Transport international des manuscrits juridiques bolonais entre 1265–1320," in *Mélanges d'histoire économique et sociale en l'honneur du professeur Antony Babel*, 2 vols. (Geneva: Imprimerie de la Tribune, 1963), 1:95–127.

15. On the legislative power of the consuls, see André Gouron, "La *Potestas statuendi* dans le droit coutumier montpelliérain du treizième siècle," in *Diritto commune et diritti locali nella storia dell'Europa*, Atti del congresso di Varenna (12–15 June 1979) (Milan: Guiffrè, 1980), 95–118. On consular development in the south of France, see André Gouron, "Diffusion des consulats méridionaux et expansion du droit romain aux XIIe et XIIIe siècles," *Bibliothèque de l'École des Chartes* 221 (1964): 26–76.

16. Gouron, *La Réglementation des métiers*, 386–88, provides a list of the occupations in the seven ladders of urban defense.

17. Ibid., 95–101.

18. On the municipal governmental setup, see ibid., and Jean Combes, "Quelques remarques sur les bourgeois de Montpellier au moyen âge," in *Recueil de mémoires et travaux publié par la société d'histoire du droit et des institutions des anciens pays de droit écrit*, fasc. 7: *Mélanges Pierre Tisset* (Montpellier: Faculté de droit et des sciences économiques de Montpellier, 1970), 93–132, at 98n41.

19. Félix Bourquelot, *Étude sur les foires de Champagne*, 2 vols. (Paris: Imprimerie Impériale, 1865), 1: 153.

20. See the chapter in Reyerson, "Commerce and Society in Montpellier," 1:197–203.

21. See Guiraud, "Recherches topographiques sur Montpellier au moyen âge."

22. Robert Ferrell, "Women in Medieval Guilds," entry on "Leather Trades," accessed January 30, 2017, at http://www.antithetical.org/restlesswind/plinth/wimguild 2.html.

23. The name R. Franc appeared in the consular lists in in 1280, 1294, 1298, 1300, 1304, 1309, 1313, and 1331.

24. A. M. Montpellier, BB 3, J. Laurentii, f. 82v. In 1342, a R. Franc served as an *ouvrier de la Commune Clôture*, one of those town leaders managing the defense organization.

25. A. M. Montpellier, BB 3, J. Laurentii, 1342–43, recorded multiple mentions of a Raymundus Franchi and his brother Bernardus, both grain merchants. Were these brothers of Martha? It is impossible to say.

26. On the transfer of information, see Reyerson, *The Art of the Deal*, Chapter 5. See also the collections Harry Kühnel, ed., *Kommunikation und Alltag in Spätmitellalter und früher Neuzeit. Internationaler Kongress Krems an der Donau (9 bis 12 Oktober 1990)* (Vienna: Oesterreichischen Akademie des Wissenschaften, 1992) and *La Circulation des nouvelles au moyen âge*, Société des Historiens Médiévistes de l'Enseignement Supérieur Public (Paris: Publications de la Sorbonne, École Française de Rome, 1994). Jean-Arnault Dérens has written on Montpellier specifically in this context: "Montpellier, ville ouverte: 1. Information, circulation et réception des nouvelles à la fin du XIVe siècle," *Bulletin historique de la ville de Montpellier* 21 (February, 1997): 37–50.

27. Pégat, Thomas, and Desmazes, eds., *Thalamus parvus*, 336. The town chronicle is included in The *Petit Thalamus*, along with many municipal regulations.

28. The chronicle stated, "fon per tot Crestianisma carestia mortal, quar lo sestier de blat velia xx s. de torn (throughout Christendom there was a mortal famine, with the setier of wheat valued at 20 sous tournois)." See ibid., 339.

29. The chronicle notation was "fo gran secaressa pertot (there was great drought everywhere)," with many processions organized, and, finally with surcease as the rain came, "e Nostre Senhor donet plueja [and our lord gave rain]." Ibid., 344.

30. On the grain trade, see Reyerson, "Montpellier et le trafic des grains en Méditerranée," in *Montpellier, la Couronne d'Aragon et les Pays de Langue d'Oc (1204–1349): Actes du XIIe Congrès d'Histoire de la Couronne d'Aragon: Mémoires de la société archéologique de Montpellier* 15 (Montpellier, 1985), 147–62.

31. R. Franc is listed as consul in 1294 and 1298, Petrus de Tornamira in 1295. R. Franc was consul again in 1309 and 1313, while Petrus was consul in 1311.

32. A. D. Hérault, II E 95/374, G. Nogareti, f. 51Rr. Jacoba was described as the daughter of the late Raymundus Franchi and the wife of the late Petrus Tornamira. See Chapter 8 below for a discussion of Cabanis real property holdings.

33. See A. D. Hérault, II E 95/368, J. Holanie, f. 143r, 18 March 1328, for mention of Guiraudus's death in a December 1326 procuration. Guillelmus Nogareti, the Cabanis family notary, recorded the procuration. For a more detailed discussion of these acts, see Reyerson, *The Art of the Deal*, 11–12.

34. See Reyerson, "Changes in Testamentary Practice at Montpellier."

35. See Reyerson, *Business, Banking and Finance*.

36. Few of these landholdings can be specified, though Martha's vineyards as an adult could well have come from her maternal family.

37. There is considerable modern scholarship on medieval children, with a particular focus on England. See Nicholas Orme, *Medieval Children* (New Haven, Conn.: Yale University Press, 2001); Barbara Hanawalt, *Growing up in Medieval London: The Experience of Childhood in History* (New York: Oxford University Press, 1993). For a broader geography,

see Frances Gies and Joseph Gies, *Marriage and the Family in the Middle Ages* (New York: Harper and Row, 1987); and Lloyd deMause, ed., *The History of Childhood* (New York: Harper and Row, 1975).

38. Orme, *Medieval Children*, 167ff.

39. A. M. Montpellier, BB 3, J. Laurentii, ff. 13r, for the will of Agnes des Bossones, two of whose granddaughters were nuns.

40. See Hilaire, *Le Régime des biens entre époux.*

41. See John Hine Mundy, *Men and Women at Toulouse in the Age of the Cathars* (Toronto: Pontifical Institute of Medieval Studies, 1990), Chapter 5, "Matrimony," 88ff.

42. No marriage-related documents have survived for Martha. On marriage in the region of Montpellier in the Middle Ages, see Jean Hilaire, *Le Régime des biens entre époux dans la région de Montpellier du début du XIIIe siècle à la fin du XVe siècle* (Montpellier: Imprimérie Causse, Graille et Castelnau, 1957). In the second half of the fourteenth century, the dowry was often in money. Kelleher, *The Measure of Woman*, 49, found a predominance of cash dowries in her period of study, though, as she stated, "Legally, dowry could consist of either moveable or immoveable goods."

43. See Chapter 8 below.

44. Kelleher, *The Measure of Woman*, 68ff, and Reyerson, "L'Expérience des plaideuses devant les cours de Montpellier."

45. The 160 wills come from four archival *fonds:* the notarial collections of the A. D. Hérault and the A. M. Montpellier, and the collections of charters in the *Grand Chartrier (Louvet)* of the A. M. Montpellier, and the Commune Clôture in the A. M. Montpellier. In contrast, Rebecca Winer, *Women, Wealth, and Community*, 20–21, worked with seventy wills for Christian lay people surviving from thirteenth-century Perpignan.

46. On Montpellier wills, see Louis de Charrin, *Les Testaments dans la région de Montpellier au moyen âge* (Ambilly: Coopérative Les Presses de Savoie, 1961. See also the Master's memoir of Isabelle Algrin, "Les Testaments dans la région montpelliéraine aux XIIe–XIVe siècles," (Université de Montpellier 3, 2011). Lucie Laumonier discusses Montpellier wills throughout *Solitudes et solidarités.* I have treated wills and marriage contracts more fully in *Women's Networks in Medieval France.*

47. See further development in Chapter 5 below. The marriage contracts come from the same archival *fonds* as the wills. The will of merchant Jacobus Brosseti gave 300 *l.p.t.* to his wife along with the use of furniture and household goods and the usufruct of all his goods unless she remarried. See A. M. Montpellier, BB 3, Johannes Laurentii, f. 36r.

48. A. D. Hérault, II E 95/374, G. Nogareti, 51Rr.

49. See Chapter 8 below.

50. Notarial registers preserve documents recording loans, partnerships, procurations, sales, recognizances (recognitions of debt to be repaid according to the terms of the contract), apprenticeship contracts, and work contracts revealing women operating at many different levels of finance, trade, real estate, and industry. On the legal support offered by notarial acts, see the useful discussion by David Herlihy, *Pisa in the Early Renaissance* (New Haven, Conn.: Yale University Press, 1958), 1–20. On the rarity of

female apprentices, see P. J. P. Goldberg, "Female Labour, Service and Marriage in the Late Medieval Urban North," *Northern History* 22 (1986): 18–38. See also Reyerson, *Business, Banking and Finance*, 15–16.

CHAPTER 3

Note to epigraph: A. D. Hérault, II E 95/368, Johannes Holanie, f. 106v, 19 January 1328 (n.s.): "Ego inquam Bertranda collocans me in dictum legitimum matrimonium cum dicta dote vobis dicto Guillelmo Audemarii meque vobis tradens in vestram legitimam uxorem et vos recipiens in meum legitimum maritum promito et convenio vobis recipienti quod ego ero vobis et vestris semper bona et legale et vos seu vestros nunquam in aliquo deciperam ymo vobis semper bonam fidem portabo." This is a rare example of a woman's perspective on marriage in Montpellier, translated in Kathryn Reyerson and Debra Salata, *Medieval Notaries and Their Acts: The 1327–1328 Register of Jean Holanie* (Kalamazoo, Mich.: Medieval Institute Publications, 2004), 60.

1. See Reyerson, *The Art of the Deal*, Introduction.

2. Laurent Mayali, *Droit savant et coutumes: L'Exclusion des filles dotées, XIIème–XVe siècles* (Frankfurt am Main: Vittorio Klostermann, 1987).

3. Hilaire, *Le Régime des biens entre époux*, 79–80.

4. Ibid., 283. See also Reyerson, *Women's Networks in Medieval France*, Chapter 4 on "Marriage."

5. On marriage models, see, for example, J. Hajnal, "European Marriage Patterns in Perspective," in D. V. Glass and David E. C. Eversley, eds., *Population in History: Essays in Historical Demography* (London: E. Arnold, 1965), 101–46.

6. See Claude Carrère, *Barcelone, centre économique au temps des difficultés, 1380–1462*, 2 vols. (Paris: Mouton, 1967). See also Winer, *Women, Wealth and Community*, 25; David Herlihy and Christiane Klapisch-Zuber, *Tuscans and Their Families: A Study of the Florentine Catasto of 1427* (New Haven, Conn.: Yale University Press, 1985); and Julius Kirshner and Anthony Molho, "The Dowry Fund and the Marriage Market in Early Quattrocentro Florence," *Journal of Modern History* 50 (1978): 403–38. For other areas of Italy beyond Florence, see Trevor Dean, ed., *Marriage in Italy, 1300–1650* (Cambridge: Cambridge University Press, 1998).

7. Tovah Bender, "Negotiating Marriage: Artisan Women in Fifteenth-Century Florentine Society," Ph.D. dissertation, University of Minnesota, 2009, has been working on a revision of this marriage model for the artisan community of late medieval Florence.

8. Winer, *Women, Wealth, and Community*, 170n61.

9. As noted in the previous chapter, the marriage contracts in this study were drawn from four archival fonds: A. D. Hérault, II E 95/368–377; A. M. Montpellier BB, 1–3; A. M. Montpellier, *Archives de la Commune Clôture*; and A. M. Montpellier, *Grand Chartier*, Louvet inventory. The practical age of majority was fourteen in the south of France, but marriage at that age for a man was unlikely. Under fourteen, a boy often had a

guardian. A boy could have a curator up to age eighteen or later. Martha was still acting as *curatrix* of Guiraudus and Jacobus into their early twenties. Jean Hilaire has studied the marriage contracts of Montpellier in *Le Régime des biens entre époux*. He stated (29) that the fifteenth-century documentary package for Montpellier included marriage contracts, donations *propter nuptias*, constitutions of a family community, and the renunciations by dowried daughters of inheritance from their parents. For a study of marriage based on rich documentation from Catalonia, see Lluis To Figueras, "Systèmes successoraux et mobilité sociale aux alentours de 1300: Les Contrats de marriage d'Amer et de Besalú en Vieille Catalogne," in Sandro Carocci, ed., *La Mobilità sociale nel medioevo* (Rome: École Française de Rome, 2010), 453–90. See also Charles Donahue, Jr., *Law, Marriage, and Society in the Later Middle Ages* (Cambridge: Cambridge University Press, 2007), 20, 99.

10. The best discussion of patterns of marriage in late medieval Europe and early modern Europe is Maryanne Kowaleski, "Singlewomen in Medieval and Early Modern Europe: The Demographic Perspective," in Judith M. Bennett and Amy M. Froide, eds., *Singlewomen in the European Past, 1250–1800* (Philadelphia: University of Pennsylvania Press, 1999), 38–81.

11. Rogozinski, *Power, Caste, and Law*, 41n4.

12. See the discussion in Chapter 4.

13. As noted earlier, record of a procuration, dated 22 December 1326, on behalf of Jacobus, called the son of the late Guiraudus de Cabanis, survives in an act of 18 March 1328. See A. D. Hérault, II E 95/368, J. Holanie, f. 143r. Guillelmus Nogareti, the Cabanis family notary, recorded the procuration, though the documents surviving in the Cabanis personal register are from a later date. For a more detailed discussion of these acts, see Reyerson, *The Art of the Deal*, 11–12.

14. A. M. Montpellier, uncatalogued notary Simon Cornaforti, f. 11ff: 1317; Archives départementales des Pyrénées Orientales, 3 E, 1, 34, f. 2: 1324); Archives Municipales de Marseille, II 38, ff. 18–19. See also Édouard Baratier, "Marseille et Narbonne au XIVe siècle d'après les sources marseillaises," *Fédération historique du Languedoc méditerranéen et du Roussillon: Narbonne archéologie et histoire*, vol. 2, *Narbonne au moyen âge* (Montpellier, 1973): 85–92. For Champagne Fair debts of merchants of Montpellier, see Eugène Martin-Chabot, *Les Archives de la cour des comptes, aides et finances de Montpellier: Avec un essai de restitution des premiers registres de la sénéchausée*, Bibliothèque de la Faculté des Lettres de l'Université de Paris 22 (Paris: Félix Alcan, 1907).

15. On wet nurses, see Leah Otis-Cour, "Municipal Wet Nurses in Fifteenth-Century Montpellier," in Barbara Hanawalt, ed., *Women and Work in Preindustrial Europe* (Bloomington: Indiana University Press, 1986), 83–93. See also Rebecca Lynn Winer, "Allaitement, esclavage et salut de l'âme dans la Couronne d'Aragon et le royaume de Majorque," in *Les femmes dans l'espace nord-méditerranéen*, under the direction of Christiane Klapisch-Zuber, *Études Roussillonnaises* 25 (2013): 107–14; and Winer, "The Mother and the *Dida* [Nanny]: Female Employers and Wet Nurses in Fourteenth-Century Barcelona," in Jutta Gisela Sperling, ed., *Medieval and Renaissance Lactations: Images, Rhetorics, Practices* (Farnham: Ashgate, 2013), 55–78.

16. Reyerson and Mummey, "Whose City Is This?" See also Reyerson, "Urban Economies."

17. On wet-nursing, see Jacques Heers, *Esclaves et domestiques au moyen-âge dans le monde méditerranéen* (Paris: Fayard, 1981). See also Otis-Cour, "Municipal Wet Nurses in Fifteenth-Century Montpellier."

18. On French queens, see Marion F. Facinger, "A Study of Medieval Queenship: Capetian France, 987–1237," *Studies in Medieval and Renaissance History* 5 (1968): 1–48.

19. Recall Kelleher, *The Measure of Woman*, 69.

20. Jean Combes, noted twentieth-century scholar of Montpellier, was skeptical regarding the possibilities of elucidating the lines of family relationship among the branches of the Cabanis family. See Combes, "L'Industrie et le commerce des toiles à Montpellier de la fin du XIIIe siècle au milieu du XVe," in *Recueil de mémoires et travaux publiés par la société d'histoire du droit et des institutions des anciens pays de droit écrit*, fasc. 9: *Mélanges Roger Aubenas* (Montpellier, 1974), 192n63. Combes calls the Cabanis mercers, linen merchants, and drapers.

21. See Reyerson, "Problems of Family Reconstruction in Medieval Montpellier," Congress on Medieval Studies, Western Michigan University, Kalamazoo, May 1982.

22. A. M. Montpellier, BB 1, J. Grimaudi, f. 66r. The name is unclear in the document. It could be interpreted as Petrus de Cabana Veteri. The former archivist of the Archives Municipales, Maurice de Dainville, in a manuscript inventory of this notarial register, "Inventaire des minutes de notaires de la ville acquis par le Consulat," gave the name as "P. de Cabanac le vieux, mercier." Editors Dainville, Marcel Gouron, and Liberto Valls, *Inventaire analytique, Série BB (Notaires et greffiers du consul.at 1293–1387)* (Montpellier: Tour des Pins, 1984), retained this interpretation as "P. de Cabanac senior, mercier." In my reading of the manuscript, I remain unconvinced of this paleographic interpretation of Cabanac. Nevertheless, the profession of mercer reinforces the family tie.

23. A. M. Montpellier, BB 2, J. Grimaudi, f. 38r. Unfortunately, no profession was associated with this mention of Petrus.

24. See Germain, *Histoire de la commune de Montpellier*, vol. 1, Appendix 19, for a list of the consuls of Montpellier.

25. Jean Hilaire, "Exercise de style: Une Affaire de succession à Montpellier au début du XIVe siècle," *Recueil de mémoires et travaux publié par la société de l'histoire du droit et des institutions des anciens pays de droit écrit*, fasc. 7: *Mélanges Pierre Tisset* (Montpellier: 1970): 283–99.

26. A. D. Hérault, II E 95/370, J. Holanie, f. 70v. Petrus did not live in that house at the time of his death.

27. A. D. Hérault, II E 95/374, G. Nogareti, passim.

28. A. D. Hérault, II E 95/370, J. Holanie, f. 66v, and Hilaire, "Exercise de style," 283–99.

29. See A. D. Hérault, II E 95/368, J. Holanie, ff. 4r, 55r, and 57v, and Hilaire, "Exercise de style."

30. See Philippe Aries, *Centuries of Childhood: A Social History of Family Life* (New York: Knopf, 1965), for a detailed discussion of family relationships.

31. Vineyard of Petrus senior: A. D. Hérault, II E 95/370, J. Holanie, f. 69v; Martha's vineyards: II E 95/374, G. Nogareti, ff. 8vR and 11rR. On prime vineyards, see Reyerson, "Land, Houses and Real Estate Investment in Montpellier: A Study of the Notarial Property Transactions, 1293–1348," *Studies in Medieval and Renaissance History* 6 (1983): 42–54.

32. For the house of Petrus near Arc Saint-Nicolas, see A. D. Hérault, II D 95/370, J. Holanie, f. 70v. Petrus lived elsewhere in a house outside the Montpelliéret gate: see f. 67r. For Martha's branch's house near Arc Saint-Nicolas, see II E 95/374, G. Nogareti, f. 16rR.

33. On clans, see Heers, *Le Clan familial au moyen âge.* On Genoa, Diane Owen Hughes, "Toward Historical Ethnography: Notarial Records and Family History in the Middle Ages," *Historical Methods Newsletter* 7 (1973): 61–71, and Hughes, "Urban Growth and Family Structure in Medieval Genoa." On Lucca, see Thomas Blomquist, "Lineage, Land and Business in the Thirteenth Century: The Guidiccioni Family of Lucca," *Actum Luce: Rivista di studi lucchesi* 9 (1980): 7–29.

34. See Reyerson, *The Art of the Deal,* Chapter 2, for a discussion of the layout of the town of Montpellier.

35. On southern French names, see H. Duffaut, "Recherches historiques sur les prénoms en Languedoc," *Annales du Midi* 12 (1900): 180–93, 329–54. There are other individuals with the surname Cabanis or Cabanas who seem less likely to have been related to Martha's in-laws, on the basis of their professional orientation, cultivator, notary, butcher.

36. On the flexibility of professional designation and multiple occupations, see Gouron, *La Règlementation des métiers en Languedoc au moyen âge,* 179, 282–83. Shennan Hutton, *Women and Economic Activities in Late Medieval Ghent,* 113, found a lack of "fixed occupational identities" in Ghent and even some men belonging to more than one guild.

37. Combes, "L'Industrie et le commerce des toiles à Montpellier," 195–96.

38. See Reyerson, *Business, Banking and Finance,* for an in-depth discussion of business partnership, and Reyerson, *The Art of the Deal,* Chapter 4, for a detailed treatment of the Cabanis brothers' partnership.

39. On procuration, see Reyerson, *The Art of the Deal,* especially 128–37.

40. A. D. Hérault, II E 95/374, G. Nogareti, f. 12v.

41. Ibid., f. 33vR.

42. A. D. Hérault, II E 95/369, J. Holanie, f. 12r.

43. A. D. Hérault, II E 95/374, G. Nogareti, f. 35rR.

44. Ibid., f. 8rR.

45. In the complex estate arrangements of 1336, a house near Arc Saint-Nicolas is mentioned for the Petrus branch (A. D. Hérault, II E 95/370, J. Holanie, f. 70r); as noted, Petrus lived in a house outside the walls, near the Montpelliéret gate where he had his wine cellar and an orchard (f. 67v). Perhaps he had retired from business before his death.

46. A. M. Montpellier BB 3, J. Laurentii, f. 24r.

47. See Rogozinski, *Power, Caste, and Law,* 163–64. See also Joseph R. Strayer, *Les Gens de justice du Languedoc sous Philippe le Bel* (Toulouse: Marc Bloch, 1970).

48. A. D. Hérault, II E 95/374, G. Nogareti, ff. 4r and 12rR.

49. A. D. Hérault, II E 95/369, J. Holanie, f. 30v.

50. See Chapter 8 below. On Bernarda de Cabanis, see Reyerson, *Women's Networks in Medieval France*, Chapter 6.

51. For a detailed discussion of the urban nobility, see ibid., Chapter 1.

52. See A. D. Hérault, II E 95/368, J. Holanie, f. 57v: Martha's son Johannes II E 95/372, J. Holanie, f. 90r: Ermessendis; II E 95/374, G. Nogareti, f. 51rR: Martha; II E 95/374, G. Nogareti, f. 44rR: wife of Martha's son Jacobus II E 95/368, J. Holanie, f. 74v: the wife of Petrus senior, sister of the mercer Nicolas Escuderii who was termed *avunculus* (uncle) by Guillelmus, son of Petrus senior; *Cartulaire de Maguelone* V, p. 816, act 1766 (1338): Na Salellas, wife of Martha's son Guiraudus. The Salellis were a family of changers; see, for example, II E 95/372, J. Holanie, f. 6v.

53. A. D. Hérault, II E 95/374, G. Nogareti, f. 44rR, for the mention of Jacobus's unnamed wife.

54. A.D. Hérault, II E 95/370, J. Holanie, ff.114r and 120r.

55. See Reyerson, "La Mobilité sociale: Réflexions sur le rôle de la femme," in Sandro Carocci, ed. *La Mobilità sociale nel medioevo* (Rome: École Française de Rome, 2010), 491–511.

56. See Reyerson, "La Participation des femmes de l'élite marchande à l'économie." Johannes Naturalis may have died about the same time as Guiraudus, as he recorded a will in 1325. See Hilaire, "Exercise de style."

57. Molho et al., "Genealogy and Marriage Alliance," 40–41.

58. Guerreau-Jalabert, "Sur les structures de parenté dans l'Europe médiévale," 1031. There is some suggestion that both patterns were present in Montpellier, as women in their burial requests retained ties to their families of origin. See Reyerson, *Women's Networks in Medieval France*, Chapter 9. Martha charted a different path with her links to the Cabanis family.

CHAPTER 4

Note to epigraph: A. D. Hérault, II E 95/374, Guillelmus Nogareti, f. 9Rv, 26 January 1338 (n.s.): "Hec acta fuerunt in Montepessulano in hospitio habitationis dicte domine Marthe."

1. See Reyerson, *The Art of the Deal*, 126–28, for a discussion of the shop in the context of a *factor* contract for the assistant who was to run it.

2. A. D. Hérault, II E 95/374, G. Nogareti, f. 47Rv where the notary explicitly stated that the act was passed in the house of the hiring parties, that is, Martha and her sons.

3. Guiraud, "Recherches topographiques sur Montpellier," 265; see Map 3 of central of Montpellier in Chapter 2 above.

4. Fabre and Lochard, *Montpellier*, 132.

5. More modest housing was termed *domus*.

6. Sournia and Vayssettes, *La Demeure médiévale*, 25–26. Sournia and Vayssettes, *L'Ostal des Carcassonne*, 45–52, discussed the Carcassonne family of drapers that can be identified with the house in the later fourteenth century.

7. See Reyerson, *Jacques Coeur*, Chapters 4 and 6.

8. Sournia and Vayssettes, *L'Ostal des Carcassonne*, 14–20. The draper's last name was Carcassonne, as noted above.

9. Ibid.

10. A. D. Hérault, II E 95/374, G. Nogareti, f. 15Rv. See the discussion in Reyerson, *The Art of the Deal*, 126–28.

11. In the late fourteenth century, Francesco di Marco Datini (1335–1410) constructed a warehouse at the back of the garden for his bourgeois home in Prato that survives today. On Datini, see Iris Origo, *The Merchant of Prato, 1335–1410* (New York: Knopf, 1957).

12. "The Allegory of Good and Bad Government in Siena," Tuscany Arts: See Beyond the Visual. February 18, 2011, http://www.turismo.intoscana.it/allthingstuscany/tuscanyarts/allegory-good-bad-government-siena, accessed 22 April 2015.

13. Reyerson, "Medieval Silks in Montpellier: The Silk Market, ca. 1250-ca.1350," *Journal of European Economic History* 11 (1982): 117–40.

14. For a discussion of the venue of Martha and her sons' acts, see Chapter 7 below.

15. The house, 3, rue de la Vieille, had a tower. A contemporary of Martha's left a house with a tower in her will. See the will of Agnes de Bossones, A. M. Montpellier, III, J. Laurentii, f. 13r ff., where there is mention of a house Agnes gave to her daughter Raymunda that incorporated a tower of the town walls. The transcription and translation of Agnes's will are found in Reyerson, *Women's Networks in Medieval France*, Appendix 5.

16. Sournia and Vayssettes, *Montpellier*, 14–181.

17. Sournia and Vayssettes, *L'Ostal des Carcassonne*, 23.

18. Paul B. Newman, *Growing Up in the Middle Ages* (Jefferson, N.C.: McFarland, 2007), 69.

19. Bensch, *Barcelona and Its Rulers*, 362. See also Batlle i Gallart, "La Casa i les béns de Bernat Durfort, cuitadà de Barcelona, a la fi del segle XIII." For an inventory of the goods of the Durfort house, see Batlle, "La Casa burguese en la Barcelona del siglo XIII," 1:9–52.

20. Sournia and Vayssettes, *L'Ostal des Carcassonne*, 56–61. The authors date the ceiling from the late thirteenth century, but there is a debate about dating, animated by Pascal Maritaux who thinks the paintings are more likely from the second half of the fourteenth century. More scientific analysis may permit greater precision in dating. See Maritaux, "Le Plafond de l'hôtel des Carcassonne à Montpellier," in Carnet de recherche, *L'Art à la loupe: Conservation-restauration au LA3M*, http://curatio.hypotheses.org/15.

21. See Sherry L. Reames, *The Legenda Aurea: A Reexamination of Its Paradoxical History* (Madison: University of Wisconsin Press, 1985); and Jacopo di Voragine, *The Golden Legend*, trans. Christopher Stace, ed. Richard Hamer (New York: Penguin, 1998).

22. See the comments by Giuseppe Mazzotta, *The Worlds of Petrarch* (Durham, N.C.: Duke University Press, 1993), 26. Paintings in terms of moveable paintings on wood and portraiture were relatively new art forms.

23. Jean Nougaret, "Autour de quelques rétables: La Peinture religieuse médiévale à Montpellier," *Fédération historique du Languedoc méditerranéen et du Roussillon* 64th Congress-1993 (Montpellier, 1994): 102.

24. See A. D. Hérault, II E 95/377, B. Egidii, ff. 164r and 292r. See also A. M. Montpellier, *Archives de la Commune Clôture*, EE 799 (1348).

25. Sournia and Vayssettes, *L'Ostal des Carcassonne*, 15. See also Bernard Sournia and Jean-Louis Vayssettes, "Trois plafonds montpelliérains du Moyen Âge," in Monique Bourin and Philippe Bernardi, eds., *Plafonds peints médiévaux en Languedoc* (Perpignan: Presses Universitaires de Perpignan, 2009), 149–71.

26. Sournia and Vayssettes, *L'Ostal des Carcassonne*, 68–69.

27. Dominique Thiébaut, "Peintures," in Françoise Baron et al., eds., *Les Fastes du Gothique: Le Siècle de Charles V* (Paris: Ministère de la Culture, Éditions de la Réunion des Musées Nationaux, 1981), 365.

28. Jérome Hayez, "La Stanza di Vignone: Identité et migration entre la Toscane et Avignon aux XIVe et XVe siècles," Doctoral thesis, Université de Paris IV-Sorbonne, 1993.

29. Thiébaut, "Peintures," 370–71.

30. See Guillemain, *La Cour pontificale*, 586–588. See also Cecilia Jannella, *Simone Martini* (Florence: Scala, Riverside, 1989), 70 and 78.

31. See Reyerson, *The Art of the Deal*, 213–14, for a discussion of the details of the transactions.

32. See ibid., for example, 213–14.

33. A. M. Montpellier, *Archives de la Commune Clôture*, EE 766: May 18, 1345. See also the discussion by Laumonier, *Solitudes et solidarities*, 63–70. For a discussion of domestic family life, see Véronique Lamazou-Duplan, "Vie familiale et univers féminins à Toulouse à la fin du Moyen Âge d'après les registres des notaires," *Études Roussillonnaises* 25 (2013): 115–25. See also Lamazou-Duplan, "Les Élites toulousaines et leurs demeures à la fin du Moyen Âge d'après les registres notaries: Entre maison possedée et maison habitée," in Maurice Scellès and Anne-Laure Napoléone, eds., *La Maison au Moyen Âge dans le Midi de la France* (Toulouse: Société archéologique du Midi de la France, 2003), 1:40–61.

34. Gies and Gies, *Marriage and the Family in the Middle Ages*, 273–74. For a detailed discussion of the household of Lapo di Giovanni, see Christiane Klapisch-Zuber, " 'Kin, Friends, and Neighbors': The Urban Territory of a Merchant Family in 1400," in Klapisch-Zuber, *Women, Family, and Ritual in Renaissance Italy*, trans. Lydia G. Cochrane (Chicago: University of Chicago Press, 1985), 68–93.

35. See Reyerson, "Prostitution in Medieval Montpellier," 226. See A. D. Hérault, II E 95/371, J. Holanie, f. 148r. See also Robert Brun, "Notes sur le commerce des objets d'art en France et principalement à Avignon à la fin du XIVe siècle," *Bibliothèque de l'École des Chartes* 65 (1934): 327–46. Brun has, in fact, traced the movements of two large coffers that he stated arrived at Aigues-Mortes, the Mediterranean port of Montpellier, in 1379.

36. A. D. Hérault, II E 95/371, J. Holanie, f. 148r and II E 95/372, J. Holanie et al., f. 42r.

37. A. D. Hérault, II E 95/371, J. Holanie, f. 25r, f. 57v and f. 102v.

38. See Appendix 2, "Monetary Problems," in Reyerson, *Business, Banking and Finance.* The year 1342 was a period of some monetary uncertainty, causing the quotation of prices in the specific money circulating at the time, that is, current money, rather than in money of account that might later, with devaluation, have translated into less valuable coins.

39. See the discussion in Gabrielle Démians d'Archimbaud et al., *Aujourd'hui le moyen âge: Archéologie et vie quotidienne en France méridionale* (Sénanque: Direction du Patrimoine, 1981–83). This ambitious series of expositions revealed the fruits of southern French medieval archeology in material culture. For the images of wooden bowls and ceramics, see *Montpellier: Vingt années de dons, acquisitions et restauration, 1968–1988* (Montpellier: Société Archéologique de Montpellier, 1988).

40. See Reyerson, "Medieval Silks in Montpellier," and Reyerson, "Le Rôle de Montpellier dans le commerce des draps de laine avant 1350," *Annales du Midi* 94 (1982): 17–40, "Les Foires en Languedoc au moyen âge."

42. See Reyerson, "Medieval Silks in Montpellier." I have also dealt in detail with the Cabanis's business operations in *The Art of the Deal.*

43. See Reyerson, "Medieval Silks in Montpellier."

44. Florence Edler de Roover, "The Silk Trade of Lucca During the Thirteenth and Fourteenth Centuries," Ph.D. dissertation, University of Chicago, 1930; and Roover, "Lucchese Silks," *Ciba Review* 80 (1950): 2902–30; see 2909 for this trade. See also Sharon Farmer, *The Silk Industries of Medieval Paris: Artisanal Migration, Technological Innovation, and Gendered Experience* (Philadelphia: University of Pennsylvania Press, 2016).

45. A. M. Montpellier, BB 3, J. Laurentii, f. 13rff.

46. A. M. Montpellier, BB 1, J. Grimaudi, f. 21r.

47. A. M. Montpellier, BB 1, J. Grimaudi, f. 63r.

48. Data come from the collections K. H. Schäfer, ed., *Vatikanische Quellen zür Geschichte der päpstlichen Hof-une-Finanzverwaltung: Die Ausgaben der apostolischen Kammer unter Johann XXII, nebst der Jahresbilanzen von 1316–1378* (Paderborn: Schöningh, 1911); Schäfer, ed., *Die Ausgaben der apostolischen Kammer unter Benedikt XII, Klemens VI und Innocenz VI* (Paderborn: Schöningh, 1914); and Schäfer, ed., *Die Ausgaben der apostolischen Kammer unter den Päpsten Urban V und Gregor XI* (Paderborn: Schöningh, 1937).

49. Schäfer, *Die Ausgaben der Apostolischen Kammer unter Johann XXII,* passim.

50. See Pégat, Thomas and Desmazes, eds., *Thalmas parvus,* 146. "Que non porton vestidura de ceda ni daur ni dargen mais cendat. Item establem que non porton vestidura deguna de ceda, ni daur ni dargen, mais cenda puescon portar en folraduras de lurs vestirs, et estiers non." Florence Edler de Roover identified *sendal (cendal),* spelled *zendadi* in her sources, as a lightweight silk. See de Roover, "The Silk Trade of Lucca," 178. See also Sarah-Grace Heller, "Sumptuary Legislation in Thirteenth-Century France, Languedoc and Italy: Limiting Yardage and Changes of Clothes," in E. Jane Burns, ed., *Medieval Fabrications: Dress Textiles, Clothwork, and Other Cultural Imaginings* (New York: St. Martin's, 2004), 181–207.

51. Sarah-Grace Heller, *Fashion in Medieval France* (Cambridge: D.S. Brewer, 2007), passim.

52. Leah Otis, *Prostitution in Medieval Society: The History of an Urban Institution in Languedoc* (Chicago: University of Chicago Press, 1985), 80; Bronislav Geremek, *Les Marginaux parisiens aux XIVe et XVe siècles* (Paris: Flammarion, 1976), 246; Rossiaud, *Medieval Prostitution*, 8, 65, for example. For information on Montpellier sumptuary law, see also Reyerson, "Medieval Silks in Montpellier." On sumptuary laws in general, see Susan Mosher Stuard, *Gilding the Market: Luxury and Fashion in Fourteenth-Century Italy* (Philadelphia: University of Pennsylvania Press, 2006).

53. A. D. Hérault, II E 95/371, J. Holanie, ff. 25r, 57v, 102v, all in 1342.

54. A. M. Montpellier, BB 2, J. Grimaudi, f. 70v. Also included in the dowry were an outfitted bed and real property, suggesting that a blacksmith possessed considerable materials goods and a landed fortune.

55. Valentina Visconti and her entourage wore black when entering Paris after the assassination of her husband Louis of Orleans. See Eric Jager, *Blood Royal: A True Tale of Crime and Detection in Medieval Paris* (New York: Little, Brown, 2014), 180.

56. Kristen M. Burkholder, "'Threads Bared': Dress and Textiles in Late Medieval English Wills," in Robin Netherton and Gale R. Owen-Crocker, eds., *Medieval Clothing and Textiles* (Woodbridge: Boydell and Brewer, 2005), 1:133–53.

57. Stuard, *Gilding the Market*, 50.

58. I have examined the workshop practices of the Montpellier silversmiths in particular in Reyerson, "The Adolescent Apprentice/Worker in Medieval Montpellier," *Journal of Family History* 17 (1992): 353–70, especially 364–66.

59. Germain, *Histoire de la commune de Montpellier*, 3:485–87. See also Jean Thuile, *L'Orfèvrerie en Languedoc du XIIe au XVIIIe siècle: Généralité de Montpellier* (Montpellier: Causse & Castelnau, 1966), 1: 43–44.

60. For examples, see A. D. Hérault, II E 95/369, J. Holanie. f. 61r: *batitor foliorum auri et argenti*; II E 95/377, B. Egidii, f. 117r, 122v; *batitor auri*: f. lv: f. 25v: *batitores foliorum auri et argenti*; II E 95/371, J. Holanie, f. 30r: *affinator argenti*; II E 95/372, J. Holanie et al, f. 33r: *aurifaber*, and II E 95/377, B. Egidii. f. 305r: *orfevre*. In fact, there were on average seven silversmiths and three goldsmiths per notarial register in the remaining archive, totaling 130 for the period 1293–1348.

61. A. D. Hérault, II E 95/372, J. Holanie, f. 33r: Petrus de Gaianis, inhabitant of Avignon.

62. A. D. Hérault, II E 95/377, B. Egidii, f. 25v. The act is incomplete. The papal accounts record an entry of August 1346 describing Salvator Salui, termed *stagnerius*, supplying Matteo Giovanetti, the painter of the pope, with *stagneolis auri*, for paintings in the papal palace. *Stannum* is an alloy of silver and lead. One possible translation for the term *stagneolum auri* would be gilded pewter.

63. A. D. Hérault, II E 95/368, J. Holanie, ff. 112v and 114v; II E 95/371, J. Holanie, f. 147r. The cost of the raw materials worked by these artists may, in turn, have assured them a higher social position than the candle makers, and perhaps than the painters, depending on the reputation of the latter. Most silversmiths and goldsmiths seem to have been completely integrated into Montpellier society and were not labeled as immigrants

by the notaries. One finds, for example, silversmiths marrying daughters of wine merchants, while daughters of silversmiths married cloth cutters and merchants. See Reyerson,
"La Mobilité sociale."

64. Teulet, ed., *Layettes du Trésor des Chartes*, I, article 27, p. 258, is reproduced as
article 28 in Pégat, Thomas, and Desmazes, eds., *Thalamus parvus*, 16. The text of this
statute as it appeared in 1190 can be found in C. Chabaneau and A. Germain, eds.,
Liber Instrumentorum Memorialium, Cartulaire des Guilhems de Montpellier (Montpellier,
1884–86), act CCXLIV.

65. This chronology represents a revision of Jean Thuile's statements in *L'Orfèvrerie
en Languedoc*, 37, where he argued that the mark appeared about 1220. Contrary to what
Thuile wrote, Majorca was incorporated into the Aragonese kingdom by James I in the
years 1229–33, and the cadet branch of the royal family, called the kings of Majorca, came
to power only at the division of the kingdom at the death of Jacme I in 1276. See Lecoy
de la Marche, *Les Relations politiques de la France avec le royaume de Majorque*. See also
Charles de Tourtoulon, *Études sur la maison de Barcelone, Jacme Ier le Conquérant, roi
d'Aragon, comte de Barcelone, seigneur de Montpellier, d'après les chroniques et les documents
inédits*, 2 vols. (Montpellier: Gras, 1863–67).

66. Pégat, Thomas, and Desmazes, eds., *Thalamus parvus*, 264–65.

67. Metalwork of Montpellier has been the focus of numerous works by Jean Thuile,
including an inventory of artisans associated with precious metalwork; see Thuile, *Histoire
de l'Orfèvrerie du Languedoc, Généralités de Montpellier et de Toulouse, Répertoire des orfèvres
depuis le moyen-âge jusqu'au début du XIXe siècle* (Paris: Théo et Florence Schmied, Aà C,
1964; D à L, 1966; M à Z, 1968). Thuile did not use notarial evidence exhaustively; hence,
there are lacunae in his work. Moreover, the emphasis in most of his work was more on
the assemblage of vast amounts of documentation and photographic evidence of surviving
objects, as well as the very significant contribution of location and identification of some
objects, thus creating a corpus, rather than an in-depth analysis of the objects themselves,
to say nothing of the workshop practices and techniques. The charters and statutes relating
to medieval metalwork in Montpellier are preserved in large measure in the A. M. Montpellier. The extant notarial sources in A. M. Montpellier, BB 1–3, and A. D. Hérault, II
E 95/368–377, were mined exhaustively for metalwork evidence in the pre-1350 period.
For the statute of 1355, see A. M. Montpellier, *Le Grand Thalamus*, f. 133v. See also *Archives
de la ville de Montpellier: Inventaires et documents* (Montpellier, 1920), III:146–47; and
Thuile, *L'Orfèvrerie en Languedoc*, 43–44.

68. See Kathryn Reyerson and Faye Powe, "Metalwork of Montpellier: Techniques
and Workshop Practices in the Fourteenth Century," International Congress on Medieval
Studies, Western Michigan University, Kalamazoo, 1984. On art in this era, see, for example, Marcel Durliat, *L'Art dans le royaume de Majorque: Les Débuts de l'art gothique en
Roussillon, en Cerdagne et aux Baléares* (Toulouse: Privat, 1962).

69. "De la façon et de l'argent de Montpellier." See Léon de Laborde, *Glossaire
français du moyen âge . . . précédé de l'inventaire des bijoux de Louis, Duc d'Anjou dressé vers
1360* (Paris: Adolphe Labitte, 1872), 104–7; and R. W. Lightbown, *Secular Goldsmiths'*

Work in Medieval France: A History (London: Society of Antiquaries of London, 1978), 9–12.

70. See the discussion of transport of jewels and enamels by Susan Mosher Stuard, *Gilding the Market*, 199–209. Enamels were part of a local commerce and of partnership investment in Montpellier. Twenty pounds of multiple colored enamels—blue, green, yellow, violet, and black—were sold by a mercer of Montpellier to a man from Todi in Tuscany on 15 December 1343. See A. D. Hérault, II E 95/372, J. Holanie et al., f. 140r.

71. On medieval jewelry, see "The Scope of Enamel," https://thescopeofenamel .wordpress.com/ . . . /medieval-jewellery-in-europe-1100–1500/, accessed April 2, 2015.

72. Reyerson and Powe, "Metalwork of Montpellier," dealt in detail with this reliquary.

73. Ibid., 12. See also Marie-Madeleine Gauthier, *Émaux du moyen âge occidental* (Fribourg: Office du Livre, 1972), cat. 197; and Lightbown, *Secular Goldsmiths' Work in Medieval France*, 91–92, plates 69–71.

74. See Bernard de Gaulejac, *Histoire de l'orfèvrerie en Rouergue* (Rodez: Société des Lettres, Sciences et Arts de l'Aveyron, 1938).

75. Reyerson and Powe, "Metalwork of Montpellier," 9.

76. Marvin Chauncey Ross, "Bassetaille Enameling at Montpellier," with "A Note on the Montpellier Reliquary in the Taft Museum," by Margaret Kremers, *Art Quarterly* 4 (1941): 32–39; and Thuile, *L'Orfèvrerie en Languedoc*, plate XV (between 68 and 69), plates XVI and XVII (between 72 and 73). See also Gauthier, *Émaux du moyen âge occidental*, 250n196, 400.

77. See l'Abbé Jacques-Rémy Antoine Texier, "Orfèvrerie du moyen âge: Écoles ou ateliers de Montpellier et de Limoges," *Annales archéologiques* 8 (1848): 264–68. For specific references, see A. D. Hérault, II E/95/369, J. Holanie, f. 49v(38v). See A. M. Montpellier, BB 1, J. Grimaudi, ff. 36r and 93r, for the involvement of merchants of Limoges in silk purchases in Montpellier.

78. A. D. Hérault, II E 95/372, J. Holanie et al, f. 32r.

79. Schäfer, *Die Ausgaben . . . Johann XXII*, 394, 398, 416, 417, 442. See also the inventory of candles made in 1342 in Montpellier, A. M. BB 3, J. Laurenti, f. 99r. There were, in addition, stonemasons and sculptors, along with bell makers, founders, forgers, and others who might be included in an artistic community. See J. Renouvier and A. Ricard, "Des maîtres de pierre et des autres artistes gothiques de Montpellier," *Mémoires de la société archéologique de Montpellier* 1st ser. 2 (1854): 135–50.

80. *The Goodman of Paris*, trans. and ed. Eileen E. Power (London: G. Routledge and Sons, 1928). See also note 107 below.

81. Leon Battista Alberti, *I Libri della Famiglia*, trans. Renee Neu Watkins as *The Family in Renaissance Florence* (Columbia: University of South Carolina Press, 1969). See also Gies and Gies, *Marriage and the Family in the Middle Ages*, Chapter 14, 217–90.

82. Klapisch-Zuber, *Women, Family, and Ritual in Renaissance Italy*.

83. On daily life of women in Catalonia, see Teresa Maria Vinyoles i Vidal, "L'Esdevenir quotidià: Treball i lleure de les dones medievals," in Mary Nash, ed., *Més enllà del*

silenci: Les dones a la història de Catalunya (Barcelona: Generalitat de Catalunya, 1988), 73–89.

84. Gies and Gies, *Women in the Middle Ages,* 193.

85. Ibid., 193. Heller, *Fashion in Medieval France,* and Stuard, *Gilding the Market,* found men were the shoppers.

86. See Chapters 5–8 below.

87. See the discussion in Chapter 9 below.

88. Gies and Gies, *Women in the Middle Ages,* 193–94.

89. Slaves were sent to municipal ovens to bake household goods in Palma di Majorca. See Kevin Mummey, "Women, Slavery, and Community in Late Fourteenth-Century Mallorca," Ph.D. dissertation, University of Minnesota, 2013.

90. Bread prices are noted in the *Petit Thalamus.* See Pégat, Thomas, and Desmazes, eds., *Thalmas parvus,* passim.

91. See Bernard H. Slicher van Bath, *The Agrarian History of Western Europe (500–1850)* (London: E. Arnold, 1963). See also Harry A. Miskimin, *The Economy of Early Renaissance Europe, 1300–1460* (Cambridge: Cambridge University Press, 1975).

92. On piracy, see Reyerson, "Identity in the Medieval Mediterranean World of Merchants and Pirates."

93. See Reyerson, "Public and Private Space in Medieval Montpellier," and Reyerson, *Women's Networks in Medieval France,* Chapter 7.

94. Madeleine Pelner Cosman, *Fabulous Feasts: Medieval Cookery and Ceremony* (New York: George Braziller, 1976).

95. Paul Freedman, *Out of the East: Spices and the Medieval Imagination* (New Haven, Conn.: Yale University Press, 2008).

96. See Reyerson, "Commerce and Society," 1: 165–76, 232–34. See also Roger Dion, *Histoire de la vigne et du vin en France des origines au XIX siècle* (Paris: Clavreuil, 1959; re-edition, Paris: Flammarion, 1991; CNRS, 2010).

97. See Schäfer, *Johann XXII,* 51, 53, 55, 66, 70, 209, 210, 323, 394, 398, 400, 408, 417, and 716.

98. Merchants of Avignon came to Montpellier for these and other products such as marzipan and for wax, wood, cloths, silks, furs, as well as paints, cotton for candlewicks, dyes, lamb skins, arms, and iron. See Avignon merchants Pierre de Orto: Schäfer, *Johann XXII,* 71, 206, 211, 415, 416, and 417; François Barralli, 81, 442, 454, 491, and 528; Guilhem Baralli, 522; Guilhem de Faueresio, 102, 103, 109, 116, 121, 161, and 346. Many of the merchants in the papal account book entries were, unfortunately, not designated by place of origin.

99. Reyerson, *The Art of the Deal,* 134.

100. A. D. Hérault, II E 95/374, G. Nogareti, f. 47Rr.

101. A. D. Hérault, II E 95/375, P. de Pena, ff. 54v and 107r.

102. Reyerson, *The Art of the Deal,* 162.

103. See Lucie Galano, "À table! Festivités et banquet au consulat de Montpellier à la fin du Moyen Âge," *Bulletin historique de la ville de Montpellier* 36 (November 2014):

60–72. The document in question is the "Libre de la Clavaria 1357–1358," A. M. Montpellier, Joffre 845. Maurice Oudot de Dainville edited a large part of the account in *Archives de la ville de Montpellier, inventaires et documents*, vol. 9, *Archives du greffe de la maison consulaire*, Armoire D *(suite)* (Montpellier: Imprimerie l'Abeille, 1949), 181–204. There has been considerable focus on food in medieval French historiography. Galano makes reference to numerous recent works.

104. Shulamith Shahar, *The Fourth Estate: A History of Women in the Middle Ages* (London: Methuen, 1983), 195. Recall the earlier comments of Régine Pernoud, *La femme au temps des cathédrales*.

105. For a discussion of Margherita Datini, see Gies and Gies, *Women in the Middle Ages*, Chapter 10, 184–209.

106. See *Le Ménagier de Paris*, French text ed. Georgine E. Brereton and Janet M. Feinley, intro. Beryl Smalley (Oxford: Clarendon, 1981), edition also in the Livre de Poche (Paris, 1994); Pernoud, *La femme au temps des cathedrals*; and Shahar, *The Fourth Estate*. See also *Le Lettere di Margherita Datini a Francesco di Marco*, and *Le lettere di Francesco Datini alla moglie Margherita*; Gies and Gies, *Women in the Middle Ages*, 184–209, and Gies and Gies, *Marriage and the Family in the Middle Ages*.

107. Hutton, *Women and Economic Activities in Late Medieval Ghent*, created an economic biography of Mergriete, 92–97.

108. Hutton, *Women and Economic Activities in Late Medieval Ghent*, 71–77, made this point in regard to the urban noblewoman, Lijsbette van Lierde, who was active in managing her property and litigating on her own behalf, while her stepdaughter was passive. Martha was active.

CHAPTER 5

Note to epigraph: A. D. Hérault, II E 95/368, Johannes Holanie, f. 143r, 18 March 1328: "Ego, Martha, uxor dicti quondam Guiraudi de Cabanis, tutrixque et nomine tutoris dicti Jacobi de Cabanis, filii mei, heredi predicti, certifficata ad plenum de predictis."

1. See Pierre Chastang, *La Ville, le gouvernement et l'écrit à Montpellier* (Paris: Publications de la Sorbonne, 2013), 364ff. This era of conflict has been treated by Jean Combes, "Finances municipales et oppositions sociales à Montpellier au commencement du XIVe siècle," in *Vivaris et Languedoc, Fédération historique du Languedoc méditerranéen et du Roussillon*, 44e Congrès, Privas, May 1971 (Montpellier: Université Paul Valéry, 1972), 99–120. See also Rogozinski, *Power, Caste and Law*, 44, who sees *populares* deriving from the Latin term *populus*, reflecting the concept of *universitas*.

2. A. M. Montpellier, *Grand Chartrier*, Louvet 3507.

3. These Fourteen were elected two per *échelle* of the *Commune Clôture* defense organization.

4. On taxation in Montpellier, see Maurice Oudot de Dainville, "Remarques sur les compoix du Languedoc méditerranéen," *Folklore* 15 (1939): 132–37; and Jacques Ellul,

"Notes sur les impôts municipaux à Montpellier aux XIIIe et XIVe siècles," *Revue Historique de Droit Français et Étranger* 17 (1938): 365–403. See also Anne-Catherine Marin-Rambier, "Montpellier à la fin du Moyen Âge d'après les compoix (1380–1450)," Thesis, École Nationale des Chartes, 1980. For a slightly later era, see the study by Lucie Laumonier, "Exemptions et dégrèvements."

5. See A. M. Montpellier, *Grand Chartrier,* Louvet 3506 and 3508.

6. Chastang, *La Ville, le gouvernement et l'écrit à Montpellier,* 369.

7. Combes, "Finances municipales et oppositions sociales à Montpellier," 106–7.

8. Pégat, Thomas, and Desmazes, eds., *Thalamus parvus,* 344.

9. Ibid., 346.

10. Combes, "Finances municipales et oppositions sociales à Montpellier," 99–120.

11. Rogozinski, *Power, Caste and Law,* 48.

12. Chastang, *La Ville, le gouvernement et l'écrit à Montpellier,* 370. The roll, Louvet 3523, is featured in a photo in Chastang, 382. Thanks are due Dr. Lucie Laumonier, my former postdoctoral fellow, for looking initially at this roll for me.

13. A. M. Montpellier, *Grand Chartrier,* Louvet 3523.

14. Chastang, *La Ville, le gouvernement et l'écrit à Montpellier,* 371.

15. Combes, "Finances municipales et oppositions sociales à Montpellier," 117–20.

16. See, for example, Elisabeth Carpentier, "Autour de la peste noire: Famines et épidémies dans l'histoire du XIVe siècle," *Annales: economies, societies, civilisations* 17 (1962): 1062–92; Jordan, *The Great Famine*; E. Perroy, "À l'origine d'une économie contractée: Les Crises du XIVe siècle," *Annales: economies, societies, civilisations* 4 (1949): 167–82; and Kathryn Reyerson, "Montpellier et le trafic des grains en Méditerranée avant 1350."

17. A. M. Montpellier, *Grand Chartrier,* Louvet 3523.

18. See A. D. Hérault, II E 95/369, J. Holanie, f. 68r, for a tutoring contract by a cleric in grammar ("in scientia gramaticali") for two sons of a silversmith in 1333.

19. On children playing, see Hanawalt, *Growing up in Medieval London,* Chapter 5, "Childrearing, Training, and Education," for a rich discussion of these dimensions of childhood in late medieval London.

20. On childhood in the Middle Ages, see Roger Virgoe, ed., *Private Life in the Fifteenth Century* (New York: Weidenfeld & Nicolson, 1989); Compton Reeves, *Pleasures and Pastimes in Medieval England* (Phonex Mill: Alan Sutton, 1995); and Hanawalt, *Growing Up in Medieval London.* See also David Nicholas, *The Domestic Life of a Medieval City, Women, Children and Families in Fourteenth Century* (Lincoln: University of Nebraska Press, 1985); and Reyerson, "The Adolescent Apprentice/Worker in Medieval Montpellier."

21. The Cabanis engaged in animal sales later in life, as did many medieval merchants. They sold a mule to a merchant in September 1342. A. D. Hérault, II E 95/374, G. Nogareti, f. 59Rr. See also Reyerson, "Commerce and Society," 1:204–11, on the sale of animals of transport and burden.

22. See Chapter 2 of this book.

23. See Chapter 2.

24. Francesco di Balduccio Pegolotti, *La Pratica della mercatura*, ed. Allan Evans (Cambridge, Mass.: Harvard University Press, 1936). See for an example, Robert S. Lopez and Irving W. Raymond, *Medieval Trade in the Mediterranean World* (New York: Columbia University Press, 2001), 109–14.

25. Franco Borlandi believed the author to be Giorgio Chiarini. See Giorgio Chiarini, *El Libro di Mercantantie et Usanze de' Paesi*, ed. Franco Borlandi (Turin: S. Lattes, 1936). See also Lopez and Raymond, *Medieval Trade in the Mediterranean World*, 348–53. See also my Ph.D. student John Manke's seminar paper, "The Usefulness of Sensory Analysis to Economic History," for my seminar "New Directions in the Middle Ages, 1100–1500," University of Minnesota, 2012. He presented a revised version of this paper, "Red Is the New Black: The Merchant Response to Changing Trends in Fifteenth-Century Culture," at the Newberry Center for Renaissance Studies: Multidisciplinary Graduate Student Conference, 24–26 January 2013.

26. See Kathryn Reyerson, "Un Exemple de micro-crédit féminin entre ville et campagne: Montpellier et ses alentours au début du XIVe siècle," in Marie Dejoux and Diane Chamboduc de Saint Pulgent, eds., *Mélanges François Menant* (Paris: La Sorbonne, forthcoming). See also Reyerson, *Women's Networks in Medieval France*, Chapter 6.

27. See discussion in Kathryn Reyerson, "Commercial Fraud in the Middle Ages: The Case of the Dissembling Pepperer," *Journal of Medieval History* 8 (1982): 63–73.

28. Ibid. 67.

29. Hutton, *Women and Economic Activities in Late Medieval Ghent*, 92ff and Chapter 5.

30. Winer, "The Mother and the *Dida* (Nanny)."

31. C. Paoli and E. Piccolomini, *Lettere volgari del secolo XIII scritte da Senesi* (Bologna, 1871), 49–58, trans. and abbrev. in Lopez and Raymond, *Medieval Trade in the Mediterranean World*, 392–94.

32. Lopez and Raymond, *Medieval Trade in the Mediterranean World*, 394.

33. See Chapters 7, 8, and 9 of this book.

34. See Chapter 8.

35. Martha's mother Jacoba's sentiment in her *donatio inter vivos* represents the exception in that it documents maternal affection. See Chapter 2, note to epigraph.

36. In one act, her sons speak of her as *"reverenda mater."* See A. D. Hérault, II E 95/374, G. Nogaretii, f. 12rR: "cum auctoritate et consensu domine Marthe reverende [matris] et curatricis." The document is missing its right edge.

37. The contentions of Philippe Aries that medieval people did not have deep feelings for their children have long since been put to rest. See Herlihy, *Medieval Households*, 125.

38. See A. D. Hérault, II E 95/368, J. Holanie, f. 143r.

39. As note earlier, the wills analyzed come from four archival *fonds*: A. D. Hérault, II E 95/368–377; A. M. Montpellier, BB 1–3; A. M. Montpellier, *Archives de la Commune Clôture*; A. M. Montpellier, *Grand Chartrier*.

40. On heirs in Montpellier, see de Charrin, *Les Testaments dans la région de Montpellier au moyen âge*, Chapter 2.

41. The latter was the case for Agnes de Bossones in her 1342 will. A. M. Montpellier, BB 3, J. Laurentii, 13r ff. See Reyerson, *Women's Networks in Medieval France*, Chapter 9.

42. See Chapters 7 and 8 below.

43. See, for example, A. D. Hérault, II E 95/368, J. Holanie, f. 106v, and its translation in Reyerson and Salata, *Medieval Notaries and Their Acts*, 59–61.

44. Teulet, ed. *Layettes du Trésor des Chartes*, vol. 1, Statutes of 1205, art. 5, 289: "Omnis mulier, puella seu vidua, potest omnia sua dare in dotem tam primo quam secundo viro, licet infantes habuerit."

45. Bensch, *Barcelona and Its Rulers*, 356. See also 372–73.

46. Winer, *Women, Wealth and Community in Perpignan*, 67ff.

47. Ibid., 47.

48. Kelleher, *The Measure of Woman*, 75.

49. Ibid.

50. Courtemanche, *La Richesse des femmes*, 252–54.

51. Ibid., 255–66. She has few examples, in fact.

52. Béghin, *"La Tentation du veuvage,"* 169–70.

53. See Reyerson, "L'Expérience des plaideuses devant les cours de Montpellier (fin XIIIe–mi-XIVe siècle)."

54. Klapisch-Zuber, " 'The Cruel Mother'."

55. Kelleher, *The Measure of Woman*, 76.

56. Ibid., 79, in regard to Béghin, "La Tentation du veuvage," 179.

57. Béghin, "La Tentation du veuvage," 164–69.

58. Ibid., 179.

59. Ibid., 180.

60. Bensch, *Barcelona and Its Rulers*, 272–75.

61. Ibid., 272–73.

62. Laumonier, *Solitudes et solidarités en ville*, 225–33.

63. Courtemanche, *La Richesse des femmes*, 251–52.

64. A. D. II E 95/374, G. Nogareti. See Appendix I below on the sources.

65. On the Cabanis business structure, see Reyerson, *The Art of the Deal*, Chapter 4.

66. See Chapters 7, 8, and 9 below.

CHAPTER 6

Notes to epigraph:

1347: Testamentary formulas can be found in Montpellier wills. See A. D. Hérault, II E 95/377, Bernardus Egidii, f. 78r, 1347: "Item confidens de legalitate dicte Gaudiose, uxori mee, dono et ordino ipsam tutricem dictorum liberorum meorum absque et quod teneatur alicui persone de administratione sua reddere rationem . . . et quod non teneatur reddere compotum nec dare cautionem aliquam de utendo et fruendo etc." See de Charrin, *Les Testaments dans la région de Montpellier au moyen âge*, 120. De Charrin stated that these are the two common formulas in use in Montpellier wills, relating to the mother as guardian.

1403: De Charrin, *Les Testaments*, 121, identified the source as A. D. Hérault, II E 95 with the notary E. de Ranc, 1403, f. 27v: "Item volo et expresse ordino quod Raymunda, uxor mea, sit domina potens ususfructuaria ac tutrix testamentaria omnium liberorum et bonorum meorum et quod non teneatur facere inventarium nec reddere compotum nec rationem alicui curie seu persone ecclesiastice vel seculari de regimine per eam facta."

1. A. D. Hérault, II E 95/374, G. Nogareti, f. 56Rr.

2. A. D. Hérault, II E 95/370, J. Holanie, ff. 42v–44v.

3. On the court system in Montpellier, see Reyerson, "Flight from Presecution," and Reyerson, "Commercial Fraud in the Middle Ages."

4. Agnes de Bossones had some trouble with the Bossones brothers that involved litigation. See Reyerson, "L'Expérience des plaideuses devant les cours de Montpellier."

5. See Kelleher, *The Measure of Woman*, chapter 1.

6. See encyclopedia articles, Kathyrn Reyerson, "Women and Law in Medieval France," in Linda E. Mitchell, ed., *Women in Medieval Western European Culture* (New York: Garland, 1999) 131–36; and Reyerson and John Bell Henneman, "Law, Southern France," in *The Dictionary of the Middle Ages* (New York: Scribner's, 1986), 7: 461–68. See also Reyerson and Salata, *Medieval Notaries and Their Acts*, and Reyerson, "Notaires et crédit à Montpellier au moyen âge," in François Menant and Odile Redon, eds., *Notaires et crédit* (Rome: École Française de Rome, 2004, appeared 2005), 241–61.

7. Pierre Tisset, "Placentin et son enseignement à Montpellier: Droit romain et coutume dans l'ancien pays de Septimanie," *Recueil de mémoires et travaux publié par la société d'histoire du droit et des institutions des anciens pays de droit écrit*, fasc. 2 (Montpellier, 1951): 67–94; see especially 79 and article 5 of the 1204 Montpellier *coutumes*: "ubi mores et consuetudines curie deficient, secundum juris ordinem." See also Tisset's concluding comments, 91.

8. See, for example, Edmond Meynial, "Des renonciations au moyen âge et dans notre ancien droit," *Revue historique de droit français et étranger* ser. 3, 25 (1901): 241–77; and André Gouron, "Diffusion des consulats méridionaux et expansion du droit romain aux XIIe et XIIIe siècles."

9. Tisset, "Placentin et son enseignement à Montpellier," 73.

10. See Roger Aubenas, "La Famille dans l'ancienne Provence," *Annales d'Histoire Économique et Sociale* 8 (1936): 523–41.

11. See Reyerson, "Women and Law in Medieval France," and Reyerson and Henneman, "Law, Southern France," where some revision of the sharply stated contrast between northern and southern France, particularly in regard to Roman law influence, is now necessary. See, for example, the findings of Marguerite Ragnow, "The Worldly Cares of Abbess Richildis," Ph.D. dissertation, University of Minnesota, 2005.

12. On *ius comune* and the different layers of law in play in southern Europe, see Kelleher, *The Measure of Woman*.

13. See Reyerson, "L'Expérience des plaideuses devant les cours de Montpellier," 522–28.

14. See Reyerson, "Women in Business."

15. Teulet, ed., *Layettes du Trésor des chartes*, 1:289: "Si deinceps aliquis, habens infantes inpuberes [*sic*], in testamento suo gadiatores aliquos fecerit, illi gadiatores intelliguntur esse tutores illorum infantum impuberum, nisi in eodem testamento aliquem esse voluerit tutorem specialiter vel expressum."

16. Winer, *Women, Wealth, and Community*, 49.

17. Quoted in ibid.

18. Ibid., 180n14. See also Heath Dillard, *Daughters of the Reconquest: Women in Castilian Town Society, 1100–1300* (Cambridge: Cambridge University Press, 1984), 109. Dillard identified the tradition of guardianship passing to a widowed mother or father as one that dated to Visigothic times.

19. Winer, *Women, Wealth, and Community*, 50.

20. Courtemanche, *La Richesse des femmes*, 266.

21. Michaud, *Un signe des temps*, 66.

22. John Pryor, *Business Contracts of Medieval Provence: Selected "Notulae" from the Cartulary of Giraud Amalric of Marseilles, 1248* (Toronto: Pontifical Institute of Mediaeval of Studies, 1981), 23–24.

23. Hilaire, "*Patria potestas* et pratique montpelliéraine au moyen âge," Symbolisme du droit écrit," in *Société pour l'histoire du droit et des institutions des anciens pays bourguignons, comtois et romands*, fasc. 30: *Mémoires Georges Chevrier* (Dijon: Faculté' de Droit et de Science Politique, 1972), 421–36, 433. Recall Chapter 2, note 5, above.

24. Pierre Petot, *Histoire du droit privé français: La Famille* (Paris: Loysel, 1992), 366–79, on *patria potestas* in both north and south.

25. Hilaire, *Le Régime des biens entre époux*, 40–42. Hilaire noted (41) that the emancipated son might still live under *patria potestas* in a familial community.

26. Petot, *Histoire du droit privé français*, 374–76.

27. Ibid., 374.

28. A. M. Montpellier, *Archives de la Commune Clôture*, EE 849: "volens et statuens quod sit domina et potens, quamdiu vixerit, in domo mea." Vesiani's support of women went beyond the reinforcement of the status of his wife to the founding endowment of the Ladies of Wednesday charity, supporting philanthropy for the poor of the hospitals of Montpellier. I treat this charity in *Women's Networks in Medieval France*, Chapter 9. See also Alexandre Germain, "La Charité publique et hospitalière à Montpellier au moyen-âge," *Mémoires de la Société Archéologique de Montpellier* 4 (1856): 481–552. I am indebted to Lucie Laumonier for the lists of recipients of this charity in 1308 (A. M. Montpellier, *Archives de la Commune Clôture*, EE 631 and 634) and 1348 (EE 568–574).

29. Hilaire, "*Patria potestas*," 429 and 429n3. See also Laure Verdon, "Les Femmes et l'exercice de la *potestas* en Provence (XIIe–XIIIe siècles): Transgression des rôles ou perméabilité des sphères de compétences?" in *Les Femmes dans l'espace nord-méditerranéen*, under the direction of Christiane Klapisch-Zuber, *Études Roussillonnaises* 25 (2013): 83–88.

30. Aubenas, "La Famille dans l'ancienne Provence," 534.

31. Courtemanche, *La Richesse des femmes*, 267.

32. On widowhood, see Mirrer, ed., *Upon My Husband's Death*.

33. Winer, *Women, Wealth, and Community*, 53.

34. Bensch, *Barcelona and Its Rulers*, 273.

35. See *Senatusconsultum Velleianum*, D 16, 1, 1.

36. Paul Gide, *Étude sur la condition privée de la femme* (Paris: L. Larose et Forcel, 1885), 159–60, made the following observation about the application of the *Senatusconsultum Velleianum*: "Le voici: c'est celui dans l'intérêt de qui la femme intervient, au lieu de lui payer une indemnité, au lieu de recevoir d'elle une liberalité, s'oblige simplement envers elle à l'indemniser du dommage qu'elle éprouvera. Dans ce cas, en effet, la femme ne *donne* rien ni ne *reçoit* rien, elle ne réalise ni perte ni acquisition actuelles, elle s'oblige et on s'oblige envers elle, et, s'exposant au danger d'un préjudice incertain et éloigné, elle obtient en échange une espérance d'indemnité incertaine et éloignée." The conditions for application of the *senatusconsultum* were thus rather complex.

37. J. A. Crook, "Feminine Inadequacy and the *Senatusconsultum Velleianum*," in Beryl Rawson, ed., *The Family in Ancient Rome: New Perspectives* (Ithaca, N.Y.: Cornell University Press, 1986), 86. The *Senatusconsultum Velleianum* evolved as an exception in that, in a suit brought against a woman, the praetor could grant "a plea of estoppel," a bar to alleging or denying a fact. Crook quotes a passage from Ulpian, D. 16,1,2,1: "Marcus Silanus and Velleus Tutor, consuls, having raised the question of the obligations of women who become liable on behalf of others, as to action to be taken the senate decided as follows. With respect to the undertakings of suretyship and the loans by which women intervene for others, although already hitherto the practice of the courts has been to forbid suit against women on such undertakings, in as much as it is not equitable that women should undertake the duties of men and become bound by obligations of such a kind, the senate is of opinion that those who are applied to in legal authority will do well and properly to see to it that in this regard the senate's wish is upheld."

38. Ibid., 90.

39. Suzanne Dixon, "Infirmitas sexus: Womanly Weakness in Roman Law," *Tijdschrift voor Rechts-Geschiedenis: The Legal History Review* 52 (1984): 343–71. An alternative interpretation by legal scholar Suzanne Dixon, 369, argued rather that a concern for "the separation of property within marriage," not a "new helplessness of women," was responsible for the emergence of the *Senatusconsultum*.

40. Gide, *Étude sur la condition privée de la femme* (l52), cited *The Digest*, D 3, 1, 1, 5, that also prohibited a woman from the act of *postulando*. Earlier in D 3, 1, 1, 2, *postulare* was defined thus: "Postulare autem est desiderium suum uel amici sui in iure apud eum, qui iurisdictioni praeest, exponere: uel alterius desiderio contradicere." See also D 50, 17, 2: "Ulpianus libro primo ad Sabinum. Feminae ab omnibus officiis ciuilibus uel publicis remotae sunt et ideo nec iudices esse possunt nec magistratum gerere nec postulare nec proalio interuenire nec procuratores existere." For an English translation of *The Digest*, see *The Digest of Justinian*, ed. and trans. Alan Watson, 2 vols. (Philadelphia: University of Pennsylvania Press, 1985).

41. Hilaire, *Le Régime des biens entre époux*, 127. Hilaire in his treatment of the alienation of dotal goods discussed renunciation of the *Lex Julia*. See Chapter 3 in this book on marriage.

42. Ibid., 90ff.

43. For this and other Roman law protections and their renunciations, see Adolf Berger, *Encyclopedic Dictionary of Roman Law* (Philadelphia: American Philosophical Society, 1953). Another common renunciation was the *exceptio non numeratae pecuniae*, which protected a debtor or a borrower from claims by a creditor to more than what was owed. It referred specifically to the counting out of money owed.

44. Ibid., 674, *ad verbum* "*renuntiare.*"

45. A. D. Hérault, II E 95/374, G. Nogareti, passim.

46. Kelleher, *The Measure of Woman*, 58–61, 75–77.

47. Scholars have traced Jacobi's movements at several junctures, as in 1291 when he witnessed in Montpellier a violent conflict between the consuls of the town and local clerics over an extraordinary financial levy. He was variously termed *legum doctor* and *legum professor* in documents of the first half of the fourteenth century. In 1312, an act stated that he was "legum egregius professor." See Louise Guiraud, *Le Collège Saint Benoît, le Collège Saint-Pierre, le Collège du Pape* (Montpellier: J. Martel aîné, 1890), xxii. The date of Jacobi's death is unknown, but legal historian Roger Grand placed it between 1351 and 1367. Roger Grand, "Un Jurisconsulte du XIVe siècle: Pierre Jacobi, auteur de la *Practica aurea*," *Bibliothèque de l'École des Chartes* 89 (1918): 101. Another legal scholar, P.-F. Fournier, drew comparisons between Philippe de Beaumanoir and Jacobi in his 1927 discussion of the latter's life and work: "through his good-naturedness, subtle and at times malicious, as much as through his qualities of person and juridical specialist, Jame [that is, Jacobi] at times calls to mind his contemporary Beaumanoir, and this comparison is not the least praise one can offer him." See P.-F. Fournier, "Pierre Jame (*Petrus Jacobi*) d'Aurillac, jurisconsulte," *Histoire Littéraire de France* 36 (1927): 481–521, 519: "par sa bonhomie fine et parfois malicieuse, autant que par ses qualités d'homme et de jurisconsulte, *Jame* [*that is, Jacobi*] *fait quelquefoi*s penser à son contemporain Beaumanoir, et cette comparaison n'est pas le moindre éloge qu'on puisse faire de lui." For the treatise, see Petrus Jacobi, *Subtilissimi et acutissimi legum interpretii Domini Petri Jacobi aurea famosissima practica* (Lyon: Martinus Lugduni du-Ry, 1527). Jacobi's digression on a mother's *tutela* is found in the *Practica aurea* under the title "De actione tutele directa," following the *libellus*, or legal accusation that was a demand for a reckoning of a guardian's actions in *tutela* by a ward now come of age. References to the Jacobi work will be by column and line in the 1527 edition. The *libellus* occurred in column 1, lines 1-38. From a statement of the case, Jacobi launched into a general discussion of *tutela*, distinguishing three possible *tutores*: the *testamentarius*, cited in a testament or codicil; the *legitimus*, whose status, in the absence of the *testamentarius*, was regulated by the *XII Tables* and other texts; and, finally, the *dativus* who was, in the absence of the above two, provided by the judge. It is from a discussion of what constituted an insufficient *tutor*, legally deficient, that Jacobi led into a treatment of abnormal *tutela*, of which the *tutela* of the mother and the grandmother is his example.

Jacobi confronted in his investigation the problem of layers of law from the *XII Tables* to the *Authenticum* and the opinions of contemporary glossators as well as the practice of his own day. Since Petrus Jacobi did not use canon law references in his discussion of *tutela*, I will not incorporate Gratian's discussion of the legal capacity of women in C 15, q 3 of the *Corpus iuris canonici*.

48. Adolf Berger, in his *Encyclopedic Dictionary of Roman Law*, defined the term *libellus*: "Written complaints in civil or criminal matters (accusations) as well as written declarations (attestations, issued by an official or a private person)." See Reyerson, "Southern French Legal Procedure and Local Practice: Legal Traditions in Dialogue," 40th International Congress on Medieval Studies, Western Michigan University, Kalamazoo, May 2005, session in honor of F. R. P. Akehurst. Jacobi's *Practica aurea* belonged in the fourteenth century to a relatively new genre presenting *libelli* or legal accusations; thirteenth-century predecessors, such as Jean Blanot and Guillaume de Ferrières, had composed formularies of *libelli*. See Fournier, "Pierre Jame," 497ff. A translation of this treatise would be valuable, but the task would be daunting, perhaps best the work of a team, on account of the myriad abbreviated legal references, used by Jacobi to justify or reference his remarks, that must be tracked down in full.

49. Grand, "Un jurisconsulte," 70, and Berger, *Encyclopedic Dictionary of Roman Law*, 561. Fournier, "Pierre Jame," 502, remarked concerning this formula: "Cette formule suppose le plus souvent un procès qui se débat à Montpellier ou dans les environs de cette ville; on y voit apparaître les juges qui siègent aux divers tribunaux de la cité et aussi les nobles, les bourgeois, les agriculteurs de la région."

50. See Joseph R. Strayer, *Les Gens de justice*. See also Rogozinski, *Power, Caste, and Law*.

51. Further on Jacobi, see Roger Grand, "Un Jurisconsulte," and "Nouveaux documents sur le jurisconsulte Pierre Jacobi et sa famille," *Bibliothèque de l'École des Chartes* 98 (1937): 221–33. See also Fournier, "Pierre Jame," for general bibliographical information. Though his treatise was known to later medieval and early modern legal scholars and enjoyed multiple print editions in the sixteenth century, Jacobi has remained underused by modern legal historians. Jacobi's thought is beginning to be exploited for his conceptions of public and administrative law by Albert Rigaudière. See Rigaudière, "État, pouvoir et administration dans la *Pratica aurea libellorum* de Pierre Jacobi (vers 1311)," in Albert Rigaudière and Jacques Krynen, eds., *Droits savants et pratiques françaises du pouvoir (XIe–XVe siècles)* (Bordeaux: Presses Universitaires de Bordeaux, 1992), 161–210; and Rigaudière, "Municipal Citizenship in Pierre Jacobi's *Practica aurea libellorum* (ca. 1311)," in Laurent Mayali and Julius Kirshner, eds., *Privileges and Rights of Citizenship. Law and the Juridical Construction of Civil Society* (Berkeley: Robbins Collection, University of California at Berkeley, 2002), 1–26.

52. One way of circumventing the problem of the will of the deceased would be to hold that it was not a legitimate desire on the part of the testator to institute a mother as guardian of minor children in his testament (Col. 11, lines 16–23). Jacobi cited C 3, 28, 35, to support this argument. Jacobi commented that, if the law had desired such a state of

affairs, it would have been easy to state as much; by the same token, since nothing was stated in the mother's favor as a testamentary guardian, such an institution should be held as omitted (Col. 11, lines 23–25).

53. Col. 11, line 54–col. 12, line 3.

54. Further on in his discussion, Jacobi repeated his embarrassment at the disparity between the law of his day and that of the *lex nova* of Justinian, and he made the interesting observation about law itself: "The correction of the law is to be avoided because that which is not changed is not prohibited from existing; that law stands, therefore, and remains, and our law is in it, and that law can be strongly sustained from law in texts lying in the *Authenticum* and in the *Novellae*." See Col. 11, lines 32–38. Yet, despite these close connections, Jacobi had to admit that doctors of great authority and glossators stated that the mother could be named guardian in the father's testament, alone or with others, and that she ought to be confirmed, although the *lex nova* did not expressly say this. See Col. 11, lines 38–41. Jacobi cited Azo's commentary on C5, 28, for confirmation of this point of view. Jacobi maintained from D 26, 1, 18, and other texts that "potest ergo dici quod mater non potest esse tutrix ex testamento etiam cum confirmatione, quia erubescimus etc., et legum correctio est euitanda, quia quod non mutatur, stare non prohibetur, stet ergo et remaneat lex illa et iure nostro in suo esse et istud forte potest sustineri de iure prout textus iacet in aut. [Authenticum] et in novellis."

55. Col. 11, lines 1–6. The last two requirements must have been an echo of the practice in Jacobi's day, since they did not occur in Justinianic legislation in the *Authenticum* passage cited by Jacobi.

56. Col. 6, lines 43–56.

57. *Novella* 118, 5, in *Iustiniani Novellae*, ed. Rudolfus Schoell and Guilelmus Kross (Berlin: Apud Weidmannos, 1912), 571. The pertinent passage is the following: "Mulieribus enim etiam nos interdicimus tutelae subire officium, nisi mater aut avia fuerit: his enim solis secundum hereditatis ordinem et tutelam subire permittimus, si inter gesta et nuptiis aliis et auxilio Velleiani senatusconsulti renuntiant." The provisions in the corresponding *Authenticum*, "Ut liceat matri et aviae de heredibus ab intestate," and in the *Constitutio* CCCXCVI, 4, of the *Iuliani Epitome Latina Novellarum Iustiniani*, ed. Gustavus Haenel (Leipzig: Reimpressio phototypica ed., 1873), are the same as the above, though with somewhat different wording.

58. Winer, *Women, Wealth, and Community*, 50. Anne-Marie Landes-Mallet, *La Famille en Rouergue au Moyen Âge 1269–1345: Étude de la pratique notariale* (Rouen: L'Université de Rouen, 1985), echoed this situation for south-central France.

59. Col. 12, lines 25–30. Because she had the father's will in her favor, she was not required to provide sureties.

60. De Charrin, *Les Testaments*.

61. Teulet, ed., *Layettes du Trésor des Chartes*, 1:255–66. See Article 38, 259: "Si mulier fidejusserit pro aliquo vel pro aliqua, tenetur in illis casibus in quibus leges permittunt. Nam secundum leges viget intercessio femine: creditoris ignorancia, obligantis se scientia, largitione, rei proprie racione, renunciatione, pignoris [vel] yppotece remissione, secundo

post biennium cautione, coram tribus testibus in instrumento premissa confessione, libertate, dote, et si exerceat officium et gratia illius intercedat, vel voluntate mariti, efficaciter obligatur."

62. Tisset, "Placentin," 87: "*Suit, secundum leges*, une énumération qui va de l'erreur du créancier et du dol de la femme (D. 16, 1, 1, 2, and 3, and 11, 11, and 12), de l'instrumentum dressé en présence de trois témoins (C. 4, 29, 23), jusqu'à la renonciation générale du D. 16, 1, 32, 4. L'article s'achève par une courte proposition: *si la femme* exerce un métier et qu'elle intercède à ce titre ou de par la volonté de son mari, elle sera valablement obligée."

63. See also Tisset, "Placentin," 87. Book 16 of the *Digest* treats the *Senatusconsultum Velleianum*. See *The Digest of Justinian*.

64. Peter Riesenberg, "Roman Law, Renunciations and Business in the Twelfth and Thirteenth Centuries," in John H. Mundy, Richard W. Emery, and Benjamin N. Nelson, eds., *Essays in Medieval Life and Thought Presented in Honor of Austin P. Evans* (New York: Columbia University Press, 1955), 207–25.

65. Pryor, *Business Contracts*, 27.

66. Riesenberg, "Roman Law," 212–14. Examining the discussion in the universities about the validity of renunciations, he discerned that "notaries and jurists adopted the general rule that those protections instituted to aid a person might be renounced, while those introduced both for one's benefit and for the protection of the commonweal might not be"; see 223.

67. Ibid., 224.

68. Ibid., 218.

69. See Kathryn Reyerson, "Rituals in Medieval Business," in Joëlle Rollo-Koster, ed., *Medieval and Early Modern Ritual. Formalized Behavior in Europe, China and Japan* (Leiden: Brill, 2002), 81–103.

70. See A. D. Hérault, II E 95/374, G. Nogareti, f. 4Rr, for the 1339 example. The remaining acts in 1340 are executed by Martha alone and concern her real property holdings (ff. 34Rv, 12r, and 12r).

71. On the *Senatusconsultum Vellianum*, see Berger, *Encyclopedic Dictionary*, 700. See also Meynial, "Des renonciations au moyen âge et dans notre ancien droit"; Riesenberg, "Roman Law, Renunciations, and Business." The earliest medieval evidence of renunciation of the *Senatusconsultum Velleianum* can be found in the first register of Giovanni Scriba in Genoa (mid-twelfth century) in a loan to a couple where the wife renounces the *senatusconsultum*. See Riesenberg, "Roman Law, Renunciations, and Business," 215 and note 30 in which he cites Scriba, I, act cciv.

72. A case in point is a sale of land and houses, recorded on 7 July 1327, in which the wife renounced this protection. A. D. Hérault, II E 95/368, J. Holanie, ff. 1r–2v. See the translated act in Reyerson and Salata, *Medieval Notaries and Their Acts*, 78–85, especially 84.

73. A. D. Hérault, II E 95/368, J. Holanie, f. 122r.

74. Thus Martha's sons' contracts contain renunciations. See A. D. Hérault, II E 95/374, G. Nogareti, passim.

75. See Hilaire, *Le Régime des biens entre époux*, 118–22.

76. Agnes de Bossones appeared frequently in the notarial register of J. Grimaudi, A. M. Montpellier, BB, 2, 1301–2, in this capacity, as did Martha de Cabanis, in A. D. Hérault, II E 95/374, G. Nogareti, 1336–43. With regard to real estate transactions, wives generally acted with the consent of their husbands. See Hilaire, *Le Régime des biens entre époux*, 112–13.

77. For an example of a woman acting without her husband's consent, see A. D. Hérault, II E 95/370, J. Holanie, f. 69r.

78. Reyerson, "L'Expérience des plaideuses devant les cours de Montpellier," 522–28.

79. See Chapter 9 below for Martha's procurations in this regard.

80. There were laywomen who did not marry but remained lifelong single women; in addition, there were life-cycle single women who remained single for a time and married later in life. For a discussion of the status of single women, see Judith Bennett and Amy M. Froide, "A Singular Past," in Bennett and Froide, eds., *Singlewomen in the European Past, 1250–1800* (Philadelphia: University of Pennsylvania Press, 1999), 1–37.

81. On Christine de Pizan, see, for example, Charity C. Willard, *Christine de Pizan: Her Life and Works* (New York: Persea, 1984); and Barbara K. Altmann, "Christine de Pizan as Maker of the Middle Ages," in Richard Utz and Elizabeth Emery, eds., *Cahier Calin: Makers of the Middle Ages: Essays in Honor of William Calin* (Kalamazoo, Mich.: Studies in Medievalism, 2011), 30–32.

CHAPTER 7

Note to epigraph: A. D. Hérault, II E 95/374, G. Nogareti, f. 12Rv, 18 March 1338 (n.s.): "Ego [Jacobus] de Cabanis, mercator Montispessulani, filius et heres universalis domini Guiraudi de Cabanis [mercatoris] Montispessulani, maior qui sum viginti annis, cum auctoritate et concensu domine Marthe reverende [matris] et curatricis mei hic presentis quod ego dicta Martha, hic presens, scio esse verum."

1. I would not make the argument of gender dependency quite so bluntly as Marie Kelleher, *The Measure of Woman*, Chapter 2.

2. See Robert Fawtier, *The Capetian Kings of France: Monarchy and Nation, 987–1328* (New York: St. Martin's, 1960), for a discussion of the inheritance of an entourage.

3. See Reyerson, *The Art of the Deal*, 129–37.

4. A. D. Hérault, II E 95/368, J. Holanie, f. 143r.

5. On Cabanis business personnel, see Reyerson, *The Art of the Deal*, Chapter 4.

6. See Reyerson, "Women in Business," and Reyerson, *Women's Networks in Medieval France*.

7. On *tutela*, see Gigliola di Renzo-Villata, "Dottrina legislation e e prassi documentaria in tema di tutela nell' Italia del duecento," *Confluence des droits savants et des pratiques juridiques, Actes du colloque de Montpellier* (1977) (Milan: A. Guiffrè, 1979), 375–434. See also Christian Bruschi, "La Tutelle des mineurs à Marseille (seconde moitié du

XIIIème s.–début du XIVème s.)," *Recueil de mémoires et travaux publié par la société d'histoire du droit et des institutions des anciens pays de droit écrit*, fasc. 13 (Montpellier: Universite de Montpellier, 1985): 61–70. Martha was still serving as *curatrix* of her sons Jacobus and Guiraudus on 10 February 1339 when she and they invested in a bilateral *commenda*. See A. D. Hérault, II E 95/374, G. Nogareti, f. 18Rr–19Rr and f 4r. In 1339, Jacobus was twenty-one and Guiraudus twenty-four. By 1340, Martha is no longer mentioned as their *curatrix*. See, for example, the procuration of f. 59Rv.

8. Bensch, *Barcelona and Its Rulers*, 272–73. See also Winer, *Women, Wealth, and Community*, 51ff.

9. On the Cabanis business structure, see Reyerson, *The Art of the Deal*, Chapter 4.

10. See Chapter 9 below.

11. Pégat, Thomas, and Desmazes, eds., *Thalamus parvus*, 348.

12. Ibid., 347. On piracy, see Fredric Cheyette, "The Sovereign and the Pirates, 1332," *Speculum* 45 (1970): 40–68.

13. See Reyerson, "Montpellier et le trafic des grains en Méditerranée," 147–62. In the 1330s and 1340s, a time of crisis, Montpellier was dependent on imports of grain in the thousands of bushels that entered the local market from sources throughout the Mediterranean world and the Black Sea.

14. Reyerson, *The Art of the Deal*, 129–137. Procurations were delegations of legal authority frequently employed in the Middle Ages.

15. A. D. Hérault, II E 95/368, J. Holanie, f. 74r.

16. A. D. Hérault, II E 95/374, G. Nogareti, f. 22Rv.

17. A. D. Hérault, II E 95/368, J. Holanie, f. 40r.

18. A. D. Hérault, II E 95/368, J. Holanie, f. 12r.

19. For calculation of the survival rate of notarial registers in Montpellier, see Reyerson (French thesis), "Montpellier de 1250 à 1350: Centre commercial et financier," Doctoral thesis, Faculté de Droit et des Sciences Économiques de Montpellier, Université de Montpellier-I, 1977. My rather dismal conclusion was that about one in three hundred registers has survived. That said, the remaining registers provide an invaluable window on the economy and society of Montpellier in Martha's era.

20. A. D. Hérault, II E 95/374, G. Nogareti. The disorder of the Nogareti register suggests that it was bound in haphazard fashion. There may have been folios lost that might fill in the gaps in the chronology. See Appendix 1: A Note on the Sources.

21. A. D. Hérault, II E 95/374, G. Nogareti, ff. 18Rr–19Rv.

22. See Reyerson, *The Art of the Deal*, 81ff, and Reyerson, "Notaires et crédit à Montpellier au Moyen Âge." See also Reyerson and Salata, *Medieval Notaries and Their Acts*.

23. A. D. Hérault, II E 95/368, 369, 370, 371, 372, J. Holanie. See also Reyerson and Salata, *Medieval Notaries and Their Acts*.

24. There are no other surviving "private" registers in the first half of the fourteenth century in Montpellier, to borrow the term of Richard W. Emery, *The Jews of Perpignan in the Thirteenth Century: An Economic Study Based on Notarial Registers* (New York:

Columbia University Press, 1959). The Nogareti records for the Cabanis are on a par with the survivals for the fourteenth-century figures Barthélémy Bonis of Montauban, the draper-notary Ugo Teralh of Forcalquier, and the merchant of Narbonne, Jacme Olivier. See Édouard Forestié, *Les Livres de comptes des frères Bonis, marchands montalbanais du XIVe siècle*, 2 vols. (Paris: Honoré Champion, 1890, 1893); Claude Cugnasse, "Activité économique et milieu humain à Montauban au XIVe siècle, d'après le registre de Barthélémy Bonis," *Annales du Midi* 69 (1957): 207–27; Paul Mayer, "Le Livre-journal de Maître Ugo Teralh, notaire et drapier à Forcalquier," *Notice et extraits des manuscrits de la Bibliothèque Nationale* 36 (1899): 129–70; and Alphonse Blanc, *Le Livre de comptes de Jacme Olivier, marchand narbonnais du XIVe siècle* (Paris: Alphonse Picard et fils, 1899).

25. She was noted in these roles in A. D. Hérault, II E 95/370, J. Holanie, f. 108v, when Johannes was fourteen, Guiraudus was twenty-one, and Jacobus eighteen.

26. I have discussed kinship in business in Reyerson, "Women in Business," and in *The Art of the Deal*, Chapter 4, the table on 108. See also Table 4 of "Women in Business."

27. See Reyerson, *The Art of the Deal*, 108, for a chart detailing kinship in business.

28. See the in-depth discussion in ibid., 109–10.

29. See A. D. Hérault, II E 95/372, J. Holanie et al., f. 38r, for the use of the term *socia* by a fisherman for his mother-in-law, the widow of a shoemaker.

30. A. D. Hérault, II E 95/369, J. Holanie, f. 12r.

31. See Chapter 8 below for a discussion of real property transactions.

32. A. D. Hérault, II E 95/368, J. Holanie, f. 143r.

33. See Reyerson, *Women's Networks in Medieval France*, Chapter 1.

34. See Reyerson, "L'Expérience des plaideuses" for the cases of Agnes and Maria.

35. McDonough, *Witnesses, Neighbors and Community in Late Medieval Marseille*, 39.

36. Winer, *Women, Wealth, and Community*, 56–62.

37. A. D. Hérault, II E 95/370, J. Holanie, f. 22v, for mention of the 1335 procuration.

38. For examples, see Reyerson, *The Art of the Deal*.

39. See ibid., Chapter 4.

40. The number of acts—327—is approximate and does not include the many internal references to other contracts and obligations—part of what would be a classic inventory of acts—that would increase the number of acts several fold.

41. Martha is also noted in acts of Holanie, II E/95/371, ff. 48r and 88r, and 370, f. 22v.

42. A. D. Hérault, II E 95/374, G. Nogareti, ff. 18Rr-19Rv, 30 May 1344.

43. See Chapter 8 below and Reyerson, "Land, Houses and Real Estate Investment."

44. A. D. Hérault, II E 95/374, G. Nogareti, f. 6vR. The local term for *commenda* is *comanda*.

45. A. D. Hérault, II E 95/374, G. Nogareti, f. 7Rr.

46. A. D. Hérault, II E 95/374, G. Nogareti, f. 16Rr.

47. A. D. Hérault, II E 95/374, G. Nogareti, f. 16Rr.

48. A. D. Hérault, II E 95/374, G. Nogareti, f. 22Rv.

49. A. D. Hérault, II E 95/374, G Nogareti, f. 12Rr: "ego dicta Martha pono curatorio nomine . . . de bonis dicti Jacobi duo milia libras turonensium parvorum." On medieval partnerships, see Lopez and Raymond, *Medieval Trade in the Mediterranean World.*

50. A. D. Hérault, II E 95/374, G. Nogareti, f. 12Rr: "in diversis mercibus et mercaturis."

51. A. D. Hérault, II E 95/374, G. Nogaretii, f. 12rR. The sums, converted to the good coinage standard of April 1330, are 1340 *l.* and 670 *l.* See Reyerson, *The Art of the Deal*, 124. See Reyerson, *Business, Banking and Finance*, Appendix 2: Monetary Problems.

52. See Chapter 1 of Reyerson, *Business, Banking and Finance.*

53. Reyerson, "Medieval Silks in Montpellier."

54. Farmer, *The Silk Industries of Medieval Paris.*

55. John Munro, *Wool, Cloth and Gold: The Struggle for Bullion in Anglo-Burgundian Trade, 1340–1478* (Toronto: University of Toronto Press, 1973). See Munro's collected articles in *Textiles, Towns, and Trade: Essays in the Economic History of Late-Medieval England and the Low Countries*, Variorum Collected Studies (Aldershot: Ashgate, 1994). See also Reyerson, "Medieval Silks in Montpellier," and "Le Rôle de Montpellier dans le commerce des draps de laine avant 1350."

56. Robert-Henri Bautier, "Les Foires de Champagne: Recherches sur une évolution historique," in *La Foire: Recueils de la société Jean Bodin, V* (Brussels: Librairie Encyclopédique, 1953), 97–148.

57. Combes, "L'Industrie et le commerce des toiles à Montpellier de la fin du XIIIe siècle au milieu du XVe." "Modern canvas is usually made of cotton or linen, though historically it was made from hemp." See "Canvas" in Wikipedia, accessed 3 July 2015.

58. Maureen Mazzaoui, *The Italian Cotton Industry in the Later Middle Ages, 1100–1600* (Cambridge: Cambridge University Press, 1981).

59. See Reyerson, "Commerce and Society in Montpellier, 1250–1350," 2: 261–67, for extant transport contracts before 1350.

60. For recent work on silks, see Sharon Farmer, "Medieval Paris and the Mediterranean: The Evidence from the Silk Industry," *French Historical Studies* 37 (2014): 383–419. On connections between the Mediterranean and the Champagne Fairs, see Robert-Henri Bautier, "Recherches sur les routes de l'Europe médiévale-1: De Paris et des Foires de Champagne à la Méditerranée par le Massif Central, " *Bulletin philologique et historique* (1960/61): 99–143; Robert S. Lopez, "The Evolution of Land Transport in the Middle Ages," *Past and Present* 9 (1956): 17–29; Jean Combes, "Transports terrestres à travers la France centrale à la fin du XIVe siècle et au commencement du XVe siècle," *Fédération historique*, 29e Congrès (Mende, 1955), 43–7; Yves Renouard, "Les Voies de communications entre pays de la Méditerranée et pays de l'Atlantique," in Charles-Edmond Perrin et al., eds., *Mélanges d'histoire du moyen âge dédiés à la mémoire de Louis Halphen* (Paris: Presses Universitaires de France, 1951), 587–94.

61. Reyerson, *The Art of the Deal*, 195–98.

62. See Chapter 2 of Reyerson, *Business, Banking and Finance.*

63. See an example in A. D. Hérault, II E 95/374, G. Nogareti, f. 2v.

64. See Reyerson, *Business, Banking and Finance*, Chapter 5.

65. See ibid., Chapter 3.

66. See the synoptic inventory of exchange contracts in Reyerson, "Commerce and Society," 2:269–78.

67. A. D. Hérault, II E 95/374, G. Nogareti, f. 41Rv.

68. A. D. Hérault, II E 95/374, G. Nogareti, ff. 11v and 39v. See Raymond de Roover, "What Is Dry Exchange? A contribution to the Study of English Mercantilism," *The Journal of Political Economy* 52 (1944): 250–66.

69. A. D. Hérault, II E 95/374, G. Nogareti, f. 31Rr.

70. A. D. Hérault, II E 95/374, G. Nogareti, f. 60Rv.

71. See Reyerson, "Le Rôle de Montpellier dans le commerce des draps de laine."

72. See Reyerson, *The Art of the Deal*, 164–66, for a discussion of the impact of the war on the Cabanis textile trade.

73. A. M. Montpellier, BB 1, J. Grimaudi, f. 63r: "in solutione et exterminatione dicti debiti duos pannos cericos quorum unus erit senhay ratus com barraturis aureis pretio xxiiii solidos melgoriensium et alius erit parvus operis montispessulani pretio xvii solidos melgoriensium." See also Reyerson, "Medieval Silks in Montpellier," 123.

74. See Reyerson, *Women's Networks in Medieval France*, Chapter 5.

75. Ibid., Chapter 6.

76. A. M. Montpellier, BB 1, J. Grimaudi, f. 64r.

77. See Reyerson, "Medieval Silks in Montpellier."

78. A. M. Montpellier, BB 1, J. Grimaudi, ff. 36r and 90v.

79. Reyerson, "Medieval Silks in Montpellier," 120–22. On the Lucchese silk industry, the major work remains Florence de Roover, "The Silk Trade of Lucca during the Thirteenth and Fourteenth Centuries." On the silk industries of Paris, see Farmer, *The Silk Industries of Medieval Paris*.

80. On Jewish activity in the silk trade in Montpellier, see A. M. Montpellier, BB 1, J. Grimaudi, ff. 7r, 21r, 27r, 28v, 47v, and 50v. On the scarlet-dyeing industry of Montpellier, see Reyerson, "Le Rôle de Montpellier dans le commerce des draps de laine," 19–21.

81. Armand O. Citarella, "A Puzzling Question Concerning the Relations Between the Jewish Communities of Christian Europe and Those Represented in Geniza Documents," *Journal of the American Oriental Society* 91 (1971): 390–97.

82. See Reyerson, "Medieval Silks in Montpellier," and Reyerson, "The Adolescent Apprentice/Worker in Medieval Montpellier." For apprenticeship contracts detailing gold thread spinning in the first half of the fourteenth century, see A. D. Hérault, II E 95/368, J. Holanie, ff. 57r, 131v, and 136r.

83. A. M. Montpellier, BB 1, J. Grimaudi, f. 80v. See William A. Bonds, "Genoese Noblewomen and Gold Thread Manufacturing," *Medievalia et Humanistica* 17 (1966): 79, mentions Montpellier, along with Genoa, Lucca, and Milan as centers of gold thread manufacture in the thirteenth century.

84. A. D. Hérault, II E 95/371, J. Holanie, f. 142v. The apprenticeship contract references no other Cabanis but Johannes the apprentice mercer, who may have had some earlier training as he earned a salary in this arrangement.

85. A. D. Hérault, II E 95/369, J. Holanie, f. 9v.

86. Reyerson, "Medieval Silks in Montpellier."

87. Reyerson, *The Art of the Deal*, 136–37. Later in the fourteenth century Robert Brun can document continued interest through Franceso di Marco Datini's trade in embroideries. The embroideries mentioned in the Datini letters were particularly destined for ecclesiastical usage, and their provenance was Lucca. Their very fine work caused Brun to categorize them as works of art, much as paintings or miniatures. See Brun, "Notes sur le commerce des objets d'art," 328, 337.

88. A. D. Hérault, II E 95/374, G. Nogareti, f. 18Rr. For a discussion of monetary matters, see Reyerson, *Business, Banking and Finance*, Appendix 2, "Monetary Problems," 139–46.

89. The sums converted to the good currency standard of 1330 are 550 *l.* and 170.5 *l.* See Appendix 2, "Monetary Problems," of Reyerson, *Business, Banking and Finance.*

90. "Et nos Jacobus et Guiraudus de Cabanis fratres et socii predicti et suprascripta [sic] sub pactis modis et formis predictis recipientes de et cum auctoritate consilio et concensu dicte domine matris et curatricis nostre, quod ego dicta Martha mater et curatrix predicta confitero esse verum."

91. A. D. Hérault, II E 95/374, G. Nogareti, f. 18Rr–19Rv.

92. A. D. Hérault, II E 95/374, G. Nogareti, ff. 37Rv and 45Rv.

93. A. D. Hérault, II E 95/374, G. Nogareti, ff. 29Rv and 55Rr.

94. See Reyerson, "Le Rôle de Montpellier dans le commerce des draps de laine."

95. A. D. Hérault, II E 95/374, G. Nogareti, ff. 26v, 18r, 23r, 24r, 50r.

96. Combes, "L'Industrie et le commerce des toiles à Montpellier de la fin du XIIIe siècle au milieu du XVe."

97. A. D. Hérault, II E 95/734, G. Nogareti, ff. 18r–19r.

98. A. D. Hérault, II E 95/374, G. Nogareti, f. 32v. Louis J. Thomas identified *candoradors* as bleachers of wool: *Montpellier, ville marchande: Histoire e'conomique et sociale de Montpellier des origines à 1870* (Montpellier: Librairie Valat, Librairie Coulet, 1936), 56.

99. On linen, see https://en.wikipedia.org/wiki/Linen, accessed 3 July 2015. Less is known of the processing of linen than of wool.

100. See the arguments in Reyerson, "Le Rôle de Montpellier dans le commerce des draps," 24–25.

101. A. D. Hérault, II E 95/374, G. Nogareti, f. 8rR and 27rR.

102. A. D. Hérault, II E 95/374, G. Nogareti, f. 32vR.

103. A. D. Hérault, II E 95/374, G. Nogareti, ff. 26vR, 27rR, 27vR, 31vR.

104. A. D. Hérault, II E 95/374, G. Nogareti, ff. 7vR 22r.

105. A. D. Hérault, II E 95/374, G. Nogareti, f. 14rR.

106. A. D. Hérault, II E 95/374, G. Nogareti, ff. 10r, 10v, 32vR.

107. A. D. Hérault, II E 95/374, G. Nogareti, f. 15r.

108. Combes, "L'Industrie et le commerce des toiles à Montpellier," 196.

109. A. D. Hérault, II E 95/374, G. Nogareti, f. 50rR.

110. Gaston Galtier, "Les Conditions géographiques de Montpellier," in *Mélanges géographiques offerts á Philippe Arbos* (Clermont-Ferrand: G. de Bussac, 1953) , 237–46.

111. Guiraud, "Recherches topographiques."

112. See Reyerson, *Business, Banking and Finance*, Chapter 1.

113. Stuard, *Gilding the Market*, invoked the emerging retail market development through her study. For another approach to the daily markets of medieval Italy, see Armando Sapori, *The Italian Merchant in the Middle Ages*, trans. Patricia Ann Kennan (New York: Norton, 1970); Sapori argued that the scarcity of fairs in medieval Italy can be explained by the operation of daily markets in towns of any significance.

114. For a discussion of these distinctions, see Reyerson, *Business, Banking and Finance*, Chapter 2, "Credit in the Market Place."

CHAPTER 8

Note to epigraph: A. D. Hérault, II E 95/374, G. Nogareti, f. 11Rv, 26 January 1338 (n.s.): "Ego Petrus Borzes, mercator vini, habitator Montispessulani pro me et meis, confiteor vobis domine Marthe, uxori Guiraudi de Cabanis, mercatoris Montispessulani condam, presenti, stipulanti, et recipienti pro vobis et vestris me a vobis tenere et velle et debere tenere in emphiteosim et sub vestro directo dominio, consilio, laudimio, et prelationis juris . . . totam quandam peciam terre vineate."

1. On dowry in Montpellier, see Hilaire, *Le Régime des biens entre époux*.

2. Mayali, *Droit savant et coutumes*.

3. For a general treatment of real estate in Montpellier, see Reyerson, "Land, Houses and Real Estate Investment."

4. To dispose of land there was often the need for approval of distant relatives, according to the *laudatio parentum*, particularly in a rural context where landholding could be very complex. See Steven D. White, *Custom, Kinship, and Gifts to Saints: The Laudatio Parentum in Western France, 1050–1150* (Chapel Hill: University of North Carolina Press, 1988). We see this operative in regard to feudal and manorial ties as early as the eleventh century.

5. Reyerson, "Land, Houses and Real Estate Investment."

6. Hélène Débax offers the most recent reassessment of the feudal/manorial situation in the south of France. See *La Féodalité languedocienne (XIe–XIIe S.): Serments, hommage, et fiefs dans le Languedoc des Trencavel* (Toulouse: Presses Universitaires du Mirail, 2003).

7. For a discussion of meteoric social ascension of a merchant with significant real property acquisition, see Reyerson, *Jacques Coeur*, Chapter 6.

8. Henri Pirenne provided an early formulation of the rise and withdrawal of capitalists from active business in his article, "The Stages in the Social History of Capitalism,"

American Historical Review 19 (1913): 494–515; see also Lucien Febvre, "Fils de riches ou nouveaux riches?" *Annales: économies, sociétés, civilisations* 1 (1946): 139–53.

9. See Robert S. Lopez, "Hard Times and Investment in Culture," *The Renaissance, a Symposium, February 8–10, 1952* (New York: Metropolitan Museum of Art, 1953), 19–34, for discussion of Genoese investment. See also Steven A. Epstein, *Genoa and the Genoese, 958–1528* (Chapel Hill: University of North Carolina Press, 1996).

10. See Johan Plesner, *L'Émigration de la campagne à la ville libre de Florence au XIIIe siècle* (Copenhagen: Gyldendal, 1934), on the case of Florence. For Genoa, see R. S. Lopez, "Aux origines du capitalisme génois," *Annales d'histoire économique et sociale* 9 (1937): 429–54.

11. A. D. Hérault, II E 95/370, J. Holanie, f. 108v. The act itself breaks off near the end.

12. A. D. Hérault, II E 95/370, J. Holanie, f. 22v.

13. Hilaire, "Exercise de style," 288, 288n14.

14. There was, in addition, the donation of real property by Jacoba, Martha's mother.

15. On rentals, see Reyerson and Salata, *Medieval Notaries and Their Acts*, 90–91.

16. On *emphyteusis*, see ibid., 91–92. See also Reyerson, "Land, Houses and Real Estate Investment," 72–77; and Pryor, *Business Contracts of Medieval Provence*, 91–92.

17. Raymond de Roover signaled the long-term financing dimension of *emphyteusis*. See the collected articles in his *Business, Banking and Economic Thought in Late Medieval and Early Modern Europe: Selected Studies of Raymond de Roover*, ed. Julius Kirshner (Chicago: University of Chicago Press, 1974). I am grateful to Kenneth Anderson for bringing this similarity to my attention.

18. See Reyerson, "Urban/Rural Exchange: Reflections on the Economic Relations of Town and Country in the Region of Montpellier Before 1350," in Kathryn Reyerson and John Drendel, eds., *Urban and Rural Communities in Medieval France: Provence and Languedoc, 1000–1500* (Leiden: Brill, 1998), 253–73. On wine and vineyards, see Reyerson, "Commerce and Society," 1:232–40.

19. A. D. Hérault, II E 95/374, G. Nogareti, f. 4Rr.

20. For a discussion of the range of the Cabanis brothers' business, see Reyerson, *The Art of the Deal*, Chapter 4.

21. See above in this chapter for more details on these leases.

22. A. D. Hérault, II E 95/374, G, Nogareti, f. 8Rv.

23. A. D. Hérault, II E 95/374, G. Nogareti, f. 9Rv.

24. A. D. Hérault, II E 95/371, J. Holanie, f. 88r.

25. A. D. Hérault, II E 95/374, G. Nogareti, ff. 11Rr, 11Rv.

26. A. D. Hérault, II E 95/374, G. Nogareti, f. 34Rv. The payment was promised in "deniers auri ad coronam."

27. A. D. Hérault, II E 95/374, G. Nogareti, 34Rv.

28. For a discussion of regional vineyards, see Gaston Galtier, *Le Vignoble du Languedoc méditerranéen et du Roussillon: Étude comparative d'un vignoble de masse*, 3 vols. (Montpellier: Causse, Graille et Castelnau, 1960).

29. See, for example, the *Liber Instrumentorum Memorialium* and the *Cartulaire de Maguelone*, ed. J. Rouquette and A. Villemagne, 5 vols. (Montpellier: Published by the editors, 1912–25).

30. See Reyerson, "Commerce and Society in Montpellier," 1: 232–40, for a discussion of vineyards and wine in this period.

31. A. D. Hérault, II E 95/374, G. Nogareti, ff. 7v, 8r, 8v, 24v, 7vR.

32. See Chapter 4 of Reyerson, *The Art of the Deal*, for a discussion of the Cabanis entourage.

33. See Reyerson, *Women's Networks in Medieval France*, Chapter 3.

34. Hutton, *Women and Economic Activities in Late Medieval Ghent*, 61. Compare Kelleher, *The Measure of Woman*, on the Crown of Aragon territories, Chapter 2, and Winer, *Women, Wealth, and Community*, Chapter 2.

35. See Reyerson, "Land, Houses and Real Estate Investment in Montpellier."

36. Guiraud, "Recherches topographiques," 156. See also A. M. Montpellier, *Grand Chartrier, Louvet* nos. 237 and 238 for the 1259 acts of the king of Aragon; and A. M. Montpellier, *Grand Chartrier, Louvet* no. 234, for the lawsuit between the Bon Amic family and the town consuls. See Reyerson, "Public and Private Space in Medieval Montpellier." The term for house used in the lawsuit dossier is *domus*. See also Guiraud, "Recherches topographiques," 157n1, for her discussion of the Bon Amic lawsuit; she quoted from the documents without specific source citation: "Locus predicte carrerie Herbarie totus est publicus, cujus fines sunt tales: confrontatur ex une parte cum macello Montispessulani, et ex alia parte cum domo liberorum Guiraudi de Cabanis et cum domibus liberorum Petri Boni Amici et Guillelmi de Conchis usque in introitu peyssonerie qui est a vento circii, et ex alia parte cum domibus que fuerunt Bernardi Lamberti et Guiraudi de Latis, et cum domo Consulatus, et ex alia parte cum domo Petri Martini, et ex alia parte cum domibus domini Guillelmi de Putheo, militis, et liberorum Petri Ymberti, campsoris quondam Montispessulani."

37. A. M. Montpellier, *Grand Chartrier, Louvet* 234, f. 42r–45r.

38. See Reyerson, "Public and Private Space in Medieval Montpellier." See also Reyerson, *Women's Networks in Medieval France*, for a detailed treatment of Agnes de Bossones.

39. A. D. Hérault, II E 95/374, G. Nogareti, f. 8Rv, for an example.

40. A. D. Hérault, II E 95/374, G. Nogareti, f. 51Rr.

41. Here is a specific instance of the relationship of Martha to the king of Majorca as a major landholder. The procuration, mentioned in Chapter 7, that empowers the payment of revenues to the king of Majorca would have been targeting holdings such as this.

42. See the detailed development in Chapter 9 below.

43. See Reyerson, "Land, Houses and Real Estate Investment," for a discussion of these matters, 72–77. See also Reyerson, *The Art of the Deal*.

44. A. D. Hérault, II E 95/374, G. Nogareti, f. 12r for both acts. The alternate transcription of Camburac is Cambuzac.

45. A. D. Hérault, II E 95/374, G. Nogareti, f. 8Rv–9Rv: 26 January 1338; f. 9Rv: 26 January 1338.

46. A. D. Hérault, II E 95/374, G. Nogareti, f. 44rR, for the mention of Jacobus's unnamed wife's transaction with her sister.

47. A. D. Hérault, II E 95/374, G. Nogareti, f. 60Rr.

48. A. D. Hérault, II E 95/374, G. Nogareti, f. 39v.

49. Compare Reyerson, "Land, Houses and Real Estate Investment in Montpellier," 80.

50. A. D. Hérault, II E 95/374, G. Nogareti, f. 47vR.

51. A. D. Hérault, II E 95/374, G. Nogareti, f. 16r.

52. On salt production in this region, see André Dupont, "L'Exploitation du sel sur les étangs de Languedoc (XIe–XIIIe siècles)," *Annales du Midi* 70 (1958): 7–22.

53. For Lunel holdings, see A. D. Hérault, II E 95/374, G. Nogareti, f. 49Rr.

54. A. D. Hérault, II E 95/374, G. Nogareti, f. 8Rr.

55. A. D. Hérault, II E 95/374, G. Nogareti, f. 19Rv.

56. See the *Liber Instrumentorum Memorialium* and the articles by Lewis, "The Development of Town Government in Twelfth-Century Montpellier," and "Seigneurial Administration in Twelfth-Century Montpellier."

57. A. D. Hérault, II E 95/374, G. Nogareti, 47rR. On such payments, see Reyerson, "Land, Houses and Real Estate Investment," 73.

58. A. D. Hérault, II E 95/374, G. Nogareti, f. 26v.

59. A. D. Hérault, II E 95/374, G. Nogareti, f. 58Rr. *Meiariam* was technically share-cropping, though here the responsibilities outstripped what would normally be understood in that context.

60. A. D. Hérault, II E 95/374, G. Nogareti, f. 29v.

61. See Reyerson, "Les Réseaux économiques entre femmes à Montpellier (fin XIIIe–mi-XIVe)."

62. See Reyerson, *Business, Banking and Finance*, 72, and Reyerson, "Italians in the Credit Networks of Early Fourteenth-Century Languedoc," paper at Medieval Academy of America, Vancouver, April 2008.

63. David Nicholas, *Town and Countryside: Social, Economic and Political Tensions in Fourteenth-Century Flanders* (Bruges: De Tempel, 1971), 287–90.

64. See Reyerson, "Land, Houses and Real Estate Investment in Montpellier."

65. A. D. Hérault, II E 95/374, G. Nogareti, f. 14v.

66. A. D. Hérault, II E 95/374, G. Nogareti, f. 15r.

67. A. D. Hérault, II E 95/374, G. Nogareti, f. 13v.

68. A. D. Hérault, II E 95/374, G. Nogareti, f. 34Rr.

69. A. D. Hérault, II E 95/374, G. Nogareti, f. f. 29v.

70. A. D. Hérault, II E 95/374, G. Nogareti, f. 26v.

71. A. D. Hérault, II E 95/374, G. Nogareti, ff. 29v, 57Rr.

72. See Georges Duby, *L'Économie rurale et la vie des campagne dans l'Occident medieval* (Paris: Aubier, 1962), 2: 632–34. See also Reyerson, "Land, Houses and Real Estate Investment in Montpellier."

73. On the *fideicommissum*, see Francis William Kent, *Household and Lineage in Renaissance Florence* (Princeton, N.J.: Princeton University Press, 1977), 136–42.

74. A. D. Hérault, II E 95/374, G. Nogareti, f. 38rR.

75. A. D. Hérault, II E 95/374, G. Nogareti, f. 108v.

76. See Hilaire, "Exercise de style."

77. See ibid.

78. See the treatment by Hilaire in ibid. See also Reyerson, "La Participation des femmes de l'élite marchande à l'économie."

79. A. D. Hérault, II E 95/370, J. Holanie, passim.

80. A. D. Hérault, II E 95/370, J. Holanie, f. 120r.

81. A. D. Hérault, II E 95/370, J. Holanie, f. 123r.

82. A. D. Hérault, II E 95/370, J. Holanie, f. 27v.

83. A. D. Hérault, II E 95/369, J. Holanie, f. 95v.

84. A. D. Hérault, II E 95/374, G. Nogareti, ff. 7r, 13v.

85. See Reyerson, "Women in Business."

86. See Reyerson, "Land, Houses and Real Estate Investment," 63–72.

87. Ibid., 70–72.

88. See ibid., 39–112, for discussion of these operations.

89. See Reyerson, "La Participation des femmes de l'élite marchande à l'économie."

90. See Reyerson, "Les Réseaux économiques entre femmes à Montpellier."

91. David Herlihy, "Land, Family, and Women in Continental Europe, 701–1200," *Traditio* 18 (1962): 89–120, found a high incidence of land ownership by women in southern France in the early Middle Ages. In urban Montpellier, such a tradition appears to have been perpetuated.

92. On the *laudatio parentum* or approval of kin, see White, *Custom, Kinship, and Gifts to Saints*. See also Amy Livingston, *Out of Love for My Kin: Aristocratic Family Life in the Lands of the Loire, 1000–1200* (Ithaca, N.Y.: Cornell Press, 2010).

93. See the discussion of Agnes's real property in Reyerson, *Women's Networks in Medieval France*, Chapter 3.

CHAPTER 9

Note to epigraph: A. D. Hérault, II E 95/374, G. Nogareti, f. 59Rr, 16 September 1342: "Ego [*sic*] hora ante tertiam nos Martha uxor Guiraudi de Cabanis condam mercatoris Montispessulani et Guiraudus de Cabanis dictorum conjugium filius [crossout] de voluntate dicte domine matris mee quod ego Martha confiteor esse verum, . . . pariter . . . facimus, ordinamus et constituimus certos veros et indubitatos [procuratores nostros] Jacobum de Cabanis filium mei dicte Marthe ac fratrem mei dicti Guiraudi presentem et recipientem et magistrum Bertholomeum Lespinhani notarium regis absentem et eorum quemlibet insolidum. Ita etc. specialiter et expresse ad petendum, fidem faciendum et requirendum pro nobis et quolibet nostrum in nos et quemlibet nostrum fieri fuisse et esse burgenses Bastide Nove Sancti Petri Belvacensis." The notary began the act with "Ego," then corrected to "Nos." I have omitted the error in the opening quote.

1. See Reyerson, *Business, Banking and Finance*, Chapter 2.

2. A. D. Hérault, II E 95/374, G. Nogareti, f. 22Rv.

3. A. D. Hérault, II E 95/374, G. Nogareti, f. 4Rr.

4. See Reyerson, *The Art of the Deal*, Chapter 4.

5. For tables detailing the activities of women in commercial transactions, see Reyerson, "Women in Business," and Reyerson, *Business, Banking and Finance*, passim.

6. A. M. Montpellier, BB 1, J. Grimaudi, ff. 7r, 21r, 27r, and 50v. In the first act of September 1293, she was described as Maria Orlhaque, wife of Bernardus; in subsequent acts of October, November, and December, she is called widow. It is highly likely that this is the same person. See also A. D. Hérault, II E 95/368, J. Holanie, ff. 114v and 142r, for the remaining acts.

7. Hutton, *Women and Economic Activities in Late Medieval Ghent*, 92ff.

8. A. M. Montpellier, BB 1, J. Grimaudi, f. 10v.

9. A. D. Hérault, II E 95/ 369, J. Holanie, f. 13v, for an example in mercery training.

10. A. M. Montpellier, BB 1, J. Grimaudi, f. 10v.

11. See Farmer, "Medieval Paris and the Mediterranean."

12. A. D. Hérault, II E 95/368, J. Holanie, f. 138v. The mother was Beatrix, wife of Raymundus de Elquerio; the mercer was Petrus de Chatnaco of Montpellier.

13. A. D. Hérault, II E 95/368, J. Holanie, f. 32v.

14. A. D. Hérault, II E 95/377, B. Edigii, f. 227r.

15. A. D. Hérault, II E 95/368, J. Holanie, f. 50r. For other examples, see II E 95/368, J. Holanie, f. 136r; II E 95/368, J. Holanie, f. 56v; II E 95/368, J. Holanie, f. 32v; II E 95/370, J. Holanie, f. 25v; II E 95/377, B. Egidii, f. 262r; and A. M. Montpellier, BB 1, J. Grimaudi, f. 80v.

16. A. D. Hérault, II E 95/368, J. Holanie, ff. 56v, 131v, 135v. See also A. D. Hérault, II E 95/368, J. Holanie, f. 135v and II E 95/ 368, J. Holanie, f. 131v.

17. See Bonds, "Genoese Noblewomen and Gold Thread Manufacturing." See also Farmer, *The Silk Industries of Medieval Paris*, and Tanya Stabler Miller, *The Beguines of Medieval Paris: Gender, Patronage, and Spiritual Authority* (Philadelphia: University of Pennsylvania Press, 2014), Chapter 3.

18. See Reyerson, "Medieval Silks in Montpellier."

19. A. D. Hérault, II E 95/ 374, G. Nogareti, f. 30r.

20. For a description of the family relationship, see A. M. Montpellier, BB 3, J. Laurentii, f. 24r.

21. A. D. Hérault, II E 95/368, J. Holanie, f. 134r. The hiring/apprenticeship document is partially illegible.

22. The statutes of the mercers are found in A. M. Montpellier, *Grand Chartrier, Louvet* 1117.

23. See Reyerson, *Women's Networks in Medieval France*, Chapters 5 and 6. See also "Les Réseaux économiques entre femmes à Montpellier."

24. A. D. Hérault, II E 95/369, J. Holanie. ff. 43v and 107v, for the mercery sales.

25. A. D. Hérault, II E 95/371, J. Holanie, f. 142v.

26. See Reyerson, "Medieval Silks in Montpellier," passim. Subsequent to the appearance of this article, I discovered additional sales of mercery of Lucca that have been used as the basis of the present calculations.

27. See the discussion in Reyerson, *The Art of the Deal*, 186–89.

28. A. D. Hérault, II E 95/374, G. Nogareti, f. 41Rv.

29. A. D Hérault, II E 95/374, G. Nogareti, f. 7v.

30. Reyerson, *The Art of the Deal*, 157. See also A. D Hérault, II E 95/374, G. Nogareti, f. 34r.

31. A. D. Hérault, II E 94/374, G. Nogareti, f. 15Rv.

32. Reyerson, *The Art of the Deal*, 126–27.

33. A. D. Hérault, II E 95/374, G. Nogareti, f. 7v.

34. See, for example, A. D. Hérault, II E 95/374, G. Nogareti, ff. 35Rv and 4v (Salamonis) and ff. 18r and 41Rv (Rodesio).

35. A. D. Hérault, II E 95/374, G. Nogareti, f. 41Rv–42Rr.

36. See Reyerson, *The Art of the Deal*, Chapter 4, for more extensive treatment of the Cabanis business entourage.

37. A. D. Hérault, II E 95/374, G. Nogareti, f. 6Rr.

38. A. D. Hérault, II E 95/374, G. Nogareti,f. 33r, dated some time after 19 February and before 2 April 1342.

39. See Reyerson, "The Adolescent Apprentice/Worker in Medieval Montpellier."

40. Reyerson, *The Art of the Deal*, 38–46.

41. See Reyerson, "Commerce and Society in Montpellier ca. 1250–ca. 1350," 2:242, for a list of the *commenda* contracts in the Nogareti register that concern the Cabanis.

42. Reyerson, *The Art of the Deal*, 42. See also Kathryn Reyerson, "Montpellier et le transport maritime: Le Problème d'une flotte médiévale," in Jean Rieucau and Gérard Cholvy, eds., *Le Languedoc, le Roussillon et la mer* (Paris: L'Harmattan, 1992), 1:98–108.

43. A. D. Hérault, II E 95/374, G. Nogareti, f. 12Rv.

44. A. D. Hérault, II E 95/374, G. Nogareti, f. 37Rv.

45. A. D. Hérault, II E 95/374, G. Nogareti, f. 43Rv.

46. A. D. Hérault, II E 95/374, G. Nogareti, f. 27r.

47. A. D. Hérault, II E 95/374, G. Nogareti, f. 45Rv.

48. A. D. Hérault, II E 95/374, G. Nogareti, f. 47Rr.

49. Reyerson, "Commerce and Society," 2:265 and 257.

50. A. D. Hérault, II E 95/374, G. Nogareti, ff. 36Rv, 18v.

51. Reyerson, *The Art of the Deal*, Introduction.

52. Reyerson, "Commerce and Society," 2:277.

53. Reyerson, *The Art of the Deal*, 197–98.

54. Ibid., 163–64.

55. On Cabanis business, see ibid., passim.

56. On Guiraudus's affairs, see ibid., Introduction.

57. See the discussion of Avignon contacts in Reyerson, "Commerce and Society," 1:146–52.

58. See Yves Renouard, *Les Relations des papes d'Avignon et des compagnies commerciales et bancaires de 1316 à 1378* (Paris: E. Boccard, 1941).

59. A. D. Hérault, II E 95/374, G. Nogareti, f. 41Rv. See the detailed discussion in Reyerson, *The Art of the Deal*, 213–14.

60. André Gouron and Jean Hilaire, "Les 'Sceaux' rigoureux du Midi de la France," *Recueil de mémoires et travaux publié par la société d'histoire du droit et des institutions des anciens pays de droit écrit*, fasc. 4 (Montpellier, 1958), 41–77, at 45.

61. A. D. Hérault, II E 95/374, G. Nogareti, ff. 36Rv–37Rv, as an example.

62. Gouron and Hilaire, "Les 'Sceaux' rigoureux," 44.

63. A. D. Hérault, II E 95/374, G. Nogareti, f. 41r.

64. See the maneuvers of Agnes de Bossones in 1301 in regard to succession challenges after the death of her husband, in Reyerson, "L'Expérience des plaideuses devant les cours de Montpellier."

65. A. D. Hérault, II E 95/374, G. Nogareti, ff. 59Rr–59Rv.

66. Abulafia, *A Mediterranean Emporium*. See also Lecoy de la Marche, *Les Relations politiques de la France avec le royaume de Majorque*.

67. Baumel, *Histoire d'une seigneurie du Midi de la France*, 2:217ff.

68. See Archives nationales, J 892, no. 9, partially transcribed in Germain, *Histoire du commerce de Montpellier anterieurement à l'ouverture du port de Cette*, 1:P. J. LXIV, 326–78. See a full treatment of the 1299 inquest in Reyerson, "Identity in the Medieval Mediterranean World of Merchants and Pirates."

69. See Reyerson, "Flight from Prosecution."

70. Reyerson, *The Art of the Deal*, 76–77.

71. Henneman, *Royal Taxation*, 110. On taxation in Montpellier, see also Jacques Ellul, "Note sur les impôts municipaux à Montpellier aux XIIIe et XIVe siècles."

72. Sumption, *The Hundred Years War*, 180–81.

73. Henneman, *Royal Taxation*, 117–19.

74. Ibid., 130.

75. Ibid., 131.

76. Ibid., 134.

77. Ibid., 136.

78. Ibid., 141–42.

79. Ibid., 142.

80. Ibid., 155–57.

81. Ibid., 159.

82. Ibid., 165, 168–69.

83. Ibid., 174.

84. Ibid., 176.

85. See Reyerson, *The Art of the Deal*, Chapter 6 and Conclusion, for my discussion of the effects of monetary manipulation on the Cabanis business.

86. Henneman, *Royal Taxation*, 179.

87. Ibid., 183.

88. Ibid., 203.

89. Sumption, *The Hundred Years War*, 378; also Reyerson, *The Art of the Deal*, 165.

90. Reyerson, "The Tensions of Walled Space."

91. For a detailed look at procuration, see Reyerson, *The Art of the Deal*, 129–38.

92. Robert S. Lopez, "Proxy in Medieval Trade," in William C. Jordan, Bruce McNab, and Teofilo F. Ruiz, eds., *Order and Innovation in the Middle Ages: Essays in Honor of Joseph R. Strayer* (Princeton, N.J.: Princeton University Press, 1976), 187–94.

93. There is no evidence in the documents of Montpellier or Marseille that women were appointed as procurators. See Reyerson, *The Art of the Deal*, 133, and Pryor, *Business Contracts*, 151.

94. A. D. Hérault, II E 95/368, J. Holanie, f. 143r. The mention of the Nogareti procuration is found in a document of 1328.

95. A. D. Hérault, II E 95/368, J. Holanie, f. 22v.

96. For a sample contract of procuration, see Reyerson and Salata, *Medieval Notaries and Their Acts,* 35–36.

97. A. D. Hérault, II E 95/374, G. Nogareti, f. 59vR, as an example.

98. A. D. Hérault, II E 95/374, G. Nogareti, f. 31v.

99. A. D. Hérault, II E 95/374, G. Nogareti, 4r.

100. A. D. Hérault, II E 95/374, G. Nogaretii, f. 51Rr.

101. A. D. Hérault, II E 95/374, G. Nogareti, f. 31v.

102. A. D. Hérault, II E 95/374, G. Nogaretii, f. 52Rv.

103. Martha's and the Cabanis' real estate fortune was discussed in Chapter 8 above.

104. A. D. Hérault, II E 95/374, G. Nogaretii, ff. 47Rv, 28r, 58Rr, 59Rv.

105. See Reyerson, *The Art of the Deal*, 129–40.

106. A. D. Hérault, II E 95/374, G. Nogaretii, ff. 59rR–59vR.

107. See the text quoted at the beginning of this chapter.

108. See Philippe Wolff, *Commerces et marchands de Toulouse (vers 1350–vers 1450)* (Paris: Plon, 1954).

109. On these courts of voluntary jurisdiction, see Gouron and Hilaire, "Les 'Sceaux' rigoureux."

110. A. D. Hérault, II E 95/374, G. Nogaretii, f. 37r.

111. See the discussion in Reyerson, *The Art of the Deal*, 165–66.

112. Cancellation in A. D. Hérault, II E 95/374, G. Nogareti, f. 19Rv.

CONCLUSION

1. Kelleher, *The Measure of Woman.*

2. Bennett, *History Matters.*

3. Bennett, *A Medieval Life*, 98–99. Cecilia Penifader was quite successful in land acquisition and management within the patriarchy of rural England.

4. The later years after 1342 contained cancellations of obligations inserted into the earlier acts. They cease in 1345.

5. See Kathryn Reyerson, "Wills of Spouses in Montpellier Before 1350: A Case Study of Gender in Testamentary Practice," in Joélle Rollo-Koster and Kathryn L. Reyerson, eds., *"For the Salvation of My Soul": Women and Wills in Early Modern France* (St. Andrews: Centre for French History and Culture, University of St. Andrews, 2012), 44–60.

6. See Reyerson, "Women in Business," 117–44.

7. Bennett, *History Matters*, 142–43, speaks of multiple distinctions among women that can be useful in teaching situations.

8. See Reyerson, "L'Expérience des plaideuses devant les cours de Montpellier."

9. On mother–daughter relationships in medieval literature, see Nikki Stiller, *Eve's Orphans: Mothers and Daughters in Medieval English Literature* (Westport, Conn.: Greenwood, 1980). Through a series of literary examples, Stiller argued that the dominant male culture co-opted mothers to perpetuate the values of patriarchal society. See also Doris Desclais Berkvam, *Enfance et maternité dans la littérature française des XIIe et XIIIe siècles* (Paris: Honoré Champion, 1981).

10. Martha's mother Jacoba's sentiment in her *donatio inter vivos* represents the exception.

11. Bensch, *Barcelona and Its Rulers*, and Winer, *Women, Wealth, and Community*.

12. David Herlihy, "Mapping Households in Medieval Italy," *Catholic Historical Review* 58 (1972): 13.

13. On the role of kinship, see Hughes, "Urban Growth and Family Structure in Medieval Genoa," 16.

14. See Reyerson, "La Participation des femmes de l'élite marchande à l'économie."

15. Pernoud, *La Femme au temps des cathédrales*, 214; Shahar, *The Fourth Estate*.

16. For synoptic tables of the transport contracts, see Reyerson, "Commerce and Society in Montpellier," 2:261–67.

17. See Reyerson, "Women in Business."

18. See Reyerson, *Women's Networks in Medieval France*, for which Agnes is the connecting thread.

APPENDIX I

1. A. D. Hérault, II E 95/368–372, J. Holanie.

2. A. D. Hérault, II E 95/374, G. Nogareti.

3. See Reyerson and Salata, *Medieval Notaries*; see also Reyerson, "Notaires et crédit à Montpellier au moyen âge."

4. Herlihy, *Pisa in the Early Renaissance*, 1–20.

APPENDIX 2

1. See Reyerson, "Women in Business." It should be noted, however, that Leah Otis Cour stated in "Municipal Wet Nurses in Fifteenth-Century Montpellier," 84, that the mere absence of a husband's or late husband's name does not automatically signify that the woman in question was single. Shennan Hutton, *Women and Economic Activities in Late Medieval Ghent*, 52, also had trouble telling in some cases whether women were married or single. However, in the local notarial evidence, the pattern I have described here is clear.

2. See, for example, the case of Bonafossia Bonela. In two acts on 29 May 1333, the notary was inconsistent in his spelling of Bonafossia's surname: A. D. Hérault, II E 95/369, J. Holanie, 1333, f. 44v: 29 May 1333: Bonela; f. 45r: 29 May 1333: Bonelhe; f. 62v: 28 August 1333: Bonela. He called her Bonafos and Bonafossia as well.

APPENDIX 3

1. On the coinage current in the region of Montpellier, see Castaing-Sicard, *Monnaies féodales et circulations monétaire en Languedoc (Xe–XIIIe siècles)*.

2. On the medieval money in general, see Étienne Fournial, *Histoire monétaire de l'Occident médiéval* (Paris: Fernand Nathan, 1970).

3. See Reyerson, *Business, Banking and Finance*, Appendix 2, "Monetary Problems."

4. See A. D. Hérault, II E 95/372, J. Holanie et al., f. 51r for details.

GLOSSARY

Accapitum. A synonym for *emphyteusis*, a long-term lease on real property.

Agnatic. Relationship through the male line.

Allod. Freehold real estate, that is, standing outside the feudal/manorial system.

Apanage. Appanage, a succession system of the French monarchy granting territories to younger sons with the expectation that they would come back to the monarchy if there were no heirs.

Apprentice. Student of an artisanal or commercial trade, having contracted with a master of a trade to receive instruction therein.

Augment. Southern French version of gift upon marriage or dower given by the groom to the bride for the support of the household.

Authenticum. Justinian's new constitutions, the fourth component of the *Corpus Iuris Civilis.*

Bayle. Bailiff, a consular legal officer.

Blancherius. A tawer/bleacher of leather.

Burgensis. Bourgeois, meaning honorific urban nobility.

Census. A form of real estate rent or dues.

Champlevé. An enameling technique in which grooves or cuts are made in metal and then filled with liquid enamel that hardens.

Chasuble. A vestment (garment) worn by a priest during the mass.

Canabasserius. Linen or hemp artisan/merchant.

Commenda. Partnership involving an investing partner and a traveling partner for one venture; the investor may put up all the capital and the traveler contribute his labor with the profits divided three-quarters and one-quarter, or there could be a division of profit according to the percentage of investment.

Consuetudines. Local urban statutes in southern France.

Consul. Municipal official of a consulate.

Cordouan. White leather product of Spain.

Corpus Iuris Civilis. The great legal collection of Emperor Justinian in the sixth century CE, comprising *The Digest*, *The Code*, and *The Institutes*, along with *The Novels* or **Authenticum**.

Curator, curatrix. Guardian of children over the age of fourteen.

Dica. A lawsuit.

Dominus/domina. Lord, lady, terms of respect for commoners, and titles for ruling nobility. The lord of Montpellier held the title *dominus*.

Donatio inter vivos. Gift of property by the donor during his or her lifetime.

Dowry. Gift to daughter in marriage by father of bride or by bride herself to support the marital household.

Emancipation. Release from ***patria potestas*** or from serfdom or slavery.

Étang. Lagoon off the Mediterranean coast of France, sometimes separating a strip of beaches from the mainland.

Emphyteusis. Long-term lease of real property with the expectation of yearly dues and other assessments.

Expertise. Official description of the state of built property.

Factor. A business representative or employee.

Familia. Extended household, including family members, servants, hangers-on.

Femme sole. Independent status permitting a married woman in England to act on her own behalf in contractual engagements.

Fideicommissum. Request from a testator to an heir that might or might not be enforceable; originating in Roman law, in Florence it took the form of entailment of an estate.

Fideiussor. A surety; someone backing up a contractual engagement of the principal.

Freresque. A joint holding of brothers who decide not to divide up their inheritance.

Garrigue. Dry brush lands, often the site of aromatic herbs.

Iuvenis/juvenis. Youth, a business assistant.

Jurisperitus. Legal specialist, university-trained.

Mansus. A landholding, *mas*.

Meiriam. A share-cropping arrangement relating to land that may carry management as well as exploitation expectations.

Mercery. Notions, decorations of ribbon, and such; sometimes included silks, brocades, and embroideries.

Namengut. Family naming pool.

Notary. Scribe invested with public authority by a political entity; in southern Europe, kept registers of acts in abbreviated form (minutes) that could serve as proof in a court of law.

Patria potestas. The power of the father over his children, descendants, and household members.

Patriarchy. A society that privileges men over women.

Patriliny. Descent through the male line.

Pignaculum. A term for "tower."

Populares. Party of protestors of consular fiscal mismanagement in Montpellier.

Procurator. Legal representative.

Rentier. Someone who lives off revenue income from real property.

Ricordanze. Memoirs of a family; a family record in medieval and Renaissance Italy.

Salines. Salt-producing exploitations.

Senatusconsultum Vellianum. Roman law action that forbade women from assuming liability for someone else, with the aim of protecting them.

Sénéchausée. French royal administrative district in the south of France, established in the thirteenth century.

Societas. A partnership lasting several years with partners investing differing percentages of the capital and receiving a division of profits that reflects the original investment.

Soler. A room in a house, usually on an upper story.

Syndic. Municipal official.

Terral. Good earth.

Turris. Tower.

Tutor, tutrix. Guardian of children, fourteen or under in age.

Usaticum. Annual dues on real property holding.

BIBLIOGRAPHY

PRIMARY SOURCES

Archives

Archives départementales de l'Hérault, II E 95/368–377, notarial registers. It is now possible to access these notaries online: http://archives-pierresvives.herault.fr/archive/recherche/Notaires/n:25.
Archives municipales de Montpellier
    BB, 1–3, notarial registers
    EE, *Fonds de la Commune Clôture*
    Le Grand Chartrier
    Le Grand Thalamus

Archival Inventories

Berthelé, Joseph, ed. *Archives de la ville de Montpellier, inventaires et documents.* V. 3. *Cartulaires de Montpellier (980–1789), cartulaire seigneurial et cartulaires municipaux.* Montpellier: Imprimerie Serre et Roumégous, 1901–1907.
Castet, Ferdinand and Joseph Bertelé, eds. *Archives de la ville de Montpellier, inventaires et documents.* V. 1. Inventaire du Grand Chartrier rédigé par Pierre Louvet, 1662–1663. Montpellier: Imprimerie Serre et Roumégous, 1895–1899.
Dainville, Maurice Oudot de, ed. *Documents omis dans l'inventaire du Grand Chartrier Inventaires et documents, Archives de La Ville de Montpellier.* V. 2. Montpellier: Imprimierie "L'Abeille" Coopérative Ouvrière, 1955.
Dainville, Maurice Oudot de, ed. *Archives de la ville de Montpellier, inventaires et documents.* V. 9. *Archives du greffe de la maison consulaire,* Armoire D *(suite).* Montpellier: Imprimerie l'Abeille, 1949.
Dainville, Maurice Oudot de, and Marcel Gouron., eds. *Archives de la ville de Montpelllier, inventaire publié par les soins de l'administration municipale.* V. 12. Série EE. *Fonds de la Commune Clôture et affaires militaires.* Montpellier: Tour des Pins, 1974.

Dainville, Maurice Oudot de, Marcel Gouron, and Liberto Valls, eds. *Archives de la ville de Montpellier.* V. 13. Inventaire analytique, Série BB. *Notaires et greffiers du consulat 1293–1387.* Montpellier: Tour des Pins, 1984.

PRINTED SOURCES

Alberti, Leon Battista. *I Libri della Famiglia.* Trans. Renee Neu Watkins as *The Family in Renaissance Florence.* Columbia: University of South Carolina Press, 1969.

Cartulaire de Maguelone. 5 vols. Ed. J. Rouquette and A. Villemagne. Montpellier: Published by the editors, 1912–25.

Chiarini, Giorgio. *El Libro di Mercantantie et Usanze de' Paesi.* Ed. Franco Borlandi. Turin: S. Lattes & C., 1936.

The Digest of Justinian. 2 vols. Trans. and ed. Alan Watson. Philadelphia: University of Pennsylvania Press, 1985.

The Goodman of Paris. Trans. and ed. Eileen E. Power. London: Routledge, 1928.

Le Guide du pèlerin de Saint-Jacques de Compostelle. 3rd ed. Ed. Jeanne Vieillard. Mâcon: Protat, 1963.

Iuliani Epitome Latina Novellarum Iustiniani. Ed. Gustavus Haenel. Leipzig: Reimpressio phototypica ed., 1873.

Iustiniani Novellae. Ed. Rudolfus Schoell and Guilelmus Kroll. Berlin: Apud Weidmannos, 1912.

Jacobi, Petrus. *Subtilissimi et acutissimi legum interpretii Domini Petri Jacobi aurea famosissima practica.* Lyon: Martinus Lugduni du-Ry, 1527.

Layettes du Trésor des Chartes. Ed. Alexandre Teulet. Vol. I. Paris: Librairie Plon, 1863.

Le Lettere di Francesco Datini alla moglie Margherita (1386–1410). Ed. Elena Cecchi. Prato: Società pratese di Storia Patria, 1990.

Le Lettere di Margherita Datini a Francesco di Marco, 1384–1410. Ed. Valeria Rosati. Prato: Archivio storico pratese, 1977.

Liber Instrumentorum Memorialium: Cartulaire des Guilhems de Montpellier. Ed. C. Chabaneau and A. Germain. Montpellier: Jean Martel ainé, imprimeur de la Société Archéologique, 1884–86.

Martin-Chabot, Eugène. *Les Archives de la cour des comptes, aides et finances de Montpellier: Avec un essai de restitution des premiers registres de la sénéchausée.* Bibliothèque de la Faculté des Lettres de l'Université de Paris 22. Paris: Félix Alcan, 1907.

Le Ménagier de Paris. French text ed. Georgine E. Brereton and Janet M. Feinley. Intro. Beryl Smalley. Oxford: Clarendon, 1981. Edition also in the *Livre de Poche* (Paris, 1994).

Paoli, C., and E. Piccolomini, eds., *Lettere volgari del secolo XIII scritte da Senesi.* Bologna, 1871, 49–58.

Pégat, F., E. Thomas, and C. Desmazes, eds. *Thalamus parvus: Le Petit thalamus de Montpellier.* Montpellier: La Société Archéologique de Montpellier, 1840.

Pegolotti, Francesco di Balduccio. *La Pratica della Mercatura*. Ed. Allan Evans. Cambridge, Mass.: Mediaeval Academy of America, 1936.

Schäfer, K. H., ed. *Die Ausgaben der apostolischen Kammer unter Benedikt XII, Klemens VI und Innocenz VI*. Paderborn: Schöningh, 1914.

———. *Die Ausgaben der apostolischen Kammer unter den Päpsten Urban V und Gregor XI*. Paderborn: Schöningh, 1937.

———. *Vatikanische Quellen zür Geschichte der päpstlichen Hof-une-Finanzverwaltung: Die Ausgaben der apostolischen Kammer unter Johann XXII, nebst der Jahresbilanzen von 1316–1378*. Paderborn: Schöningh, 1911.

Teulet, Alexandre, ed. *Layettes du Trésor des Chartes*. Vol. 1. Paris: Librairie Plon, 1863.

Tierney, Brian, ed. *The Crisis of Church and State: 1050–1300*. Englewood Cliffs, N.J.: Prentice-Hall, 1964.

Voragine, Jacopo di. *The Golden Legend*. Trans. Christopher Stace. Ed. Richard Hamer. New York: Penguin, 1998.

Watt, Diane. *The Paston Women: Selected Letters. Translated from the Middle English with Introduction, Notes and Interpretative Essay*. Cambridge: D.S. Brewer, 2004.

SECONDARY SOURCES

Abulafia, David. *A Mediterranean Emporium: The Catalan Kingdom of Majorca*. Cambridge: Cambridge University Press, 1994.

Algrin, Isabelle. "Les Testaments dans la région montpelliéraine aux XIIe–XIVe siècles." Master's memoir I, Université de Montpellier 3, 2011.

Altmann, Barbara K., "Christine de Pizan as Maker of the Middle Ages." In Richard Utz and Elizabeth Emery, eds., *Cahier Calin: Makers of the Middle Ages: Essays in Honor of William Calin*. Kalamazoo, Mich.: Studies in Medievalism, 2011, 30–32.

Aries, Philippe. *Centuries of Childhood: A Social History of Family Life*. New York: Knopf Doubleday, 1965.

Aubenas, Roger. "Le Contrat d'*affrairamentum* dans le droit provençal du moyen âge." *Revue historique de droit français et étranger* 4th ser. 12 (1933): 477–524.

———. "La Famille dans l'ancienne Provence." *Annales d'Histoire Économique et Sociale* 8 (1936): 523–41.

Aubrun, Michel. *La Paroisse en France des origines au XVe siècle*. Paris: Picard, 1986.

Baratier, Édouard. *Histoire du commerce de Marseille*. Vol. 2. Paris: Librairie Pion, 1952.

——— "Marseille et Narbonne au XIVe siècle d'après les sources marseillaises." *Fédération historique du Languedoc méditerranéen et du Roussillon: Narbonne archéologie et histoire*, vol. 2, *Narbonne au moyen âge*. Montpellier, 1973, 85–92.

Bardsley, Sandy. *Women's Roles in the Middle Ages*. Westport Conn.: Greenwood Press, 2007.

Baron, Françoise et al. *Les Fastes du Gothique: Le Siècle de Charles V*. Paris: Ministère de la Culture. Éditions de la Réunion des Musées Nationaux, 1981.

Barron, Caroline. *London in the Later Middle Ages: Government and People, 1200–1500.* Oxford: Oxford University Press, 2004.

Batlle i Gallart, Carme. "La Casa burguesa en la Barcelona del siglo XIII." In *La Societat barcelonina a la baixa edat mitjana: Annexos d'història medieval.* Barcelona: Universitat de Barcelona, 1983, 1:9–52.

———. "La Casa i les béns de Bernat Durfort, cuitadà de Barcelona, a la fi del segle XIII." *Acta Historica et Archaeologica Mediaevalia* 9 (1988): 9–51.

———. "La Vida y las actividades de los mercaderes de Barcelona dedicados al comercio marítimo (siglo XIII)." In Luigi de Rosa, ed., *Le Genti del mare mediterraneo.* Naples: Lucio Pironti Editore, 1981, 1:291–339.

Baumel, Jean. *Histoire d'une seigneurie du Midi de la France, Naissance de Montpellier (985–1213).* Vol. 1. Montpellier: Éditions Causse, 1969.

———. *Histoire d'une seigneurie du Midi de la France: Montpellier sous la seigneurie de Jacques le Conquérent et des rois de Majorque: Rattachement de Montpelliéret et de Montpellier à la France, 1213–1349.* Vol. 2. Montpellier: Éditions Causse, 1971.

Bautier, Robert-Henri. "Les Foires de Champagne: Recherches sur une évolution historique." In *La Foire: Recueils de la société Jean Bodin, V.* Brussels: Éditions de la Librairie Encyclopédique, 1953, 97–148.

———. "Recherches sur les routes de l'Europe médiévale–1: De Paris et des Foires de Champagne à la Méditerranée par le Massif Central." *Bulletin Philologique et Historique* (1960/61): 99–143.

Beech, Georges. "Prosopography." In James M. Powell, ed., *Medieval Studies: An Introduction.* 2nd ed. Syracuse, N.Y.: Syracuse University Press, 1992, 185–226.

Béghin-LeGourriérec, Cécile. "Le Rôle économique des femmes dans les villes de la Sénéchaussée de Beaucaire à la fin du moyen âge (XIVe–XVe siècles)." 3 vols. Ph.D. dissertation, École des Hautes Études en Sciences Sociales-Paris, 2000.

———. "La Tentation du veuvage: Patrimoine, gestion et travail des veuves dans les villes du Bas-Languedoc aux XIVe et XVe siècles." In *La Famille, les femmes et le quotidien (XIVe–XVIII siècles).* Textes offerts à Christiane Klapisch-Zuber et rassemblés par Isabelle Chabot, Jérôme Hayez, et Didier Lett. Paris: Publications de la Sorbonne, 2006, 163–80.

Bender, Tovah. "Negotiating Marriage: Artisan Women in Fifteenth-Century Florentine Society." Ph.D. dissertation, University of Minnesota, 2009.

Bennett, Judith M. *History Matters: Patriarchy and the Challenge of Feminism.* Philadelphia: University of Pennsylvania Press, 2006.

———. *A Medieval Life: Cecilia Penifader of Brigstock, c. 1295–1344.* Boston: McGraw-Hill, 1999.

Bennett, Judith M., and Amy M. Froide, eds. *Singlewomen in the European Past, 1250–1800.* Philadelphia: University of Pennsylvania Press, 1999.

Bennett, Judith M., and Ruth Mazo Karras, eds. *Oxford Handbook on Medieval Women and Gender.* Oxford: Oxford University Press, 2013.

Bensch, Stephen P. *Barcelona and Its Rulers, 1096–1291.* Cambridge: Cambridge University Press, 1995.

Berger, Adolf. *Encyclopedic Dictionary of Roman Law.* Philadelphia: American Philosophical Society, 1953.

Berkvam, Doris Desclais. *Enfance et maternité dans la littérature française des XIIe et XIIIe siècles.* Paris: Honoré Champion, 1981.

Berlow, Rosalind. "The Sailing of the 'Saint-Esprit'." *Journal of Economic History* 39 (1979): 345–62.

Bernard, Antoine. *La Sépulture en droit canonique du décret de Gratien au concile de Trente.* Paris: Domat-Montchrestien, 1933.

Bisson, Thomas N. *Conservation of Coinage: Monetary Exploitation and Its Restraint in France, Catalonia, and Aragon (c. A.D. 1000–c. 1225).* Oxford: Oxford University Press, 1979.

Blanc, Alphonse. *Le Livre de comptes de Jacme Olivier, marchand narbonnais du XIVe siècle.* Paris: Alphonse Picard et fils, 1899.

Blomquist, Thomas. "Lineage, Land and Business in the Thirteenth Century: The Guidiccioni Family of Lucca." *Actum Luce: Rivista di studi Lucchesi* 9 (1980): 7–29.

Bompaire, Marc. "L'Atelier monétaire royale de Montpellier et la circulation monétaire en Bas Languedoc jusqu'au milieu du XVe siècle." Thesis, École des Chartes, 1980.

Bonds, William A. "Genoese Noblewomen and Gold Thread Manufacturing." *Medievalia et Humanistica* 17 (1966): 79–81.

Bonnet, Émile. "Les Séjours à Montpellier de Jacques le Conquérant roi d'Aragon." *Mémoires de la société archéologique de Montpellier* 2nd ser. 9 (1927): 153–232.

Boriès, Marcel. "Les Origines de l'Université de Montpellier." In *Les Universités du Languedoc au XIIIe siècle.* Cahiers de Fanjeaux 5. Toulouse: Privat, 1970, 92–107.

Bourdieu, Pierre. *The Logic of Practice.* London: Blackwell, 1990.

Bourin, Monique, John Drendal, and François Menant, eds. *Les Disettes dans la conjuncture de 1300 en Méditerranée occidentale.* Rome: École Française de Rome, 2011.

Bourquelot, Félix. *Étude sur les foires de Champagne.* 2 vols. Paris: Imprimerie Impériale, 1865.

Brown, Judith C., and Jordan Goodman. "Women and Industry in Florence." *Journal of Economic History* 40 (1980): 73–80.

Brun, Robert. "Notes sur le commerce des objets d'art en France et principalement à Avignon à la fin du XIVe siècle." *Bibliothèque de l'École des Chartes* 95 (1934): 327–46.

Bruschi, Christian. "La Tutelle des mineurs à Marseille (seconde moitié du XIIIème s.–début du XIVème s.)." In *Recueil de mémoires et travaux publié par la société d'histoire du droit et des institutions des anciens pays de droit écrit,* fasc. 13. Montpellier: Universite de Montpellier, 1985, 61–70.

Burkholder, Kristen M. "'Threads Bared': Dress and Textiles in Late Medieval English Wills." In Robin Netherton and Gale R. Owen-Crocker, eds., *Medieval Clothing and Textiles.* Vol. 1. Woodbridge: Boydell and Brewer, 2005, 133–53.

Burnham, Louisa A. *So Great a Light, So Great a Smoke: The Beguin Heretics of Languedoc.* Ithaca, N.Y.: Cornell University Press, 2008.

Caille, Jacqueline. "Emengarde, Viscountess of Narbonne (1127/29–1196/97): A Great Female Figure of the Aristocracy of the Midi." In Kathryn L. Reyerson, ed., *Medieval*

Narbonne: A City at the Heart of the Troubadour World. Aldershot: Ashgate, 2005, X:1–46. Also published as "Ermengarde, vicomtesse de Narbonne (1127/29–1196/97): Une grande figure féminine du Midi aristocratique." *Narbonne: Fédération Historique du Languedoc Méditerranéen et du Roussillon* (1994): 9–50.

———. *Hôpitaux et charité publique à Narbonne au Moyen Âge*. Toulouse: Privat, 1977.

———. "Urban Expansion in Languedoc from the Eleventh to the Fourteenth Century: The Example of Narbonne and Montpellier." In Kathryn Reyerson and John Drendel, eds., *Urban and Rural: Communities in Medieval France: Provence and Languedoc, 1000–1500*. Leiden: Brill, 1998, 51–72.

Carpentier, Elisabeth. "Autour de la peste noire: Famines et épidémies dans l'histoire du XIVe siècle." *Annales: economies, sociétés, civilisations* 17 (1962): 1062–92.

Carrère, Claude. *Barcelone, centre économique au temps des difficultés, 1380–1462*. 2 vols. Paris: Mouton, 1967.

Casey, Kathleen. "The Cheshire Cat: Reconstructing the Experience of Medieval Women." In Berenice A. Carroll, ed., *Liberating Women's History: Theoretical and Critical Essays*. Urbana: University of Illinois Press, 1976, 224–49.

Castaing-Sicard, Mireille. *Monnaies féodales et circulation monétaire en Languedoc (Xe–XIIIe siècles)*. Toulouse: Marc Bloch, 1961.

Chabot, Isabelle. "Widowhood and Poverty in Late Medieval Florence," *Continuity and Change* 3 (1988): 291–311.

Charrin, Louis de. *Les Testaments dans la région de Montpellier au moyen âge*. Ambilly: Coopérative Les Presses de Savoie, 1961.

Chastang, Pierre. *La Ville, le gouvernement et l'écrit à Montpellier*. Paris: Publications de la Sorbonne, 2013).

Cheyette, Fredric L. *Ermengard of Narbonne and the World of the Troubadours*. Ithaca, N.Y.: Cornell University Press, 2001.

———. "The Sovereign and the Pirates, 1332." *Speculum* 45 (1970): 40–68.

Chiffoleau, Jacques. *La Comptabilité de l'au-delà: Les hommes, la mort et la religion dans la région d'Avignon à la fin du moyen âge (vers 1320–vers 1480)*. Rome: École Française de Rome, 1980.

Chojnacki, Stanley. *Women and Men in Renaissance Venice. Twelve Essays on Patrician Society* (Baltimore: Johns Hopkins University Press, 2000).

Cholvy, Gérard., ed. *Le Diocèse de Montpellier*. Paris: Éditions Beauchesne, 1976.

———. *Histoire de Montpellier*. Toulouse: Privat, 1984.

La Circulation des nouvelles au moyen âge. Société des Historiens Médiévistes de l'Enseignement Supérieur Public. Paris: Publications de la Sorbonne, École Française de Rome, 1994.

Citarella, Armand O. "A Puzzling Question Concerning the Relations Between the Jewish Communities of Christian Europe and Those Represented in Geniza Documents." *Journal of the American Oriental Society* 91 (1971): 390–97.

Combes, Jean. "Finances municipales et oppositions sociales à Montpellier au commencement du XIVe siècle." In *Vivarais et Languedoc, Fédération historique du Languedoc méditerranéen et du Roussillon,* 44e Congrès, Privas, May 1971. Montpellier: Université Paul Valéry, 1972, 99–120.

———. "Les Foires en Languedoc au moyen âge." *Annales: économies, societies, civilisations* 13 (1958): 231–59.

———. "L'Industrie et le commerce des toiles à Montpellier de la fin du XIIIe siècle au milieu du XVe." In *Recueil de mémoires et travaux publié par la société de l'histoire du droit et des institutions des anciens pays de droit écrit,* fasc. 9: *Mélanges Roger Aubenas.* Montpellier: Faculté de droit et des sciences économiques de Montpellier, 1974, 181–212.

———. "Un marchand de Chypre bourgeois de Montpellier." In *Études médiévales offertes à Augustin Fliche.* Montpellier, 1950, 33–39.

———. "La Monnaie de Montpellier et les gisements d'or et d'argent dans les Cévennes méridionales au XVe siècle." *Mines et mineurs en Languedoc-Roussillon et régions voisines de l'Antiquité à nos jours, Fédération historique du Languedoc méditerranéen et du Roussillon* 49e congrès, Alès. Montpellier, 1977, 145–55.

———. "Quelques remarques sur les bourgeois de Montpellier au moyen âge." In *Recueil de mémoires et travaux publié par la société d'histoire du droit et des institutions des anciens pays de droit écrit,* fasc. 7: *Mélanges Pierre Tisset.* Montpellier: Faculté de droit et des sciences économiques de Montpellier, Narbonne: Fédération Historique du Languedoc Méditerranéen, 93–132.

———. "Transports terrestres à travers la France central à la fin du XIVe siècle et au commencement du XVe siècle." *Fédération historique,* 29e Congrès, Mende, 1955, 43–47.

Cosman, Madeleine Pelner. *Fabulous Feasts: Medieval Cookery and Ceremony.* New York: George Braziller, 1976.

Courtemanche, Andrée. *La Richesse des femmes: Patrimoines et gestion à Manosque au XIVe siècle.* Paris: Vrin, 1993.

———. "Women, Family, and Immigration in Fifteenth-Century Manosque: The Case of the Dodi Family of Barcelonnette." In Kathryn Reyerson and John Drendel, eds., *Urban and Rural Communities in Medieval France: Provence and Languedoc, 1000–1500.* Leiden: Brill, 1998, 101–27.

Crook, J. A. "Feminine Inadequacy and the *Senatusconsultum Velleianum.*" In Beryl Rawson, ed., *The Family in Ancient Rome: New Perspectives.* Ithaca, N.Y.: Cornell University Press, 83–92.

Cugnasse, Claude. "Activité économique et milieu humain à Montauban au XIVe siècle, d'après le registre de Barthélémy Bonis." *Annales du Midi* 69 (1957): 207–27.

Dean, Trevor, ed. *Marriage in Italy, 1300–1650.* Cambridge: Cambridge University Press, 1998.

Débax, Hélène. *La Féodalité languedocienne (XIe–XIIe S.): Serments, hommage, et fiefs dans le Languedoc des Trencavel.* Toulouse: Presses Universitaires du Mirail, 2003.

deMause, Lloyd, ed. *The History of Childhood.* New York: HarperTorchbook, 1975.

Démians d'Archimbaud, Gabrielle et al. *Aujourd'hui le moyen âge: Archéologie et vie quotidienne en France méridionale.* Sénanque: Direction du Patrimoine, 1981–83.

Dérens, Jean-Arnault. "Montpellier, ville ouverte: 1. Information, circulation et réception des nouvelles à la fin du XIVe siècle." *Bulletin Historique de la Ville de Montpellier* 21 (1997): 37–50.

————. "Les Ordres mendiants à Montpellier: 'Religieux de la ville nouvelle' ou religieux du consulat?" *Annales du Midi* 107 (1995): 277–98.

Dillard, Heath. *Daughters of the Reconquest: Women in Castilian Town Society, 1100–1300.* Cambridge: Cambridge University Press, 1984.

Dion, Roger. *Histoire de la vigne et du vin en France des origines au XIX siècle.* Paris: Clavreuil, 1959; re-edition, Paris: Flammarion, 1991; Paris, CNRS, 2010.

Dixon, Suzanne. "Infirmitas Sexus: Womanly Weakness in Roman Law." *Tijdschrift voor Rechts-Geschiedenis: The Legal History Review* 52 (1984): 242–71.

Dognon, Paul. *Les Institutions politiques et administratives du pays de Languedoc du XIIIe siècle aux guerres de religion.* Toulouse: Privat, 1895.

————. "De quelques mots employés au moyen âge dans le midi pour désigner des classes d'hommes: *platerii, platearii.*" *Annales du Midi* 11 (1899): 348–58.

Donahue, Charles, Jr. *Law, Marriage, and Society in the Later Middle Ages.* Cambridge: Cambridge University Press, 2007.

Duby, Georges. *L'Économie rurale et la vie des campagnes dans l'Occident medieval.* 2 vols. Paris: Aubier, 1962.

————. *La Société aux XIe et XIIe siècles dans la région mâconnaise.* Paris: A. Colin, 1953.

Duffaut, H. "Recherches historiques sur les prénoms en Languedoc." *Annales du Midi* 12 (1900): 180–93, 329–54.

Dugrand, Roger. "La Garrigue montpelliéraine." *Bulletin de la société languedocienne de géographie* 2nd ser. 34 (1963): 3–266.

Duhamel-Amado, Claudie. *Genèse des lignages méridionaux.* Toulouse: CNRS-Université de Toulouse-Le Mirail, 2001.

Dulieu, Louis. *La Médicine à Montpellier.* Vol. 1, *Le Moyen Âge.* Avignon: Les Presses Universelles, 1975.

Dupont, André. "L'Exploitation du sel sur les étangs de Languedoc (XIe–XIIIe siècles)." *Annales du Midi* 70 (1958): 7–22.

Durliat, Marcel. *L'Art dans le royaume de Majorque: Les Débuts de l'art gothique en Roussillon, en Cerdagne et aux Baléares.* Toulouse: Privat, 1962.

Elder, Glen. "Family History and the Life Course." In Tamara K. Hareven, ed., *Transitions: The Family and the Life Course in Historical Perspective.* New York: Academic Press, 1978, 17–64.

Ellul, Jacques. "Notes sur les impôts municipaux à Montpellier aux XIIIe et XIVe siècles." *Revue historique de droit français et étranger* 17 (1938): 365–403.

Emery, Richard W. "The Black Death of 1348 in Perpignan." *Speculum* 42 (1967): 611–23.

————. *The Friars in Medieval France: A Catalogue of French Mendicant Convents, 1200–1550.* New York: Columbia University Press, 1962.

————. *The Jews of Perpignan in the Thirteenth Century: An Economic Study Based on Notarial Registers.* New York: Columbia University Press, 1959.

Elliott, Dyan. "The Three Ages of Joan Scott." In "AHR Forum: Revisiting 'Gender: A Useful Category of Historical Analysis'." *American Historical Review* 113 (2008): 1390–1403.

Epstein, Steven A. *Genoa and the Genoese, 958–1528.* Chapel Hill: University of North Carolina Press, 1996.

———. *Wills and Wealth in Medieval Genoa, 1150–1250.* Cambridge, Mass.: Harvard University Press, 1984.

Evergates, Theodore, ed. *Aristocratic Women in Medieval France.* Philadelphia: University of Pennsylvania Press, 1999.

Fabre, Ghislaine, Daniel Le Blévec, and Denis Menjot, eds. *Les Ports et la navigation en Mediterranée au Moyen Âge.* Montpellier: DRAC, 2009.

Fabre, Ghislaine, and Thierry Lochard. *Montpellier: La Ville médiévale.* Paris: Imprimerie Nationale, 1992.

Facinger, Marion F. "A Study of Medieval Queenship: Capetian France, 987–1237." *Studies in Medieval and Renaissance History* 5 (1968): 1–48.

Famille et parenté dans l'Occident medieval: Actes du colloque de Paris (June 1974), organized by L'École Pratique des Hautes Études (VIe section) en collaboration avec le Collège de France et l'École Française de Rome. Communications et débats présentés par Georges Duby et Jacques Le Goff. Rome: École Française de Rome, 1977.

Farmer, Sharon. "Medieval Paris and the Mediterranean: The Evidence from the Silk Industry." *French Historical Studies* 37 (2014): 383–419.

———. *The Silk Industries of Medieval Paris: Artisanal Migration, Technological Innovation, and Gendered Experience.* Philadelphia: University of Pennsylvania Press, 2016.

Favreaux, Robert. "Les Changeurs du royaume de France sous le règne de Louis XI." *Bibliothèque de l'École des Chartes* 122 (1964): 216–51.

Fawtier, Robert. *The Capetian Kings of France: Monarchy and Nation, 987–1328.* London: Macmillan, 1960.

Febvre, Lucien. "Fils de riches ou nouveaux riches?" *Annales: économies, sociétés, civilisations* 1 (1946): 139–42.

Figueras, Lluis To. "Systèmes successoraux et mobilité sociale aux alentours de 1300: Les Contrats de marriage d'Amer et de Besalú en Vieille Catalogne." In Sandro Carocci, ed., *La Mobilità sociale nel medioevo.* Rome: École Française de Rome, 2010, 453–90.

Forestié, Édouard. *Les Livres de comptes des frères Bonis, marchands montalbanais du XIVe siècle.* 2 vols. Paris: Honoré Champion, 1890, 1893.

Fournial, Étienne. *Histoire monétaire de l'Occident medieval.* Paris: Fernand Nathan, 1970.

Fournier, P.-F. "Pierre Jame (*Petrus Jacobi*) d'Aurillac, jurisconsulte." *Histoire littéraire de France* 36 (1927): 481–521.

Freedman, Paul. *Out of the East: Spices and the Medieval Imagination.* New Haven, Conn.: Yale University Press, 2008.

Gaillard, Bernardin. *La Tutelle maternelle.* Montpellier: Firmin et Montane, 1897.

Galano, Lucie. "À table! Festivités et banquets au consulat de Montpellier à la fin du Moyen Âge." *Bulletin historique de la ville de Montpellier* 36 (2014): 60–72.

Galtier, Gaston. "Les Conditions géographiques de Montpellier," in *Mélanges géographiques offerts á Philippe Arbos* (Clermont-Ferrand: Impr. G. de Bussac, 1953), 237–46.

———. *Le Vignoble du Languedoc méditerranéen et du Roussillon: Étude comparative d'un vignoble de masse.* 3 vols. Montpellier: Causse, Graille et Castelnau, 1960.

Gaulejac, Bernard de. *Histoire de l'orfèvrerie en Rouergue.* Rodez: Société des Lettres, Sciences et Arts de l'Aveyron, 1938.

Gauthier, Marie-Madeleine. *Émaux du moyen âge occidental.* Fribourg: Office du Livre, 1972.

Geremek, Bronislav. *Les Marginaux parisiens aux XIVe et XVe siècles.* Paris: Flammarion, 1976.

Germain, Alexandre. "La Charité publique et hospitalière à Montpellier au moyen-âge." *Mémoires de la société archéologique de Montpellier* 4 (1856): 481–552.

———. *Histoire de la commune de Montpellier.* 3 vols. Montpellier: Imprimerie J. Martel ainé, 1851.

———. *Histoire du commerce de Montpellier antérieurement à l'ouverture du port de Cette.* 2 vols. Montpellier: Imprimerie de Jean Martel ainé, 1861.

———. "La Paroisse à Montpellier au moyen âge." *Mémoires de la société archéologioque de Montpellier* 5 (1860–69): 1–56.

Géze, J.-B. "Les Drailles du Départment de l'Hérault." Montpellier: Office Agricole Départemental de l'Hérault, 1926.

Gide, Paul. *Étude sur la condition privée de la femme.* Paris: L. Larose et Forcel, 1885.

Gies, Frances and Joseph. *Marriage and the Family in the Middle Ages.* New York: Harper and Row, 1987.

———. *Women in the Middle Ages.* New York: Thomas Y. Crowell, 1978; Barnes and Noble, 1980.

Given, James B. *Inquisition and Medieval Society: Power, Discipline, and Resistance in Languedoc.* Ithaca, N.Y.: Cornell University Press, 1997.

Goldberg, P. J. P. "Female Labour, Service and Marriage in the Late Medieval Urban North." *Northern History* 22 (1986): 18–38.

Gouron, André. "Diffusion des consulats méridionaux et expansion du droit romain aux XIIe et XIIIe siècles." *Bibliothèque de l'École des Chartes* 121 (1964): 26–76.

———. "Les Étapes de la pénétration du droit romain au XIIe siècle dans l'ancienne Septimanie." *Annales du Midi* 69 (1957): 103–20.

———. "Grands bourgeois et nouveaux notables: L'Aspect social de la révolution montpelliéraine de 1204." *Recueil de mémoires et travaux de la société d'histoire du droit et des institutions des anciens pays de droit écrit,* 15 (1991): 27–48.

———. "L'Origine du Tribunal du Petit-Scel de Montpellier." *Fédération historique du Languedoc méditerranéen et du Roussillon,* Mende (Montpellier, 1955), 55–70.

———. "La *Potestas statuendi* dans le droit coutumier montpellirain du treizième siècle." In *Diritto commune et diritti locali nella storia dell'Europa.* Atti del congress di Varenna (June 12–15, 1979). Milan: Guiffrè, 1980, 95–118.

———. *La Réglementation des métiers en Languedoc au moyen âge.* Geneva: Droz, 1958.

Gouron, André, and Jean Hilaire. "Les 'sceaux' rigoureux du Midi de la France." *Recueil de mémoires et travaux publié par la société d'histoire du droit et des institutions des anciens pays de droit écrit*, fasc. 4 (Montpellier, 1958), 41–77.

Grand, Roger. "Un jurisconsulte du XIVe siècle: Pierre Jacobi, auteur de la *Practica aurea*." *Bibliothèque de l'École des Chartes* 58 (1918): 68–101.

———. "Nouveaux documents sur le jurisconsulte Pierre Jacobi et sa famille," *Bibliothèque de l'École des Chartes* 98 (1937): 221–33.

Guerreau-Jalabert, Anita. "Sur les structures de parenté dans l'Europe médiévale," *Annales: histoire sciences sociales* 36 (1981): 1028–49.

Guillemain, Bernard. *La Cour pontificale d'Avignon (1309–1376): Étude d'une société*. Paris: Boccard, 1966.

Guillerme, André E. *The Age of Water: The Urban Environment in the North of France, A.D. 300–1800*. College Station: Texas A&M University Press, 1988.

Guiraud, Louise. *Le Collège Saint Benoît, le Collège Saint-Pierre, le Collège du Pape*. Montpellier: J. Martel aîné, 1890.

———. *La Paroisse de Saint-Denis de Montpellier: Étude historique*. Montpellier: Librairie J. Calas, 1887.

———. "Recherches topographiques sur Montpellier au moyen âge." *Mémoires de la société archéologique de Montpellier* 2nd ser. 2 (1895): 89–335.

Hajnal, J. "European Marriage Patterns in Perspective." In D. V. Glass and David E. C. Eversley, eds., *Population in History: Essays in Historical Demography* (London: E. Arnold, 1965), 101–46.

Haluska-Rausch, Elizabeth. "Family, Property, and Power: Women in Medieval Montpellier, 985–1213." Ph.D. dissertation, Harvard University, 1998.

———. "Unwilling Partners: Conflict and Ambition in the Marriage of Peter II of Aragon and Marie de Montpellier." In Theresa Earenfight, ed., *Queenship and Political Power in Medieval and Early Modern Spain*. Aldershot: Ashgate, 2005, 3–20.

Hanawalt, Barbara A. *Growing Up in Medieval London: The Experience of Childhood in History*. New York: Oxford University Press, 1993.

———. *"Of Good and Ill Repute": Gender and Social Control in Medieval England*. New York: Oxford University Press, 1998.

———. *The Wealth of Wives: Women, Law, and Economy in Late Medieval London*. Oxford: Oxford University Press, 2007.

Hareven, Tamara. "L'Histoire de la famille et complexité du changement social." *Cahiers d'Histoire* 45 (2000): 9–34, 205–32.

Hayez, Jérome. "La Stanza di Vignone: Identité et migration entre la Toscane et Avignon aux XIVe et XVe siècles." Doctoral thesis, Université de Paris IV-Sorbonne, 1993.

Heers, Jacques. *Le Clan familial au moyen âge*. Paris: Presses Universitaires de France, 1974.

———. *Esclaves et domestiques au moyen-âge dans le monde méditerranéen*. Paris: Fayard, 1981.

Heller, Sarah-Grace. *Fashion in Medieval France*. Cambridge: D.S. Brewer, 2007.

————. "Sumptuary Legislation in Thirteenth-Century France, Languedoc and Italy: Limiting Yardage and Changes of Clothes." In E. Jane Burns, ed., *Medieval Fabrications: Dress Textiles, Clothwork, and Other Cultural Imaginings* (New York: St. Martin's, 2004), 181–207.

Henneman, John Bell. *Royal Taxation in Fourteenth-Century France: The Development of War Financing, 1322–1356.* Princeton, N.J.: Princeton University Press, 1971.

Herlihy, David. "Land, Family, and Women in Continental Europe, 701–1200." *Traditio* 18 (1962): 89–120.

————. "Mapping Households in Medieval Italy." *Catholic Historical Review* 58 (1972): 1–19.

————. *Medieval Households.* Cambridge, Mass.: Harvard University Press, 1985.

————. *Pisa in the Early Renaissance.* New Haven, Conn.: Yale University Press, 1958.

Herlihy, David, and Christiane Klapisch-Zuber. *Tuscans and Their Families: A Study of the Florentine Catasto of 1427.* New Haven, Conn.: Yale University Press, 1985.

Hilaire, Jean. "Exercise de style: Une affaire de succession à Montpellier au début du XIVe siècle." *Recueil de mémoires et travaux publié par la société de l'histoire du droit et des institutions des anciens pays de droit écrit,* fasc. 7: *Mélanges Pierre Tisset* (Montpellier, 1970): 283–99.

————. "*Patria potestas* et pratique montpelliéraine au moyen âge: Symbolisme du droit écrit." *Société pour l'histoire du droit et des institutions des anciens pays bourguignons, comtois et romands* 30: *Mémoires Georges Chevrier.* Dijon: Faculté de droit et des sciences politiques, 1972. 421–36.

————. *Le Régime des biens entre époux dans la région de Montpellier du début du XIIIe siècle à la fin du XVe siècle.* Montpellier: Imprimérie Causse, Graille et Castelnau, 1957.

Hoffman, Richard C. "Medieval Fishing." In Paolo Squatriti, ed., *Working with Water in Medieval Europe: Technology and Resource Use.* Leiden: Brill, 2000, 331–93.

Hohenberg Paul M., and Lynn Hollen Lees. *The Making of Urban Europe.* Cambridge, Mass.: Harvard University Press, 1985.

Howell, Martha C. "Fixing Movables: Gifts by Testament in Late Medieval Douai." *Past and Present* 150 (1996): 3–45.

————. *The Marriage Exchange: Property, Social Place, and Gender in Cities of the Low Countries, 1300–1550.* Chicago: University of Chicago Press, 1998.

Hughes, Diane Owen. "Domestic Ideals and Social Behavior: Evidence from Medieval Genoa." In Carol Neel, ed., *Medieval Families: Perspectives on Marriage, Household, and Children.* Toronto: University of Toronto Press and Medieval Academy of America, 2004, 125–56.

————. "Toward Historical Ethnography: Notarial Records and Family History in the Middle Ages." *Historical Methods Newsletter* 7 (1973): 61–71.

————. "Urban Growth and Family Structure in Medieval Genoa." *Past and Present* 66 (1975): 3–28.

Hutton, Shennan. *Women and Economic Activities in Late Medieval Ghent.* New York: Palgrave-Macmillan, 2011.

Jager, Eric. *Blood Royal: A True Tale of Crime and Detection in Medieval Paris.* New York: Little Brown, 2014.

Jannella, Cecilia. *Simone Martini.* Florence: Scala, Riverside, 1989.

Jehel, Georges. *Aigues-Mortes: Un port pour un roi; Les Capétiens et la Méditerranée.* Roanne/Le Coteau: Horvath, 1985.

Jordan, William Chester. *The French Monarchy and the Jews from Philip Augustus to the Last Capetians.* Philadelphia: University of Pennsylvania Press, 1989.

———. *The Great Famine: Northern Europe in the Early Fourteenth Century.* Princeton, N.J.: Princeton University Press, 1996.

Juifs et judaïsme de Languedoc. Cahiers de Fanjeaux 12. Toulouse: Privat, 1977.

Karras, Ruth Mazo. *Common Women: Prostitution and Sexuality in Medieval England.* New York: Oxford University Press, 1996.

Kelleher, Marie A. *The Measure of Woman: Law and Female Identity in the Medieval Crown of Aragon.* Philadephia: University of Pennsylvania Press, 2010.

Kelly-Gadol, Joan. "Did Women Have a Renaissance?" In Renate Bridenthal, Claudia Koonz, and Susan Stuard, eds., *Becoming Visible: Women in European History.* 2nd ed. Boston: Houghton Mifflin, 1987, 174–201.

Kent, Francis William. *Household and Lineage in Renaissance Florence.* Princeton, N.J.: Princeton University Press, 1977.

Kirshner, Julius. "Wives' Claims Against Insolvent Husbands in Late Medieval Italy." In Julius Kirshner and Suzanne F. Wemple, eds., *Women of the Medieval World: Essays in Honor of John Mundy.* Oxford: Blackwell, 1985, 256–303.

Kirshner, Julius, and Anthony Molho. "The Dowry Fund and the Marriage Market in Early Quattrocentro Florence." *Journal of Modern History* 50 (1978): 403–38.

Klapisch-Zuber, Christiane. "'The Cruel Mother': Maternity, Widowhood, and Dowry in Florence in the Fourteenth and Fifteenth Centuries." In Klapisch-Zuber, *Women, Family, and Ritual in Renaissance Italy,* 117–31.

———. "'Kin, Friends, and Neighbors': The Urban Territory of a Merchant Family in 1400." In Klapisch-Zuber, *Women, Family, and Ritual in Renaissance Italy,* 68–93.

———. *Women, Family, and Ritual in Renaissance Italy.* Trans. Lydia G. Cochrane. Chicago: University of Chicago Press, 1985.

Kowaleski, Maryanne. "The History of Urban Families in England." *Journal of Medieval History* 14 (1988): 47–63.

———. "Singlewomen in Medieval and Early Modern Europe: The Demographic Perspective." In Judith M. Bennett and Amy M. Froide, eds., *Singlewomen in the European Past, 1250–1800.* Philadelphia: University of Pennsylvania Press, 1999, 38–81.

Kowaleski, Maryanne, and Judith M. Bennett. "Crafts, Gilds, and Women in the Middle Ages: Fifty Years After Marian K. Dale." *Signs: Journal of Women in Culture and Society* 14 (1989): 474–88. Reprinted in Judith M. Bennett, Elizabeth A. Clark, Jean

F. O'Barr, B. Anne Vilen, and Sarah Westphal-Wihl, eds., *Sisters and Workers in the Middle Ages*. Chicago: University of Chicago Press, 1989, 11–25.

Krueger, Hilmar. "Genoese Merchants, Their Partnerships and Investments, 1155–1164." *Studi in onore di Armando Sapori*. Milan: Istituto Editoriale Cisalpino, 1957, 1: 259–71.

Kühnel, Harry, ed. *Kommunikation und Alltag in Spätmitellalter und früher Neuzeit: Internationaler Kongress Krems an der Donau (9 bis 12 Oktober 1990)*. Vienna: Oesterreichischen Akademie des Wissenschaften, 1992.

Laborde, Léon de. *Glossaire français du moyen âge . . . précédé de l'inventaire des bijoux de Louis, Duc d'Anjou dressé vers 1360*. Paris: A. Labitte, 1872.

Laborderie-Boulou, P. "La Viguerie de Montpellier au XIIe siècle." *Archives de la ville de Montpellier, Inventaires et documents*, vol. 4. Montpellier: Imprimerie Roumégous et Déhan, 1920.

Laclotte, Michel. *Les Fastes du Gothique: Le Siècle de Charles V. Catalogue de l'exposition*. Paris: Grand Palais, 1981–82.

Lamazou-Duplan, Véronique. "Les Élites toulousaines et leurs demeures à la fin du Moyen Âge d'après les registres notariés: Entre maison possedée et maison habitée." In Maurice Scellès and Anne-Laure Napoléone, eds., *La Maison au Moyen Âge dans le Midi de la France*, vol. 1. Toulouse: Société archéologique du Midi de la France, 2003, 40–61.

———. "Vie familiale et univers féminins à Toulouse à la fin du Moyen Âge d'après les registres des notaires." *Études Roussillonnaises* 25 (2013): 115–25.

Landes-Mallet, Anne-Marie. *La Famille en Rouergue au Moyen Âge 1269–1345: Étude de la pratique notariale*. Rouen: L'Université de Rouen, 1985.

Laumonier, Lucie. "Exemptions et dégrèvements: Les Montpelliérains face à la fiscalité (fin XIVe et XVe siècles)." *Bulletin historique de la ville de Montpellier* 35 (2013): 34–47.

———. *Solitudes et solidarités en ville: Montpellier, mi XIIIe–fin XVe siècles*. Turnhout: Brepols, 2015.

———. "Vivre seul à Montpellier à la fin du Moyen Âge." Doctoral thesis, Université de Sherbrooke (QC) and Université de Montpellier 3, 2013.

Laumonier, Lucie, and Lucie Galano. *Montpellier au Moyen Âge: Bilan et approches nouvelles*. Turnhout: Brepols, forthcoming.

Lecoy de la Marche, Albert. *Les Relations politiques de la France avec le royaume de Majorque*. 2 vols. Paris: E. Leroux, 1892.

LeRoy Ladurie, Emmanuel. *Les Paysans de Languedoc*. Paris: SEVPEN, 1966.

———. "Systèmes de coutume: Structures familiales et coutume d'héritage en France au XVIème siècle." *Annales: économies, sociétés, civilisations* 27 (1972): 825–46. Trans. as "A System of Customary Law: Family Structures and Inheritance Customs in Sixteenth-Century France," in Robert Forster and Orest Ranum, eds., *Family and Society: Selections from the Annales*. Baltimore, Md.: Johns Hopkins University Press, 1976, 75–103.

Lewis, Archibald R. *The Development of Southern French and Catalan Society, 718–1050*. Austin: University of Texas Press, 1965.

———. "The Development of Town Government in Twelfth-Century Montpellier." *Speculum* 22 (1947): 51–67.

———. "Popular Assemblies and the Charter of Liberties of Montpellier in 1202." In *Album Elemér Malyusz*. Brussels: Librairie Encyclopédique, 1976, 49–59.

———. "Seigneurial Administration in Twelfth-Century Montpellier." *Speculum* 22 (1947): 562–77.

Lightbown, R. W. *Secular Goldsmiths' Work in Medieval France: A History*. London: Society of Antiquaries of London, 1978.

Lightfoot, Dana Wessel. "The Projects of Marriage: Spousal Choice, Dowries and Domestic Service in Early Fifteenth-Century Valencia." *Viator: Medieval and Renaissance Studies* 40, 1 (2009): 333–53.

Livingston, Amy. *Out of Love for My Kin: Aristocratic Family Life in the Lands of the Loire, 1000–1200*. Ithaca, N.Y.: Cornell University Press, 2010.

Lopez, Robert S. "Aux origines du capitalisme génois." *Annales d'histoire économique et sociale* 9 (1937): 429–54.

———. "The Evolution of Land Transport in the Middle Ages." *Past and Present* 9 (1956): 17–29.

———. "Hard Times and Investment in Culture." In *The Renaissance, a Symposium, February 8–10, 1952*. New York: Metropolitan Museum of Art, 1953, 19–34.

———. "Proxy in Medieval Trade." In William C. Jordan, Bruce McNab, and Teofilo F. Ruiz, eds., *Order and Innovation in the Middle Ages: Essays in Honor of Joseph R. Strayer*. Princeton, N.J.: Princeton University Press, 1976, 187–194.

Lopez , Robert S., and Irving W. Raymond. *Medieval Trade in the Mediterranean World*. New York: Columbia University Press, 1955.

Lorcin, Marie-Thérèse. "Les Clauses religieuses dans les testaments du plat pays lyonnais aux XIVe et XVe siècles." *Moyen Âge* (78 no. 2) 4th ser. 27 (1972): 301–10.

Lynch, Joseph H. *Godparents and Kinship in Early Medieval Europe*. Princeton, N.J.: Princeton University Press, 1986.

Mafart, Bertrand-Yves. "Approche de la mortalité maternelle au moyen âge en Provence." In *La femme pendant le moyen âge et l'époque moderne*. Dossiers de documentation archéologique 17. Nice: Université de Nice, 1994, 207–19.

Manke, John. "Red Is the New Black: The Merchant Response to Changing Trends in Fifteenth-Century Culture." Conference paper, Newberry Center for Renaissance Studies: Multidisciplinary Graduate Student Conference, January 24–26, 2013.

———. "The Usefulness of Sensory Analysis to Economic History." Seminar paper, "New Directions in the Middle Ages, 1100–1500," University of Minnesota, 2012.

Marin-Rambier, Anne-Catherine. "Montpellier à la fin du Moyen Âge d'après les compoix (1380–1450). Thesis, École Nationale des Chartes, 1980.

Maritaux, Pascal. "Le Plafond de l'hôtel des Carcassonne à Montpellier." In Carnet de Recherche, *L'Art à la loupe: Conservation-restauration au LA3M*. http://curatio.hypotheses.org.15. Accessed 24 July 2016.

Martines, Lauro. *Power and Imagination: City-States in Renaissance Italy*. New York: Vintage Books-Random House, 1979.

Mayali, Laurent. *Droit savant et coutumes: L'Exclusion des filles dotées–XVème siècles*. Frankfurt am Main: Vittorio Klostermann, 1987.

Mayer, Paul. "Le Livre-journal de Maître Ugo Teralh, notaire et drapier à Forcalquier." *Notice et extraits des manuscrits de la Bibliothèque Nationale* 36 (1899): 129–70.

Mazzaoui, Maureen. *The Italian Cotton Industry in the Later Middle Ages, 1100–1600*. Cambridge: Cambridge University Press, 1981.

Mazzotta, Giuseppe. *The Worlds of Petrarch*. Durham, N.C.: Duke University Press, 1993.

McDonough, Susan Alice. *Witnesses, Neighbors, and Community in Late Medieval Marseille*. New York: Palgrave Macmillan, 2013.

McIntosh, Marjorie K. "The Benefits and Drawbacks of *Femme Sole* Status in England, 1300–1630." *Journal of British Studies* 44 (2005): 410–38.

McNamara, Jo-Ann, and Suzanne Wemple, "The Power of Women Through the Family in Medieval Europe: 500–1100." *Feminist Studies* 1 (1972): 126–41.

Meynial, Edmond. "Des renonciations au moyen âge et dans notre ancien droit." *Revue historique de droit français et étranger* ser. 3 25 (1901): 241–77.

Michaud, Francine. *Un signe des temps: Accroissement des crises familiales autour du patrimoine à Marseille à la fin du XIIIe siècle*. Toronto: Pontifical Institute of Mediaeval Studies, 1994.

Miller, Tanya Stabler. *The Beguines of Medieval Paris: Gender, Patronage, and Spiritual Authority*. Philadelphia: University of Pennsylvania Press, 2014.

Mirrer, Louise, ed. *Upon My Husband's Death: Widows in the Literature and Histories of Medieval Europe*. Ann Arbor: University of Michigan Press, 1992.

Miskimin, Harry A. *The Economy of Early Renaissance Europe, 1300–1460*. Cambridge: Cambridge University Press, 1975.

Molho, Anthony, R. Barducci, G. Battista, and F. Donnini. "Genealogy and Marriage Alliance: Memories of Power in Late Medieval Florence." In S. K. Cohn, Jr., and S. A. Epstein, eds., *Portraits of Medieval and Renaissance Living: Essays in Honor of David Herlihy*. Ann Arbor: University of Michigan Press, 1990, 39–70.

Montel, Achille. "Le Catalogue des chapellenies." *Revue de Langues Romanes* 3 (1872): 292–310; 4 (1873): 5–43.

Montpellier: Vingt années de dons, acquisitions et restauration, 1968–1988. Montpellier: Société Archéologique de Montpellier, 1988.

Moreau, Marthe. *L'Âge d'or des religieuses: Monastères féminins du Languedoc méditerranéen au moyen âge*. Montpellier: Presses du Languedoc, 1988.

———. "Les Moniales du diocèse de Maguelone au XIIIe siècle." In *La Femme dans la vie religieuse du Languedoc*. Cahiers de Fanjeaux 23. Toulouse: Privat, 1988, 241–60.

Mummey, Kevin. "Women, Slavery, and Community in Late Fourteenth-Century Mallorca." Ph.D. dissertation, University of Minnesota, 2013.

Mundy, John Hine. *Men and Women at Toulouse in the Age of the Cathars*. Toronto: Pontifical Institute of Medieval Studies, 1990.

Munro, John H. *Textiles, Towns, and Trade: Essays in the Economic History of Late-Medieval England and the Low Countries*. Variorum Collected Studies. Aldershot: Ashgate, 1994.

———. *Wool, Cloth and Gold: The Struggle for Bullion in Anglo-Burgundian Trade, 1340–1478*. Toronto: University of Toronto Press, 1973.

Murray, James A. *Bruges, Cradle of Capitalism, 1280–1390*. Cambridge: Cambridge University Press, 2005.

Newman, Paul B. *Growing Up in the Middle Ages*. Jefferson, N.C.: McFarland, 2007.

Nicholas, David. *The Domestic Life of a Medieval City: Women, Children and Families in the Fourteenth Century*. Lincoln: University of Nebraska Press, 1985.

———. *The Growth of the Medieval City: From Late Antiquity to the Early Fourteenth Century*. New York: Longman, 1997.

———. *Town and Countryside: Social, Economic and Political Tensions in Fourteenth-Century Flanders*. Bruges: De Tempel, 1971.

Nougaret, Jean. "Autour de quelques rétables: La Peinture religieuse médiévale à Montpellier." *Fédération historique du Languedoc méditerranéen et du Roussillon*, 64th Congress-1993 (Montpellier, 1994): 101–26.

Nucé de Lamothe, Marie-Simone. "Piété et charité publique à Toulouse de la fin du XIIIe siècle au milieu du XVe siècle d'après les testaments." *Annales du Midi* 76 (1964): 5–39.

O'Faolain, Julia, and Lauro Martines, eds. *Not in God's Image*. New York: Harper & Row, 1973.

Origo, Iris. *The Merchant of Prato, 1335–1410*. New York: Knopf, 1957.

Orme, Nicholas. *Medieval Children*. New Haven, Conn.: Yale University Press, 2001.

Otis-Cour, Leah. "Municipal Wet Nurses in Fifteenth-Century Montpellier." In Barbara A. Hanawalt, ed., *Women and Work in Preindustrial Europe*. Bloomington: Indiana University Press, 1986, 83–93.

———. *Prostitution in Medieval Society: The History of an Urban Institution in Languedoc*. Chicago: University of Chicago Press, 1985.

Oudot de Dainville, Maurice. "Remarques sur les compoix du Languedoc méditerranéen." *Folklore* 15 (1939): 132–37.

Paterson, Linda M. *The World of the Troubadours: Medieval Occitan Society, c. 1100–c. 1300*. Cambridge: Cambridge University Press, 1993.

Pawlowski, Krzysztof. *Circulades languedociennes de l'an mille: Naissance de l'urbanisme européen*. Montpellier: Presses du Languedoc, 1994.

Pegg, Mark. *A Most Holy War: The Albigensian Crusade and the Battle for Christendom*. Oxford: Oxford University Press, 2008.

Pernoud, Régine. *La Femme au temps des cathédrales*. Paris: Éditions Stock, 1980.

Perroy, Édouard. "À l'origine d'une économie contractée: Les Crises du XIVe siècle." *Annales: economies, sociétés, civilisations* 4 (1949): 167–82.

Petot, Pierre. *Histoire du droit privé français: La Famille*. Paris: Loysel, 1992.

Peyron, Jacques. "Montpellier médiévale, urbanisme et architecture." *Annales du Midi* 91 (1979): 255–72.

Pirenne, Henri. "The Stages in the Social History of Capitalism." *American Historical Review* 19 (1913): 494–515.

Plesner, Johan. *L'Émigration de la campagne à la ville libre de Florence au XIIIe siècle.* Copenhagen: Gyldendal, 1934.

Prat, Geneviève. "Albi et la peste noire." *Annales du Midi* 94 (1952): 15–25.

Pryor, John, H. *Business Contracts of Medieval Provence: Selected "Notulae" from the Cartulary of Giraud Amalric of Marseilles, 1248.* Toronto: Pontifical Institute of Mediaeval of Studies, 1981.

Ragnow, Marguerite. "The Worldly Cares of Abbess Richildis." Ph.D. dissertation, University of Minnesota, 2005.

Reames, Sherry L. *The Legenda Aurea: A Reexamination of Its Paradoxical History.* Madison: University of Wisconsin Press, 1985.

Reeves, Compton. *Pleasures and Pastimes in Medieval England.* Phoenix Mill: Sutton, 1995.

Renouard, Yves. *Les Relations des papes d'Avignon et des compagnies commerciales et bancaires de 1316 à 1378.* Paris: E. Boccard, 1941.

———. "Les Voies de communications entre pays de la Méditerranée et pays de l'Atlantique." In Charles-Edmond Perrin et al., eds., *Mélanges d'histoire du moyen âge dédiés à la mémoire de Louis Halphen.* Paris: Presses Universitaires de France, 1951, 587–94.

Renouvier, J. and A. Ricard. "Des maîtres de pierre et des autres artistes gothiques de Montpellier." *Mémoires de la société archéologique de Montpellier* 1st ser. 2 (1854): 135–50.

Renzo Villata, Gigliola di. "Dottrina legislation e prassi documentaria in tema di tutela nell' Italia del duecento." *Confluence des droits savants et des pratiques juridiques, Actes du colloque de Montpellier* (1977). Milan: A. Guiffrè, 1979, 375–434.

———. *La Tutela, Indagini sulla scuola dei glossatori.* Milan: A. Guiffrè, 1975.

Reyerson, Kathryn L. "The Adolescent Apprentice/Worker in Medieval Montpellier." *Journal of Family History* 17 (1992): 353–70. Reprinted in *Society, Law, and Trade in Medieval. Montpellier.*

———. *The Art of the Deal: Intermediaries of Trade in Medieval Montpellier.* Leiden: Brill, 2002.

———. *Business, Banking and Finance in Medieval Montpellier.* Toronto: Pontifical Institute of Mediaeval Studies, 1985.

———. "Changes in Testamentary Practice at Montpellier on the Eve of the Black Death." *Church History* 47 (1978): 253–69. Reprinted in *Society, Law, and Trade in Medieval Montpellier.*

———. "Commerce and Society in Montpellier: 1250–1350." 2 vols. Ph.D. dissertation, Yale University, 1974.

———. "Commercial Fraud in the Middle Ages: The Case of the Dissembling Pepperer." *Journal of Medieval History* 8 (1982): 63–73. Reprinted in *Society, Law, and Trade in Medieval Montpellier.*

———. "Un exemple de micro-crédit féminin entre ville et champagne: Montpellier et ses alentours au début du XIVe siècle." In Marie Dejoux and Diane Chamboduc de

Saint Pulgent, eds. *Mélanges François Menant.* Paris: Publications de la Sorbonne, forthcoming.

————. "L'Expérience des plaideuses devant les cours de Montpellier (fin XIIIe–mi-XIVe siècle)." In Julie Claustre, Olivier Mattéoni, and Nicolas Offenstadt, eds., *Un Moyen Âge pour aujourd'hui: Mélanges offerts à Claude Gauvard.* Paris: Presses Universitaires de France, 2010, 522–528.

————. "Flight from Prosecution: The Search for Religious Asylum in Medieval Montpellier." *French Historical Studies* 17 (1992): 603–26. Reprinted in *Society, Law, and Trade in Medieval Montpellier.*

————. "Identity in the Medieval Mediterranean World of Merchants and Pirates." *Mediterranean Studies* 20 (2012, appeared 2013): 129–46.

————. "Italians in the Credit Networks of Fourteenth-Century Languedoc." Paper at Medieval Academy of America, Vancouver, April 2008.

————. *Jacques Coeur: Entrepreneur and King's Bursar.* New York: Pearson Longman, 2005.

————. "Land, Houses and Real Estate Investment in Montpellier: A Study of the Notarial Property Transactions, 1293–1348." *Studies in Medieval and Renaissance History* 6 (1983): 39–112. Reprinted in *Society, Law, and Trade in Medieval Montpellier.*

————, ed. *Medieval Narbonne: A City at the Heart of the Troubadour World.* Aldershot: Ashgate, 2005.

————. "Medieval Silks in Montpellier: The Silk Market, ca. 1250–ca.1350." *Journal of European Economic History* 11 (1982): 117–40. Reprinted in *Society, Law, and Trade in Medieval Montpellier.*

————. "The Merchants of the Mediterranean: Merchants as Strangers." In F. R. P. Akehurst and Stephanie Cain Van D'Elden, eds., *The Stranger in Medieval Society.* Minneapolis: University of Minnesota Press, 1997, 1–13.

————. "La Mobilité sociale: Réflexions sur le rôle de la femme." In Sandro Carocci, ed., *La Mobilità sociale nel medioevo.* Rome: École Française de Rome, 2010, 491–511.

————. "Montpellier de 1250 à 1350: Centre commercial et financier." Doctoral thesis, Faculté de Droit et des Sciences Économiques de Montpellier, Université de Montpellier-1, 1977.

————. "Montpellier et le trafic des grains en Méditerranée avant 1350." *Montpellier, la Couronne d'Aragon et les Pays de Langue d'Oc (1204–1349): Actes du XIIe Congrès d'Histoire de la Couronne d'Aragon, Mémoires de la société archéologique de Montpellier* XV (Montpellier, 1985), 147–62. Reprinted in *Society, Law, and Trade in Medieval Montpellier.*

————. "Montpellier et le transport maritime: Le Problème d'une flotte médiévale." In Jean Rieucau and Gérard Cholvy, eds., *Le Languedoc, le Roussillon et la mer.* 2 vols. Paris: L'Harmattan, 1992, 1:98–108.

————. "Notaires et crédit à Montpellier au moyen âge." In François Menant and Odile Redon, eds., *Notaires et crédit.* Rome: École Française de Rome, 2004, appeared 2005. 241–61.

————. "Les Opérations de crédit dans la coutume et dans la vie des affaires à Montpellier au moyen âge: Le Problème de l'usure." In *Diritto comune et diritti locali nella storia dell'Europa*. Milan: A. Guiffrè, 1980, 189–209. Reprinted in *Society, Law, and Trade in Medieval Montpellier*.

————. "La Participation des femmes de l'élite marchande à l'économie: Trois exemples montpelliérains de la première moitié du XIVe siècle." In *Les Femmes dans l'espace nord-méditerranéen*, under the direction of Christiane Klapisch-Zuber. *Études Rousillonnaises* 25 (2013): 129–35.

————. "Patterns of Population Attraction and Mobility: The Case of Montpellier, 1293–1348." *Viator* 10 (1979): 257–81. Reprinted in *Society, Law, and Trade in Medieval Montpellier*.

————. "Problems of Family Reconstruction in Medieval Montpellier." Paper at Congress on Medieval Studies, Western Michigan University, Kalamazoo, May 1982.

————. "Prostitution in Medieval Montpellier: The Ladies of Campus Polverel." *Medieval Prosopography* 18 (1997): 209–28.

————. "Public and Private Space in Medieval Montpellier: The Bon Amic Square." *Journal of Urban History* 24 (1997): 3–27.

————. "Les Réseaux économiques entre femmes à Montpellier (fin XIIIe–mi-XIVe)." In Lucie Laumonier and Lucie Galano, eds., *Montpellier au Moyen Âge: Bilan et approches nouvelles*. Turnhout: Brepols, forthcoming.

————. "Rituals in Medieval Business." In Joëlle Rollo-Koster, ed., *Medieval and Early Modern Ritual: Formalized Behavior in Europe, China and Japan*. Leiden: Brill, 2002, 81–103.

————. "Le Rôle de Montpellier dans le commerce des draps de laine avant 1350." *Annales du Midi* 94 (1982): 17–40.

————. *Society, Law, and Trade in Medieval Montpellier*. Aldershot: Variorum, 1995.

————. "Southern French Legal Procedure and Local Practice: Legal Traditions in Dialogue," 40th International Congress on Medieval Studies, Western Michigan University, Kalamazoo, May 2005.

————. "Le Témoignage des femmes (à partir de quelques enquêtes montpelliéraines du XIVe siècle)." In Claude Gauvard, ed., *L'Enquête au moyen âge*. Rome: École Française de Rome, 2008, 153–68.

————. "The Tensions of Walled Space: Urban Development Versus Defense." In James D. Tracy, ed., *City Walls: The Urban Enceinte*. Cambridge: Cambridge University Press, 2000, 88–116.

————. "Urban Economies." In Judith M. Bennett and Ruth Mazo Karras, eds., *Oxford Handbook on Medieval Women and Gender*. Oxford: Oxford University Press, 297–310.

————. "Urban/Rural Exchange: Reflections on the Economic Relations of Town and Country in the Region of Montpellier Before 1350." In Kathryn Reyerson and John Drendel, eds., *Urban and Rural Communities in Medieval France: Provence and Languedoc, 1000–1500*. Leiden: Brill, 1998, 253–73.

———. "Urban Sensations: The Medieval City Imagined." In Richard Newhauser, ed., *A Cultural History of the Senses*. Vol. 2. Oxford: Berg, 2014. 45–65.

———. "Wills of Spouses in Montpellier Before 1350: A Case Study of Gender in Testamentary Practice." In Joëlle Rollo-Koster and Kathryn L. Reyerson, eds., *"For the Salvation of My Soul": Women and Wills in Early Modern France*. St. Andrews: Centre for French History and Culture, University of St. Andrews, 2012, 44–60.

———. "Women and Law in Medieval France." In Linda E. Mitchell, ed., *Women in Medieval Western European Culture*. New York: Garland, 1999, 131–36.

———. "Women in Business in Medieval Montpellier." In Barbara A. Hanawalt, ed., *Women and Work in Preindustrial Europe*. Bloomington: Indiana University Press, 1986, 117–44.

———. *Women's Networks in Medieval France: Gender and Community in Montpellier, 1300–1350* New York: Palgrave Macmillan, 2016.

Reyerson, Kathryn, and Barbara A. Hanawalt, eds. *City and Spectacle in Medieval Europe*. Minneapolis: University of Minnesota Press, 1994.

Reyerson, Kathryn, and John Bell Henneman. "Law, Southern France." *Dictionary of the Middle Ages*. Vol. 7. New York: Scribner's, 1986, 461–68.

Reyerson, Kathryn, and Kelly Morris. "Debt Among Religious Women in Medieval Southern France." Paper at Center for Medieval Studies, University of Minnesota, April 2005.

Reyerson, Kathryn, and Kevin Mummey, "Whose City Is This? Hucksters, Domestic Servants, Wet Nurses, Prostitutes, and Slaves in Late Medieval Western Mediterranean Urban Society." *History Compass* 9, 12 (2011): 910–22.

Reyerson, Kathryn, and Faye Powe. "Metalwork of Montpellier: Techniques and Workshop Practices in the Fourteenth Century." Paper at International Congress on Medieval Studies, Western Michigan University, Kalamazoo, 1984.

Reyerson, Kathryn, and Debra Salata. *Medieval Notaries and Their Acts: The 1327–1328 Register of Jean Holanie*. Kalamazoo, Mich.: The Medieval Institute, 2004.

Richard, Jean-Claude. "Le Problème des origines de Montpellier." *Revue archéologique de Narbonne* 2 (1969): 49–62.

Richardot, H. "Le Fief roturier à Toulouse aux XIIe et XIIIe siècles." *Revue historique du droit français et étranger* 4th ser. 14 (1935): 307–59, 495–569.

Riesenberg, Peter. "Roman Law, Renunciations and Business in the Twelfth and Thirteenth Centuries." In John H. Mundy, Richard W. Emery, and Benjamin N. Nelson, eds., *Essays in Medieval Life and Thought Presented in Honor of Austin P. Evans*. New York: Columbia University Press, 1955, 207–25.

Rigaudière, Albert. "État, pouvoir et administration dans la *Pratica aurea libellorum* de Pierre Jacobi (vers 1311)." In Albert Rigaudière and Jacques Krynen, eds. *Droits savants et pratiques françaises du pouvoir (XIe–XVe siècles)*. Bordeaux: Presses Universitaires de Bordeaux, 1992, 161–210.

———. "Municipal Citizenship in Pierre Jacobi's *Practica aurea libellorum* (ca. 1311)." In Laurent Mayali and Julius Kirshner, eds., *Privileges and Rights of Citizenship: Law and the Juridical Construction of Civil Society*. Berkeley: Robbins Collection, University of California at Berkeley, 2002, 1–26.

Rogozinski, Jan. "The Counsellors of the Seneschal of Beaucaire and Nîmes, 1250–1350." *Speculum* 44 (1969): 421–39.

———. "Ordinary and Major Judges." *Studia Gratiana* 15 (1972): 589–611.

———. *Power, Caste, and Law: Social Conflict in Fourteenth-Century Montpellier*. Cambridge, Mass.: Medieval Academy of America, 1982.

Rollo-Koster, Joëlle. *Avignon and Its Papacy, 1309–1417: Popes, Institutions, and Society*. Lanham, Md.: Rowman & Littlefield, 2015.

———, ed. *Medieval and Early Modern Ritual: Formalized Behavior in Europe, China and Japan*. Leiden: Brill, 2002.

Rollo-Koster, Joëlle, and Kathryn L. Reyerson, eds. *"For the Salvation of my soul": Women and Wills in Early Modern France*. St. Andrews: Centre for French History and Culture, University of St. Andrews, 2012.

Romestan, Guy. "Sous les rois d'Aragon et de Majorque (1204–1349)." *Histoire de Montpellier*. Toulouse: Privat, 1974, 39–69.

Roover, Florence Edler de. "Lucchese Silks." *Ciba Review* 80 (1950): 2902–30.

———. "The Silk Trade of Lucca During the Thirteenth and Fourteenth Centuries." Ph.D. dissertation, University of Chicago, 1930.

Roover, Raymond de. *Business, Banking and Economic Thought in Late Medieval and Early Modern Europe: Selected Studies of Raymond de Roover*. Ed. Julius Kirshner. Chicago: University of Chicago Press, 1974.

———. *Money, Banking and Credit in Medieval Bruges: Italian Merchant-Bankers, Lombards and Money-Changers*. Cambridge, Mass.: Mediaeval Academy of America, 1948.

———. "What Is Dry Exchange? A Contribution to the Study of English Mercantilism." *Journal of Political Economy* 52 (1944): 250–66.

Ross, Marvin Chauncey. "Bassetaille Enameling at Montpellier." With "A Note on the Montpellier Reliquary in the Taft Museum" by Margaret Kremers. *Art Quarterly* 4 (1941): 32–39.

Rossiaud, Jacques. *Medieval Prostitution*. Trans. Lydia G. Cochrane. Oxford: Blackwell, 1988.

Rouquette, Jean. *Histoire du diocèse de Maguelone*. 2 vols. Montpellier: J. Rouquette, 1921–27.

Sapori, Armando. *The Italian Merchant in the Middle Ages*. Trans. Patricia Ann Kennan. New York: Norton, 1970.

Sautel, Gérard. "Une juridiction paroissiale dans le Midi de la France au Moyen Âge: La Cour de Saint-Firmin à Montpellier." *Recueil et mémoires et travaux publié par de la société d'histoire du droit et des institutions des anciens pays de droit écrit* 2 (Montpellier, 1951), 47–65.

Shahar, Shulamith. *The Fourth Estate: A History of Women in the Middle Ages*. London: Methuen, 1983.

Slicher van Bath, Bernard H. *The Agrarian History of Western Europe (500–1850)*. London: E. Arnold, 1963.

Smail, Daniel Lord. *The Consumption of Justice: Emotions, Publicity, and Legal Culture in Marseille, 1264–1423.* Ithaca, N.Y.: Cornell University Press, 2003.

———. "Démanteler le patrimoine: Les Femmes et les biens dans la Marseille médiévale, 1337–1362." *Annales: histoire, sciences sociales* 52 (1997): 343–68.

———. *Imaginary Cartographies: Possession and Identity in Late Medieval Marseille.* Ithaca, N.Y.: Cornell University Press, 1999.

———. "Mapping Networks and Knowledge in Medieval Marseille, 1337–1362: Variations on a Theme of Mobility." Ph.D. dissertation, University of Michigan, 1994.

———. "Notaries, Courts, and the Legal Culture of Late Medieval Marseille." In Kathryn L. Reyerson and John Drendel, eds., *Medieval Urban and Rural: Communities in France: Provence and L.anguedoc, 1000–1500.* Leiden: Brill, 1998, 23–50.

Sournia, Bernard, and Jean-Louis Vayssettes. *La Demeure médiévale.* Paris: Imprimerie Nationale, 1991.

———. *L'Ostal des Carcassonne: La Maison d'un drapier montpelliérain du XIIIe siècle.* Montpellier: DRAC, 2014.

———. "Trois plafonds montpelliérains du Moyen Âge." In Monique Bourin and Philippe Bernardi, eds. *Plafonds peints médiévaux en Languedoc.* Perpignan: Presses Universitaires de Perpignan, 2009, 149–71.

Squatriti, Paolo. *Water and Society in Early Medieval Italy, AD 400–1000.* Cambridge: Cambridge University Press, 1998.

Staples, Kate Kelsey. *Daughters of London: Inheriting Opportunity in the Late Middle Ages.* Leiden: Brill, 2011.

Stelling-Michaud, Swen. "Le Transport international des manuscrits juridiques bolonais entre 1265–1320." In *Mélanges d'histoire économique et sociale en l'honneur du professeur Antony Babel.* 2 vols. Geneva: Imprimerie de la Tribune, 1963, 1:95–127.

Stiller, Nikki. *Eve's Orphans: Mothers and Daughters in Medieval English Literature.* Westport, Conn.: Greenwood, 1980.

Strayer, Joseph R. *The Albigensian Crusades.* Ann Arbor: University of Michigan Press, 1971.

———. *Les Gens de justice du Languedoc sous Philippe le Bel.* Toulouse: Marc Bloch, 1970.

Stuard, Susan Mosher. *Gilding the Market: Luxury and Fashion in Fourteenth-Century Italy.* Philadelphia: University of Pennsylvania Press, 2006.

———. *A State of Deference: Ragusa/Dubrovnik in the Medieval Centuries.* Philadelphia: University of Pennsylvania Press, 1992.

———. "Women in Charter and Statute Law: Medieval Ragusa/Dubrovnik." In Susan Mosher Stuard, ed., *Women in Medieval Society.* Philadelphia: University of Pennsylvania Press, 1976, 199–208.

Sumption, Jonathan. *The Albigensian Crusade.* London: Faber, 1978.

———. *The Hundred Years War: Trial by Battle.* Philadelphia: University of Pennsylvania Press, 1991.

Texier, Abbé Jacques-Rémy Antoine. "Orfèvrerie du moyen âge: Écoles ou ateliers de Montpellier et de Limoges." *Annales Archéologiques* 8 (1848): 260–68.

Thiébaut, Dominique. "Peintures." In Françoise Baron et al., eds., *Les Fastes du gothique: Le Siècle de Charles V.* Paris: Ministère de la Culture. Éditions de la Réunion des Musées Nationaux, 1981.

Thomas, Louis J. "Montpellier entre la France et l'Aragon pendant la première moitié du XIVe siècle." In *Monspeliensia, Mémoires et documents relatifs à Montpellier et à la région montpelliéraine* 1, fasc. 1. Montpellier: Impr. de E. Montane, 1929, 1–56.

———. *Montpellier, ville marchande: Histoire économique et sociale de Montpellier des origines à 1870.* Montpellier: Librairie Valat, Librairie Coulet, 1936.

———. "Note sur l'origine de Montpellier." *Cahiers d'Histoire et d'Archéologie* 1st ser. 2 (1931): 126–35.

Thuile, Jean. *Histoire de l'Orfèvrerie du Languedoc, Généralités de Montpellier et de Toulouse, Répertoire des orfèvres depuis le moyen-âge jusqu'au début du XIXe siècle.* Paris: Théo et Florence Schmied, A à C, 1964; D à L, 1966; M à Z, 1968.

———. *L'Orfèvrerie en Languedoc du XIIe au XVIIIe siècle: Généralité de Montpellier.* Vol. I. Montpellier: Causse & Castelnau, 1966.

Tisset, Pierre. "Placentin et son enseignement à Montpellier: Droit romain et coutume dans l'ancien pays de Septimanie." *Recueil de mémoires et travaux publié par la société d'histoire du droit et des institutions des anciens pays de droit écrit* 2 (1951): 67–94.

Tourtoulon, Charles de. *Études sur la maison de Barcelone, Jacme Ier le Conquérant, roi d'Aragon, comte de Barcelone, seigneur de Montpellier, d'après les chroniques et les documents inédits.* 2 vols. Montpellier: Gras, 1863–67.

Verdon, Laure. "Les Femmes et l'exercice de la *potestas* en Provence (XIIe–XIIIe siècles): Transgression des roles ou perméabilité des spheres de compétences?" *Les femmes dans l'espace nord-méditerranéen,* under the direction of Christiane Klapisch-Zuber, *Études Roussillonnaises* 25 (2013): 83–88.

Vidal, Henri. "Les Mariages dans la famille des Guillems." *Revue historique du droit français et étranger* 62 (1984): 231–45.

Vincent, Catherine. *Les Confréries médiévales dans le royaume de France XIIIe–Ve siècle.* Paris: Albin Michel, 1994.

Vinyoles i Vidal, Teresa-Maria. *Les Barcelonines e les darrieres de l'Edat Mitjana (1370–1410).* Barcelona: Fundació Salvador Vives Casajuana, 1976.

———. "L'Esdevenir quotidià: Treball i lleure de les dones medievals." In Mary Nash, ed., *Més enllà del silenci: Les Dones a la història de Catalunya.* Barcelona: Generalitat de Catalunya, 1988, 73–89.

Virgoe, Roger, ed. *Private Life in the Fifteenth Century.* New York: Weidenfeld & Nicolson, 1989.

Wakefield, Walter, *Heresy, Crusade, and Inquisition in Southern France, 1100–1250.* Berkeley: University of California Press, 1974.

Walker, Sue Sheridan, ed. *Wife and Widow in Medieval England.* Ann Arbor: University of Michigan Press, 1993.

White, Steven. *Custom, Kinship, and Gifts to Saints: The Laudatio Parentum in Western France, 1050–1150.* Chapel Hill: University of North Carolina Press, 1988.

Willard, Charity C. *Christine de Pizan: Her Life and Works.* New York: Persea, 1984.

Winer, Rebecca Lynn. "Allaitement, esclavage et salut de l'âme dans la Couronne d'Aragon et le royaume de Majorque." *Les Femmes dans l'espace nord-méditerranéen,* under the direction of Christiane Klapisch-Zuber, *Études Roussillonnaises* 25 (2013): 107–14.

———. "The Mother and the *Dida* [Nanny]: Female Employers and Wet Nurses in Fourteenth-Century Barcelona." In Jutta Gisela Sperling, ed., *Medieval and Renaissance Lactations: Images, Rhetorics, Practices.* Farnham: Ashgate, 2013, 55–78.

———. *Women, Wealth, and Community in Perpignan, c. 1250–1300.* Aldershot: Ashgate, 2006.

Winroth, Anders. *The Making of Gratian's Decretum.* Cambridge: Cambridge University Press, 2000.

Wolff, Philippe. *Commerces et marchands de Toulouse (vers 1350–vers 1450).* Paris: Plon, 1954.

Wood, Charles. *The French Apanages and the Capetian Monarchy, 1224–1328.* Cambridge, Mass.: Harvard University Press, 1966.

Yver, Jean. *Égalité entre héritiers et exclusion des enfants dotés: Essai de géographie coutumière.* Paris: Sirey, 1966.

Zerner, Monique. ed. *Inventer l'hérésie: Discours polémiques et pouvoirs avant l'Inquisition.* Nice: Centre d'Études Médiévales, 1998.

Ziegler, Philip. *The Black Death.* New York: Harper and Row, 1969.

Zupko, Ronald E., and Robert A. Laures. *Straws in the Wind: Medieval Urban Environmenal Law—The Case of Northern Italy.* Boulder, Colo.: Westview, 1996.

INDEX

Page references in italics refer to illustrations.

ACKNOWLEDGMENTS

I am grateful to the University of Minnesota and to the Department of History for a single-semester leave in spring 2015 and for earlier leaves that permitted me time to finish this book, as well as for McKnight and McMillan fellowships. I owe much to the archivists of the Archives Départementales de l'Hérault and the Archives Municipales de Montpellier for assistance in my research over many decades. Mark Lindberg of the Cartography Laboratory of the University of Minnesota deserves my thanks for drawing the maps, as does the Interlibrary Loan service at the University of Minnesota for its help over the years.

I am grateful to the audiences who heard versions of this project in France and Italy, where I spoke at the invitation of my colleagues Claude Gauvard, professor emerita of the Université de Paris Panthéon-Sorbonne and François Menant, professor emeritus of the École Normale Supérieure, rue d'Ulm, Paris. I thank Monique Bourin, professor emerita of the Université de Paris Panthéon-Sorbonne, for her feedback on medieval houses and painted ceilings. And I owe a tremendous debt of thanks to Jean-Louis Vayssettes, ingénieur de recherche of the DRAC of Languedoc-Roussillon, for his assistance with images of the Carcassonne house, 3 rue de la Vieille.

I thank my many colleagues at the University of Minnesota, specialists in the history of women and gender, for feedback on this study over many years. I also want to thank the anonymous readers of the manuscript version of this book for their invaluable suggestions and criticisms. I am grateful to my friend Marlys Harris for her comments. I owe a great debt to Marguerite Ragnow and Ruth Karras for their comments, and to Maggie, in particular, my gratitude for her patience and encouragement over the years. Finally, thanks go to Jerry Singerman and his colleagues at the University of Pennsylvania Press for their support.

Any remaining errors are my responsibility alone.